D0521147

# GENERATION ECCH!

**JASON COHEN AND MICHAEL KRUGMAN**

COMIX BY EVAN DORKIN

A FIRESIDE BOOK    Published by Simon & Schuster

New York London Toronto Sydney Tokyo Singapore

**F**

FIRESIDE
Rockefeller Center
1230 Avenue of the Americas
New York, New York 10020

Designed by Bonni Leon

Manufactured in the United States of America

10  9  8  7  6  5  4  3  2

Library of Congress Cataloging-in-Publication Data

Cohen, Jason.
     Generation Ecch!: the backlash starts here/by Jason Cohen and Michael Krugman; comix [sic] by Evan Dorkin.
          p.      cm.
     "A Fireside book."
     1. Mass media and young adults—United States—Humor. 2. United States—Popular culture—Humor. I. Krugman, Michael. II. Dorkin, Evan. III. Title
P94.5.Y68C65   1994
305.23′5′0973—dc20                                    94–11306
                                                                   CIP

ISBN 0-671-88694-0

*To our sisters, Julie Cohen and Michele Krugman*

*"Was it Kierkegaard
or Dick Van Patten
who said, 'If you
label me, you negate me'?"*

*—Wayne Campbell*

# Table of Malcontents

*Generation X*
*Slackers*
*twentysomethings*
*Grunge Kids*
*13ers*
*Busters*
*The Motorbooty Generation*
*Tweeners*
*Late Bloomers*
*Postboomers*
*Boomlets*
*The Boomerang Generation*

**W**ho are these people, and why is everybody saying such terrible things about them? The above is an abbreviated selection of the barrage of cognomina for an age-group united by nothing more than alienation, irony, overlong immaturity and a love/hate relationship with Anthony Michael Hall. The horrifying afterbirth of the baby boom, today's eighteen-to-twenty-nine-year-olds have been simultaneously condemned and pursued by the American establishment, making them the subject of the most excessive publicity overload since, well . . . the baby boom.

# The

# Hatching of the

# Ecch

# or

# Baby Boom

# Bye-Bye

This mass media hand-wringing has seen dozens of writers, ad men and so-called thinkers trying to make sense of the motives and mores of "kids today." In response, supposedly representative members have given their inflated and enfeebled explanations of what their generation thinks and feels *ad infinitum*.

As members of this ubiquitous pigeonhole, we find ourselves distrustful of the categorizations and dissatisfied with the multitude of self-appointed spokespeople. Ergo, we have decided to anoint ourselves Debunkers of the Realm.

This book will put to rest the allegations that this generation is lazy, dysfunctional and anti-intellectual. It most certainly is. It's also fixated on show business, naively delusional about the past and onanistically obsessed with its own fiscal and psychological well-being.

So, for our entry into the moniker derby, we've chosen to dub the phenomenon *Generation Ecch*. Because, quite frankly, it makes us sick.

Lookit: Since when is the possibility of being less affluent than our parents a problem on the order of world hunger, the federal deficit and Courtney Love? Why are millions of college graduates working at Carl's Jr. when what they really want to do is direct? When did R.E.M. become classic rock? Is John Hughes our generation's Joseph L. Mankiewicz? Was the cancellation of *thirtysomething* directly related to the emergent popularity of *Beverly Hills 90210*? Is it healthy to have eight different grandparents? Is sex without a condom a revolutionary act? How did *The Brady Bunch* become the best the American theater has to offer? And is it possible that most people think David Copperfield is the name of a TV illusionist, and can't figure out how Charles Dickens wrote a book about him?

Conventional wisdom holds that *GenEcch* is entirely a media creation, devised by demographic-driven advertisers desperate to pick the pockets of a group with a small—but fully disposable—income. This is most decidedly the way *Ecch* fever began, but now there's something going on that's far creepier than old-fashioned capitalist greed. All the hubbub has prompted a self-absorbed and self-important generation to rationalize its own existence, ascribing significance to meaninglessness. Haunted by the spectre of the beats and the boomers and the hippies and the punks, today's youth have eagerly accepted the glib labels foisted upon them, good or bad. *Ecch* has been content with anything that will give it a generational self-image, whether it's that of rebel or loser.

Which leaves nothing more than a bunch of rebellious losers. It's no accident that the phrase "rebel without a clue" has become a bigger cliché than "rebel without a cause."

It's sad to say, but looking at *GenEcch* through the pop culture that formed them, as well as the books, movies and music the generation has produced itself, seems to validate conservative old fart Allan Bloom's bellyaching about the accelerating vapidity of post-TV youth and their complete lack of depth, smarts, feeling or history. (The late Dr. Bloom was also correct when he said that rock'n'roll moves to the beat of sexual intercourse, but that's another story.) If a modern-day Allen Ginsberg were to write a *Howl* for the age of *Ecch*, the minute he saw the best minds of the generation he'd drop the poesy and go back to the *schmatte* business. The Beat Generation went out looking for America; we're sitting at home chatting about it.

In the postatomic years, after Kerouac and Elvis, the moral and intellectual fiber of American society really did begin to crumble. Now the members of *Generation Ecch* sit among the rubble, fiddling with the remote control, the only way they know to effect change.

**E***cch* is as much about critical interpretations of a social phenomenon as it is about the people participating in it. The generation as we know it today was conceived, carried and delivered by the media, whose recklessly absurd series of generalizations, think pieces and psychographic marketing ploys can be likened to a prenatal diet of Chianti and Marlboros. *Ecch* was plucked from the womb of invisible individualism on July 16, 1990, with *Time*'s cover story C-section of this confusing, contradictory and little understood group.

**twentysomething,** the familiar red-bordered cover whispered, copping the soft-spoken tag from the baby boom's favorite TV show. Five distressed-looking, diverse and decidedly multicultural youths stood listlessly in the cover photo, while a subhead queried: "Laid back, late blooming or just lost? Overshadowed by the baby boomers, America's next generation has a hard act to follow." The first salvo in the new generational name game had been fired.

*Time* put the generation at forty-eight million folks between the ages of eighteen and twenty-nine, all petulant and empty-headed, so torn up by divorce, Republicanism and economic strife that it didn't care about anything except its own well-being. Being *Time*, the magazine commissioned a survey, which revealed, among other things, that 58 percent of the selfish bastards believed there is no point in staying in a job unless you are completely satisfied.

Using that 58 percent statistic, *Time* very somberly concluded that there would be a severe labor shortage and that "during the next several years, employers will have to double their recruiting efforts" simply to put together a passable workforce from this hapless generation of demanding do-nothings. The continuing recession provided a quick fix to that dilemma, and now *Ecch*-analyzing essays focus on how difficult it is for the generation to find good work. It's one thing to make coffee for the head of literary acquisitions at Paramount until you hit the next step of the ladder—it's quite another to make coffee for the *Frasier* production assistants at the Burbank Starbucks franchise.

The weekly newsmagazine also predicted that, as children of divorce, *Ecch*sters will be the ones who make the nuclear family great again. Actually, it looks as though this generation has bypassed the nuclear family altogether, viewing it as inherently explosive. We're perfectly happy with our nontraditional families, like *90210* and *The Real World*.

Among the other useless info gleaned from *Time*'s insightful research was how the generation feels about the sixties. *Time* asked, "Which aspects of the sixties do you find attractive?" The survey says . . .

**"The easygoing lifestyle":** 77 percent attractive, 21 percent not attractive, 2 percent not sure

**"The music":** 70 percent attractive, 28 percent not attractive, 2 percent not sure

**"The drugs":** 17 percent attractive, 79 percent not attractive, 4 percent not sure

**"The chance to go to a country you've never heard of and kill your friends with friendly fire, then watch the rest of them go nuts from posttraumatic stress disorders or get cancer from Agent Orange":** 26 percent attractive, 57 percent not attractive, 17 percent not sure

Clearly, the answer to the generational problem circa 1990 was simple—twentysomethings couldn't compare to the boomers because they hadn't yet developed the proper respect for the art of getting wasted.

The initial "twentysomething" tag may well have been the best one—simple and descriptive without any sneaky connotations or extra implications. It continues to show up in articles today despite the dozens of new entries. But the term is inherently problematic because it automatically expires in the year 2000 or so, by which time even the youngest of *Ecch*sters will have hit the ripe old age of thirty. By then they'll have moved on to more mature life experiences, like infidelity, starting their own ad agencies, breast cancer and getting run over while riding a bicycle.

The trouble with *Time*'s getting the jump on this bandwagon before it got rolling was that the "twentysomethings" were so unformed that they couldn't be documented accurately. The piece was far below Nostradamus level in its cultural forecast. "They have few heroes, no anthems, no style to call their own," the piece lamented. In the next year or so, the new activism and so-called grunge fashion would come along, as would the Lollapalooza tour and Nirvana's "Smells Like Teen Spirit"—a snide, ironic antianthem to be sure, but that only made it more *Ecch*, not less. Douglas Coupland's novel(ty) *Generation X* was published, a handy-dandy guide to the new postgrad crowd, with pseudoanthropological descriptions of *Ecch*'s styles and living habits in its margins and, as a bonus, a little story to illustrate his points. Between Coupland's pretense to social chronicling and Richard Linklater's film *Slacker,* a hyperintellectual comedy about life on the fringe that was quickly interpreted as a definitive generational statement, more fun names entered the zeitgeist.

The floodgates of *Ecch* mania were open, and a deluge of stupid articles flowed unabated. *Psychology Today* had a piece, called "A Generation of Gripers . . . and How They Grew," blaming the generational anomie on "America's collective stress level," which began rising in 1967 and hit an all-time high in 1987 (the last year for which figures were available, though it's obviously gotten worse, as the success of *Listening to Prozac* attests).

Yes, those anxious decades were the years in which *Ecch* came of age. The headshrinkers also chipped in with the staggering observation that *Ecch* "tends to hang out in groups." Whoa! Just like street gangs or the Algonquin Round Table (aka the "Quips"). An unprecedented development in the life of America's youth! Alert the media! Oh, somebody already did.

*U.S. News & World Report*'s cover story came three years after that of *Time,* its major competition (Mort must be slipping). Updated to reflect new developments in *Ecch* society and culture, the piece was a little more optimistic, suggesting that *Ecch* could be "the Repair Generation," a "generation of janitors" committed to cleaning up what's wrong with America. We are indeed a generation of janitors—and busboys and temps and bicycle messengers. And it's not "janitors"—call us "custodial engineers."

*U.S. News* also suggested that "twentysomethings are in need of a press agent." Huh?

All of the mainstream media articles about *Ecch* were exactly the same—the requisite pictures of bespectacled drummers/substitute teachers, the same old statistics, the condescending interpretations of popular culture and the addition of token activists and shallow deep thinkers for "balance." They might have been saying bad things about the generation, but what the articles really did was alert advertisers, marketers and fellow publishers to a demographic they hadn't discovered yet. The baby-boom-age journalists only served to popularize their object of derision.

When it comes to *Ecch*, the baby-boom-age journalists on everybody's Rolodex are Neil Howe and Bill Strauss. Howe is an economist, while Strauss is the director of the Capitol Steps political-satire troupe. (That would make Howe the funny one.) They are the resident boomer *Ecch*perts, quoted in these articles freely and frequently as a result of their authorship of an *Atlantic Monthly* cover story on the "new generation gap" and a deceptively hip-looking sociology tome called *13th Gen: Abort, Retry, Ignore, Fail?*

Howe and Strauss's *nom de gen* comes from the notion that, "counting back to the peers of Benjamin Franklin, this generation is, in point of fact, the thirteenth to know the American nation, flag, and Constitution." Presumably, they use the term "know" loosely.

Their methodology only serves to point out the greater superflousness of the name game, as only a few American generations had nicknames and unifying cultural goals. Not all of them felt compelled to answer to a dopey sobriquet. Were the teenagers who came of age after the Civil War known as "postslavies?" Today's media demands that everything have a label, and since most kids get everything they know from the media, they have no qualms about playing along.

What sets these two apart from their fellow geezers is that Howe and Strauss have come to praise *Ecch*, not to bury it. Actually, they bury their subject with faint praise, spewing out page after page of analysis that attempts to put the generation into a historical context while committing all sorts of mistakes and misreadings. To compensate for their ascending age, they cram the margins of their book with *Ecch*-related media quotes and engage in an ostensibly spontaneous BBS exchange with "Crasher," a twenty-one-year-old North Carolinian. Crasher serves as Howe and Strauss's "voice of the generation" with his angst-ridden responses to their blah-blah-blah.

They're fortunate that Crasher feeds them firsthand info about *Ecch* habits, because in spite of their quote-happy margins, these two dads don't seem to know much about *Ecch* culture. They have a habit of picking up on meaningless cultural artifacts—"evil child movies," an obscure They Might Be Giants song, the "'70s era period piece" *Alice's Restaurant* (which was released in 1969)—merely because the works in question hew to their own flimsy analogies. Analyzing pop music and videos, they proclaim that 13ers watch MTV "for only an average of 12 minutes at a time, but those are high-intensity minutes that leave indelible memories." Yeah, those girls in "Hot for Teacher" are impossible to forget. So much for defending this generation.

They dismiss Dan Cortese in a regurgitative *New York Times* piece published post–*13th Gen . . .* as Burger King's "congenially dumb, monosyllabic, backward-capped young spokesman." Hell, *Entertainment Tonight* says that Cortese and MTV's Daisy Fuentes are *the* spokespeople for this generation. How can these two clowns call themselves scholars if they don't even watch *Entertainment Tonight*?

**S**unday, May 3, 1992. A date which will live in infamy. Under the direction of executive editor Max Frankel and then deputy publisher Arthur "Pinch" Sulzberger, Jr., *The New York Times* introduced its new Sunday section, Styles of the *Times*. The paper of record meant to capture *Ecch* readers by giving them a section which related to their interests—you know, clothes, pop stars, that kind of thing. Styles was supposed to be a sort of old gray *Interview*, full of exciting new fashion trends and ultrahip celebrity profiles. Instead, the section became one of those wonderful events in the NYC publishing world: a complete laughingstock.

The Styles of the *Times'* debut was one of the most ridiculous moments in *NYT* history. "The Arm Fetish," the headline read, heralding the arrival of "the body part as fashion accessory." There to enjoy with your mimosas and bagels was an enormous photo of a pumped-up appendage and a fifteen-hundred-word essay featuring prose like "It is sinewy and outstretched, relaxed and yearning, like the arm Michelangelo gave Adam. But what is it reaching for?" *A razor, to cut the wrist's translucent skin guarding the blue veins through which courses the blood of life itself?*

Never before had there been such an instantaneous register of "what's hot and what's not." On a given Saturday, designers, musicians, models could be on top of the downtown world, known only to those who made them happening. But after an appearance in Sunday's Styles, it was over, done, finito. By Monday, they were merely victims of scorn and mockery.

Further weeks saw revealing exposés on why people were wearing Birkenstocks or distressed plaid, as well as hard-hitting investigative reporting on such earthshaking events as the Don't Bungle the Jungle II rain forest benefit, which had raised only $150,000 (*Heavens!*) because of an abundance of cheap seats and an excessive guest list (*Shocking!*).

Of the many Styles low points, the best-loved classic remains its big grunge feature, which appeared on November 15, 1992—well over a year after Nirvana's *Nevermind* success. A full-size action photo of Kurt Cobain and shots of designer Marc Jacobs's goofy grunge fashion adorned the front page, while inside the section, a picture of a couple of *Ecch* types bore the caption "In downtown Manhattan, the flannel shirt is becoming an accessory as common as the baseball cap worn backwards." Proving the planned obsolescence of any fashion trend, grunge or otherwise, the bottom of the page contained an ad for a new department of Macy's devoted to goods inspired by Francis Ford Coppola's awful *Bram Stoker's Dracula.* Nuff said.

As if Styles' belated bandwagon-hopping wasn't enough, there was also the infamous sidebar "Lexicon of Grunge: Breaking the Code." The *Times'* intrepid reporter had discovered Seattle's exciting new grunge lingo, which included definitions like "harsh realm" for the outdated "bummer," and "cob nobbler" for anyone who could be described as a loser. Unfortunately for the *Times,* the new jive was a hoax perpetrated by Megan Jasper, a twenty-five-year-old ex–Sub

Pop employee (which, in the *Times'* eyes, makes her a grunge "expert"). The *Times* took a beating in the underground media, but let's be fair: How exactly do you fact-check the correct usage of an expression like "swingin' on the flippity flop?"

If it's true that Styles put the kibosh on hipitude—and it is—then this generational thing should have peaked on Valentine's Day 1993, when Styles joined the *Ecch* fray. As always, its efforts were too little, too late. The piece, creatively titled "The Name Game," contributed no new thoughts to the information waste stream apart from an unprecedented assortment of proposed *Ecch* nomenclature, including, amidst the usual "Generation X," "slackers" and "twentysomethings": "technobabies," "videos," "boomernots," "cyborgs," "posties," "protos" (for "proto-adults"), "borders," "downbeats," "mall rats," "nowheres," "burn-outs," "remotes," "steroids," "junkies," "the cable generation," "metamorphs," "Bradys," and "sparse."

Sparse?!?

In fact, *Ecch* is the second-largest group of young people in American history, after you-know-who. We purchase $125 billion worth of goods and services every year, a statistic that marketers and advertisers were bound to take note of.

Sho'nuff, the business and advertising publications were the next segment of the media to leech onto the Story of *Ecch*. Both *Business Week* and *Advertising Age* checked in with cover articles unashamedly aimed at corporate America. "The busters are here, and they're angry," *Ad Age* declared. What are they angry about? Apparently, that there aren't enough commercials directed at them.

Quoted in almost all the *Ecch* marketing articles is Karen Ritchie, senior vice-president and director of media services at the McCann-Erickson ad agency. Her speech at a magazine publishers' convention in the fall of 1992 was single-handedly responsible for Madison Ave.'s *Ecch* wake-up call. She suggested that the cultural dominance of boomers is, like the boomers themselves, old and tired: "Lately, when

I look at my little brother the baby boomer, I see a forty-five-year-old man with a potbelly, a bald spot and his own corporation." It was time for advertisers to pay attention to the generation whose wallets will drive American culture for the next thirty years. Ritchie jokingly refers to *Ecch* as "purple-haired people," but what she's really saying is, *Ecch* money is still green.

To help marketers along, Condé Nast fashion mag *Mademoiselle* commissioned a Roper Group study, *Twentysomething: The New Individual*, which is where most articles get their fountain of *Ecch* statistics from. The magazine, which has attempted to remodel itself as an *Ecch* version of *Cosmo*, also began publishing *Twenty Twenty Insight*, a trade newsletter providing "news and information about marketing to 20–29 year olds," which contains such crucial information as "advertiser-friendly alternatives" to the usual *Ecch* labels, like "voracious shoppers" instead of "mall rats," and "active" instead of "skate punks."

*Twenty Twenty Insight* says that, according to the Roper Group, the Twentysomething generation (which, by the way, is capitalized here) "actually *enjoys* advertising and are *less cynical* towards marketers and advertisers than baby boomers were in the '60s." Judith Langer, the president of Langer Associates, claims that "rather than rejecting marketers and the media as manipulators, as the young did during the 1960s, some twentysomethings enjoy being part of the game themselves. They *enjoy* advertising which says, in effect, 'Yeah, we know this is dopey, but isn't it fun?'"

These observations totally contradict the standard take on *Ecch*'s relationship with advertising. *Business Week* characterized *Ecch* as "far more knowledgeable about and suspicious of advertising than earlier generations passing through their twenties ... they're tremendously cynical because they know the media is most often talking to them to sell them something." Allegedly, *Ecch* is just too bright and too cool to be suckered by the usual Mad. Ave. inveiglement. "If anything is seen as mainstream, they lose interest," one shiller told the advertising columnist in the New York *Daily News*.

So how does one market to *Ecch*? Subaru tried with a now infamous ad featuring a slovenly *Ecch*ster pitching the 1993 Impreza. Circling the vehicle as if caught in a slow mosh, the kid denounced other automobiles as "boring and corporate" and proclaimed that "*this* car . . . is like *punk rock.*" *Yeah, in its first year they only sold five thousand of 'em, but in fifteen years it'll go to #1.* The campaign turned out to be a one-car pileup, and Subaru even fired ad biggies Wieden & Kennedy, the geniuses behind Nike's "Just Do It" campaigns.

Merely marketing a car wasn't enough, so Chrysler decided to make one specifically for *Ecch*: the Neon. (Hi!) "This car is targeted for people in their mid to late twenties and their early thirties," Chrysler chairman Robert Eaton told *The New York Times.* "People who are now in the market with a different values system. And I can't imagine a better name for this vehicle with the generation we're going after."

Oh yeah? How about The Chrysler *Nirvana*—just fill the tank up with heroin (*Talk about horse power!*) and sink back into a lush interior of rich Corinthian flannel. . . .

As you tool about the 'burbs in your new Nirvana, you'll probably want to drink. Schiefellin & Somerset, the American importer of Dewar's White Label Scotch, is hoping that you'll forgo the brewskies in favor of its elegant intoxicant. It seems that *Ecch*sters shun the so-called "brown goods" (bourbon, Scotch, rye) in favor of vodka, gin, beer and wine coolers. So, like everybody else, Dewar's commenced with an *Ecch*centric magazine ad campaign. "You thought girls were yucky once too," the ad taunts, adjacent to a shot of an unattainable beauty. Geez, if you're in your twenties and the word "yucky" still appeals to you, you should probably stick to wine coolers.

If the Scotch manufacturers were smart, they'd bypass the "brown" problem entirely. Clearly, the booze of the future will be Dewar's Crystal Ultimate. Or Johnnie Walker Clear. Or maybe Jack Daniel's Lite. We can see the ad slogans now: *Your judgment may be clouded, but your drink won't be.*

There's no straight answer on how marketers can reach *Ecch*, but spokesman/cob nobbler Douglas Coupland has a suggestion, despite his previously stated intentions to remove himself from this debate.

He told *Twenty Twenty Insight* that "it comes as a great shock to me that advertisers have failed to tap the one genuine icon of the Xers—the Brady Bunch—as spokespeople. I would buy dirt if Maureen McCormick endorsed it. I would buy used tea bags if Eve Plumb said I should." Obviously, Doug is a little loopy from all that chicken fried in Wesson oil. "I Am Not a Target Market," a chapter title in *Generation X* proclaims. Yeah, right.

The mass media's mercenary *Ecch* frenzy was both reductionist and generalistic in its constant kvetching. Unfortunately, the only people who took the trendy magazines to task were the many *Ecch*sters working in the media biz themselves. Their attempts at intellectual self-defense were so whiny and simpleminded that they merely hammered home the arguments made by *Time* et al.

Writing in that well-known *Ecch* journal, the Op-Ed page of *The New York Times*, Alexander Abrams and David Lipsky, a writer and lawyer, respectively, pitched a conniption fit. Why? Because they, as two upstanding aspiring postyups, have been lumped in with the younger soldiers of *Ecch*, aka the "grunge kids" (a term they use no fewer than four times).

According to them, the matter most troubling to the elder end of *Generation Ecch* is their inability to be boomers—to live the boomer lifestyle, to drive Saabs instead of Civics, to work on Wall Street instead of at Wal-Mart. "Call us boomlets, if you have to call us anything. . . ." *Just don't call us late for dinner.*

The "boomlets" are a bunch with "easily identifiable tastes and . . . irresistible purchasing power," and Messrs. Dave and Alex are peeved that they're getting passed over. "No one we know listens to Pearl Jam and Nirvana . . . [or] read Douglas Coupland's *Generation X*," they continue. Actually, "boomlets" prefer 10,000 Maniacs and R.E.M., Abrams & Lipsky insist, claming that it's impossible for the same generational image to encompass both George Stephanopoulos and Marky Mark. "Imagine George Stephanopoulos showing up for work with Soundgarden blasting out of a Walkman." No, but we can imagine him cranking up the White House stereo with the garage rock of Gumball, the band managed by George's brother Andrew.

Equally out of touch at another end of the *Ecch* spectrum is the Northern California magazine *Soma*, whose Phil Busse and Rebecca Paoletti are very angry about the name game's suggestion that *Ecch* has no identity, "no distinctive qualities or attitude."

"Piss off!" they swear, distinctively and attitudinally. Hey, kids, lighten up! Two words for you: Pro-zac.

Busse and Paoletti ought to realize that if they want to defend a generation that's considered to be trite and stupid, they should learn how to spell first, particularly when their misspellings include "Wily E. Coyote," for "Wile E. Coyote" and "Dali Llama" for "Dalai Lama." Discussing a superhero conglomerate called the "League of Justice" instead of the "Justice League of America," they even screw up their pop-culture references, which in some circles is grounds for *Ecch*-communication. C'mon, guys, everyone knows the League of Justice was that international organization formed by Woodrow Wilson after the First World War. These guys may live in the valley called Soma, but it looks to us as if they've been taking it.

Tom Frank and Keith White, writing in the obscure culture journal *The Baffler*, are annoyed that all the labels are boomer-generated. They claim it's the boomers who are worrying about this stuff, not *Ecch*. True enough, but too many *Ecch*sters have taken it lying down, tacitly supporting the whole scam by complaining about it, or by writing articles (or books) opposing it.

Frank and White go on to speak for what appears to be their little world of nonconformist indie-rock slackers, claiming that "our youthful vision of the world was more influenced by Minor Threat than the Partridge Family." In this case, "our" would only apply to the 1 percent of *Ecch*sters who know who Minor Threat is. *The Baffler* asserts that punk and 1977 changed the way *Ecch* looked at the world forever, so that "we could no longer buy the mainstream American dream." But you can bet there are millions more *Ecch*sters buying the "mainstream American dream" than *The Baffler*.

"We are *twentynothing!*" they avow, "forever lost to your suburban platitudes, lost to the simple blather of your TV"—*Say it!*—"deaf to your non-politics, hopelessly estranged from your cult of professionalism, the brain deadening architecture of your office complexes . . ." *Testify, brother!*—"Our youth has been a classroom of resistance in which we have learned how to free ourselves from the grasp of understanding your manipulation." *Hallelujah!*

*Exsqueeze me? Baking powder?* What is this bullshit? Most people of *Ecch* wouldn't know a platitude from a platypus, although "blather" is something they're quite familiar with.

These *Ecch* rebutters are nothing but obscure and elite media children defending *themselves*, perhaps successfully, but without any relevance to the forty-seven and a half million members of the generation who aren't as "cool" as they are. It's as if these writers say, "Hey, I'm not like that, so my generation isn't either and they shouldn't say these things," a generalization as specious as anything from *Time* or *Business Week.*

A word of advice to all you yo-yos wasting precious TV time thinking about this nonsense: Get over it. Go live your life. Is it worth expending what little energy you have worrying what friggin' *U.S. News & World Report* says about people your age? Just worry about yourself, one of the few things the generation is supposed to be good at, and chill out. Okay? It's not that big a deal.

Try to imagine a world where everybody's dreams and desires are geared around success in show biz. There are no architects or plumbers or appliance salesmen here, only artists and comedians, rockers and rappers, dancers and music critics. In this world, regular jobs are in short supply, but real problems hardly ever arise, since everyone is preoccupied with the pettier aspects of day-to-day existence. You know, important crises like who's attracted to whom, whose self-esteem is wounded, who likes what kind of music. This is of course, a multicultural place, with blacks and whites, straights and gays, Evangelicals and Muslims, crackers and city kids, all occupying the same space, though not always in perfect harmony. But everyone looks really cool and life, filled with exciting adventures like auditions and recording sessions, is a never-ending roller-coaster ride of melodrama and excitement.

This may sound like some bizarre flight of fancy or exercise in imagination—but this is the world where *Generation Ecch* resides. Yes folks, this is the real world. More precisely, this is *The Real World.*

The first season of MTV's mockudramedy chronicled five months in the life of seven *Ecch* strangers who opted to reside together in a spacious Manhattan loft under the watchful eye of MTV's camera. It was like a bizarre lab test on a grand scale, the objective being to document either a diverse group's discovery, appreciation and increased understanding of Others or the abject, willing self-humiliation of a bunch of jerks.

But what would drive someone to live every moment in front of millions of television viewers? Is it the idea of shacking up (*rent-free!*) in truly bitchin' digs, if only for a few months? Or is it the desire to participate in a noble experiment to get under the skin of a generation? Fact is, only *Ecch* kids lusting for (career) exposure would be willing to be so (personally) exposed.

Though *Ecch*'s forty-eight million include lawyers and stockbrokers, bricklayers and secretaries, homeless people and drug addicts, true *Ecch*sters are creatures certain that they were born and raised to bask in the cathode spotlight. As such, the first *Real World* crew consisted of a rapper, a poet/rock critic, a grunge-band loser, a female folkie, a bisexual artist, a heterosexual model, and a ballet dancing naïf. Utter perf-*Ecch*-tion, no?

When *The Real World* debuted in 1992, nabobs and pundits wailed that the network's chosen cross-section of young America was, on the one hand, tokenistic—among the group were two black characters (one male, one female), a gay man and an innocent Southern belle—and on the other, elitist and unrepresentative—all the kids were *artistes* of one kind of another, living the hep Soho-Boho existence while the majority of young Americans toiled in classrooms and offices, fast food chains and antiseptic malls.

As with the hype over *Ecch* ennui, this is where criticisms of the show really jumped off the rails. Once again, the media kvetching and handwringing missed the big truths, the ones that lie at the heart of *The Real World*, at the heart of MTV, and, most importantly, at the heart of *Ecch*. *The Real World* is a complete expression of the universe the generation lives in. Our modern world is one where people routinely reveal their most intimate and perverse secrets before the eye of the camera for Montel, Oprah or, God help us, Richard Bey. Where news is entertainment and entertainment news is the best news of all—as rap music is to the African-American community (that is, as Chuck D once said, the black man's CNN), E! Entertainment Television is to *Ecch*. Where every single member of the generation can dream that they're just a phone call from Lorne Michaels away from nabbing a late night talk show. There is no nobler pursuit for *Ecch* than pseudo-celebrity.

*T*he *Real World* is truly a TV show about TV: Take a bunch of people who watch a lot of TV, people that desperately want to *be* on TV, and ... *put them on TV*. (Oddly, despite living together in the same apartment and spending so much time hanging around, the *Real* kids barely watched the tube. This is a common feature of the American television show—*All in the Family* aside, TV didn't really discover TV until the working class clans of *Roseanne*, *Married with Children*, and *The Simpsons* came along. People sitting around watching television just doesn't make very good television.)

*The Real World* #1 was also a very, very real deconstruction of *Ecch* multiculturalism. "What happens when people stop being polite and start being real?" the show's voice-over tantalizes. Well, black or white, it would seem that they show their true bigoted colors. This gang moved into their happening Soho loft with gigundo ethnic chips on their shoulder. In the first episode, when rapper Heather's beeper goes off (she had important business with hip-hop star KRS-One), JuliefromAlabama asks, "Are you a drug dealer?" From there on, every typical roommate squabble—essentially all the show is ever about, as in "Who's turn is it to do the dishes," "Get off the phone," and "I need the bathroom"—became a portentous racial conflict. The show's producers (not to mention the *Ecch* stars themselves) did everything they could to portray the battles between Eric the model and Kevin the angry black poet as a heavy-duty cultural misunderstanding. It never seemed to occur to anyone that the real problem was that hot'n'shallow Eric was an annoying asshole, and so, for that matter, was Kevin.

Needless to say, *The Real World* was lambasted by critics and viewers alike for violating the sanctity of its video *vérité* objective. Hundreds of hours of footage were compressed and distorted into weekly twenty-two-minute packages, and the corrupt producers manipulated the lives of the subjects to stimulate sexual and racial sparks. *Shocking!* Critiquing *The Real World*'s media-massaged artifice is pointless—no one has ever confused MTV with Frederick Wiseman. And even if there was good reason to hold *The Real World* to the exacting standards of the serious documentarian, the verisimilitude of all documentaries is automatically a few degrees removed from "objective reality." Put some people in front of a camera and what you get is not a record of people doing things, but a record of people doing things in front of a camera.

In fact, the show's producers threw out any pretense of *vérité* reality right off the bat, choosing to cut the shows together with a combination of in-house action and talking heads interviews. This technique makes the show seem more like a documentary and less like uninterrupted video eavesdropping. More importantly, it allowed the characters to ramble on about their injured egos and innermost thoughts for the camera.

MTV enabled these kids to become true artist/slackers for a few months, and everything about their world—the way they acted, the way they dressed, the political correctness and cultural differences, the way they made a living and the size of their brains—was 100 percent certified *Ecch*. It is life MTV-style, lived by the MTV generation in front of viewers yearning for the MTV lifestyle.

For all the gorgeous magazine layouts and nonstop attention this crowd received as the first citizens of *The Real World*, the New York crew really hasn't gotten much mileage out of their time on MTV. Becky the folkie is a bartender—she recently formed a new band, *Les Enfants Terribles*, but they "aren't ready to play out yet." Andre, the rockin' frontman of Reigndance, and Heather the rapper, are working at pretty much the same level of fame as they were before, i.e., none. Norman still paints, as obscure as he was before moving into *The Real World*—even in real life situations, TV producers couldn't figure out what to do with the gay character. Kevin the poet/critic has been lucky enough to preserve his credibility as a writer, currently working at the African American culture mag *Vibe*. Only male model Eric, who, not coincidentally, is even less liked by the cast now than he was then, has made out, getting hired by MTV to host its afternoon flesh fest/dance party *The Grind*. He's very, very happening, especially if you ask him. Hey Eric, what do you suppose happened to Downtown Julie Brown? (Actually, she's on MTV-ish ESPN2, undoubtedly the closest thing to purgatory in a cable box.)

**A**t this point, it was our most sincere intention to quote Neil Postman, the perspicacious writer and thinker noted for his savage, skeptical critiques of television. But we accidentally taped over his most recent *Charlie Rose* appearance. Aw, who are we kidding—we haven't watched Charlie Rose since he stopped working the *Nightwatch* graveyard shift—his new gig is way too highbrow (it's a salon, y'know).

It's not exactly news that the baby boomers were the first generation to be raised in the age of TV, while *Ecch* is the first generation to be raised *by* TV. The electronic babysitter, the glass nipple, *Amusing Ourselves to Death*—you know the drill. The picture tube was our womb, the screen our placenta, the cable box our teat.

And the milk that flowed into *Ecch*'s growing minds and bodies was pure, unhomogenized MTV. The basic take on the vid net is that it was the final nail in the coffin of *Ecch*'s short attention span. You didn't have to concentrate on it for more than a minute. It ruined music by providing prefabricated images for every popular song. It was always *on*, its images rushing through the brainpan, demanding that you make it part of your life rather than a simple viewing experience.

But that was the MTV of old, the MTV of all music videos all the time, the MTV of Martha Quinn and Cyndi Lauper, the MTV where you never saw any African Americans except for J. J. Jackson (and, let's face it, he wasn't all that black to begin with), the MTV of "Rio" and "Karma Chameleon" and Billy Squier singing that really stupid Christmas song. In the '90s, MTV has become much more than just a dopey video channel. It has become the agenda-setter for *Ecch*'s life, the main conduit of style, culture and politics for a generation.

For example, sometime in the mid '80s, the network wised up and introduced black music to their programming. As hip-hop took over the pop consciousness, MTV loaded up their rotation with rap and r'n'b. One assumes that demographic studies told the MTV bigwigs that a) white people dig the stuff in a big way, and b) that black people indeed possessed cable, and not only that, they bought stuff, too!

Anyway, now there are MTV game shows, MTV talk shows, MTV cartoon shows and, most importantly, MTV News, which is not just for rock'n'rollers anymore.

*Ecch*'s anchorperson of choice isn't some blow-dried Peter, Tom, or Connie. Our Murrow didn't make his bones covering any war. For Kurt Loder, MTV's dashing and intrepid newsreader, the warzone was the offices of *Rolling Stone* magazine, where he toiled for years as a rock critic. But his good looks and charm made him a star at the video network, an earth-toned Walter Cronkite for the new generation: "This week, Billy Idol filmed the seventh video from his *Cyberpunk* lp, and *you are there!*"

"The Week In Rock" became a *MacNeil-Lehrer Report* for a demographic group disinterested in economic summits or political roundtables. Millions of *Ecch* viewers saw history unfold during the weekly wrap-up. Who among us can forget Loder's famous grilling of Axl Rose over his involvement in Iran-Contra? (Actually, MTV News did help elect a president—but more on that later.)

When not busy chronicling the continuing adventures of Whitney and Bobby, the MTV news department has branched out into the documentary arena, producing socially significant *Ecch* infotainment about guns, racism, sex and the other Seven Deadly Sins (Avarice and Sloth are big MTV favorites), tackling the big issues with that special MTV combination of simplemindedness, zealousness, and hip 'tude.

That with-it point of view is visualized through that most irritating of MTV innovations, the constantly moving camera, or, the "Dockers"-cam. *Whoosh! Look over There!* It's hard to trace the origin of the style, though it seemed to take hold with *Miami Vice*, which for all intents and purposes *was* MTV. *Zoom! Now look up!* From there on in, all commercials, all videos—hell, just about everything—looked like it was photographed by Michael Ballhaus with a head full of 'ludes. *Swish! Now look over there, on the floor!* This spastic, agitated viewpoint became the *Ecch* way of seeing, as if their heads were constantly lolling about on their shoulders like slobbering imbeciles.

Every news division needs a vapid, unctuous sportscaster, and MTV has the horror-show *Ecch* hero, Dan Cortese. *MTV Sports* (creative name, huh?) follows our boy Dan's escapades in "extreme" athletics like bungee jumping, sky surfing, or dating. The wacky camera made Cortese a star of sorts, starring in irritating Burger King commercials and an irritating TV remake of a classic series. (C'mon. Surely you remember his stirring performance in 1993's *Route 66.*) Subsequently, he co-starred in a CBS cop drama, *Traps,* with George C. Scott, marking the all-time low point in a career (Scott's, that is) that's had its fair share of potholes. (Maybe they should have teamed up with Trish Van Devere for a sequel to the Scotts' classic incest movie *The Savage is Loose.*)

MTV today, then, is not just a part of the *Ecch* lifestyle. It *is* the *Ecch* lifestyle. News, information, vicarious thrills and *Unplugged*—what more does a person need?

The New York *Real World* kids may have been the frontiersmen of *Ecch* reality-TV, but the second season was where the show really articulated the MTV/*Ecch* lifestyle to the fullest, with a perfect mesh of somber social commentary and completely frivolous entertainment. The action moved to Los Angeles for the next go-round—we know this because the show opens with shots of the Capitol Records building and girls in bikinis. The L. A. *Real World* bunch were placed in a

$2 million house in Venice Beach, but aside from the geographical transplant, the formula didn't change much.

This group numbered among them one black female diva, one black male comedian, one grungy alcoholic Irish music and TV critic, one female wannabe actress, one Hispanic policewoman, one heterosexual surfer Republican, and one Southern country singing naïf. The balance was off a little bit, so they married off the only normal person, the policewoman, and replaced her with a lesbian (the black male comedian didn't last either, but that's a whole other story).

The season actually began in Kentucky, where Tami, the En Vogue wannabe and perhaps the world's only homophobic HIV clinic worker, joined up with Dominic, the Irish rock critic. Like the other members of the cast, Dominic was picked largely because of his heritage—accents are *cool*. The Dommer, as he's affectionately known, really was one of the cooler members of either *Real World*—he goes skiing in his leather jacket and his spiky hair could qualify as the eighth wonder of the world. He's like a cross between one of *The Commitments* and the evil *Leprechaun*. As the resident alternative music expert on the show, he can't help but remind you of the dreadful former *120 Minutes* host Dave Kendall. He's said to be under contract to MTV since the end of the show, and if there's any justice they're grooming him to replace Lewis Largent.

The hipster mick and the vapid black beauty were given the keys to a Winnebago and sent down South to pick up Jon, eighteen years old, fundamentally Christian and a local country music sensation, complete with his own line of Jon sweatshirts and big hats and autographed pictures. Even this early on, viewers can tell that it's not going to be the same for Jon when he's sharing the stage at the Palomino with stripper-turned-belter Candye Kane.

The evil genius of the show is all laid out in advance—it doesn't take an Einstein to figure out what kind of conflicts will arise for this heroic trio. Jon, being the good monotheist that he is, is derisive when he finds out Tami is a chanting Buddhist as well as an Afrocentric Muslim. Partly because of this, and partly out of pure preconception, Tami assumes that Jon, being a good ol' Southern monotheist, is a racist. Dominic manages to stay above the fray, ethnocentrically speaking. (Later, because he's Irish and likes beer, everyone thinks that Dom's a drunk. Also, the cast became annoyed because every time it's Dominic's turn to cook all he ever makes is potatoes: new potatoes,

potatoes *au gratin*, mashed potatoes, potato *souffle*, stuffed potatoes, baked potatoes, *stuffed baked* potatoes—even potato latkes.)

Upon arriving in Venice, we get to meet the rest of the housemates. There's Aaron, the blonde surfer boy who's majoring in economics at UCLA, which makes him something like a cross between Eddie Vedder and Mick Jagger. Except he doesn't sing and is really dull. Then there's Beth, the *zaftig* movie-biz hanger-on: "I do production work, a lot of PA work," she explains. "I love the entertainment industry. I want to direct, and I want to produce. I'm interested in acting, too." (Note to those of you expecting an actual joke here—do you really think one is necessary?)

Irene is a Chicana cop, who's far too normal and well-adjusted for her to be of any use to the series. (Later, she marries and moves out, to be replaced by Beth Anthony, a crewcut lesbian. *Aah, that's better!*) Finally, there's David, an angry black stand-up comic, who instantly gets on everyone's nerves with his loud, obnoxious demeanor and all-around bad manners.

For these kids of Cali (and Dom), Jon is a person totally outside their usual frame of reference. But their first reaction is not to view him as a new and unusual human being—instead, Dominic says he finds Jon to be "such a cliché . . . a Hollywood creation." The punch line, of course, is that *everyone* on *The Real World* is. Jon, for his part, finds Tami and Dominic to be "strange." Translation, *Ecch* and *Real World* style: Jon *is* a racist! But he's also a sweet, well-meaning kid who rarely imposes his own old-fashioned beliefs on the others. "I don't mean to stereotype people," he explains in one of those helpful interview segments.

Hey, Jon, don't worry about it—MTV has taken care of that for you in advance. The show asks the multicultural question on everyone's mind since the Rodney King incident: "Can we all get along?" Apparently, the answer is "No."

When Dominic asks angry black stand-up comic David where he was from, David says "Africa." Later, David's Malcolm X shirt prompts Jon to put a Confederate flag up in the bedroom the two of them were sharing. No one was as amused as they should have been.

The difference between *The Real World* #1 and *The Real World* #2 is that the second cast was aware of the first one's experiences. Serendipitously, David's beeper goes off in the second episode and Jon, right in character and right on time, asks, "Do you sell drugs?"

David freaks out, before it's explained to him that Jon was actually making a playful reference to the first episode of the first *Real World*. Jon's a postmodernist and he doesn't even know it. They don't teach Fredric Jameson at many Kentucky high schools.

Structurally, there was one major revelation/addition in the second year—in order to better facilitate the personal monologues that tie together the so-called action, one room in the house is a "confession room," a solitary space with a single camera and some cloudy wallpaper that looks like the backdrop of a Sears photography studio. The roomies are expected to go to confession once a week, and amazingly, when they go, they actually reveal their deepest thoughts and emotions. Hey, there might be an agent watching!

The star of the show, of course, is the omnipresent camera. Amazingly, the reality of constant observation and thirty-six crew members in a back room rarely intrudes when the cast is at the house. But outside, in the um, er . . . world, the MTV tagalongs are much more problematic. F'rinstance, David finds that they make for an excellent icebreaker when you're hitting on scantily clad women strolling up and down Melrose Ave. At one point, Beth takes the gang to a fancy-shmancy Beverly Hills party that they weren't exactly invited to. Ordinarily, it's easy to do such a thing—you walk in, grab a drink, act as if you belong, and chat some people up. But it's hard to crash an exclusive *soiree* when you're carrying a camera crew with ya. Our heroes wind up getting kicked out by the party's hostess, who is obviously far too sensible to be living in L.A. She could've been on MTV, but maybe she didn't want her parents to know she was having a party. Other situations—an Inspiral Carpets gig, Jon and Irene's night out at the suburban shitkicker bar, an evening of bowling— seem more natural, but of course arrangements had to be made with these places in advance to accomodate the camera corps.

Any multiple-roommate situation automatically resembles college life, and as such, childish fraternity-style hijinks abound on *The Real World*. Dom is fond of telling Beth that her cat fell down the stairs, while Beth slips into Dominic's room one late drunken night to peek at his boxers. Jon and Aaron steal Dom's car and tell him it got towed. Dom catches Jon fucking his dog while Beth watches. (Alright, you caught us. We made that one up. Happy now?) Aaron and Dominic load Jon's Kool-Aid with extra sugar. You keep praying for some angry viewer to turn up and spike the Kool-Aid with something that smells like almonds: *Stay tuned to MTV for* The Real World: The Afterlife. *Where people stop being polite, and start being dead. On tonight's episode, Jon makes fun of Tami because he has a better view in heaven, but she gets the last laugh when it turns out that Jesus really* was *black! Sorry, Jon. Also, Dominic gets fired from his job at Celestial Variety when he gives Jack Benny a bad review!*

College life also means Spring Break!, and if there's one thing MTV knows about, it's Spring Break! The first season, the female cast members jetted down to Jamaica, but things fell apart when Becky had an affair with the director, who was fired from the show, only to return as a peripheral cast member: Becky's boyfriend. For the second year, the entire group went on an Outward Bound excursion deep in Joshua Tree Memorial Park, as well as a long weekend in Cozumel. Nice work if you can get it.

The magical hand of the MTV editors plays its role in instigating audience involvement. At one point, Tami remarks that her sex life is going to be a problem while she's living in the house. Cut to: no, not Aaron or Dominic—the most taboo kind of love is *too* real for this show—but to David. Now ignore the obvious racial pairing. What's truly hysterical about this bit of drama is that every cut has been made with the benefit of hindsight. The episodes are put together after the kids have already moved out and on. For this moment, the director set up this little taste of titillation and tension knowing full well that a few weeks later David would be accused of sexually harassing Tami.

Everything that makes *The Real World* #2 so damned fascinating is apparent in the way this very confused, very PC-sensitive, very *Ecch* group of seven strangers react when the nonstop entertainment, fratboy antics and low-grade sexual tension finally explode. The Troubles begin (*Calm down, Dom*) when David, a self-confessed chronic masturbator who is seen jonesing for Tami in the early episodes, is goofing around in the girls' bedroom and decides to pull the covers off Tami, who sleeps in her underwear. Tami protests and screams, albeit with some good humor. Beth, giggling, joins the fray as well, jumping on Tami to protect her. The problem, of course, is not so much that Tami doesn't want David to see her skivvies—she doesn't want millions of MTV viewers to see them. David, who has proved himself to be a hostile jerk time and again, takes things a little too far, getting more physical than today's woman will tolerate. Tami feels harassed and humiliated. Mostly humiliated—her ego is bruised more than anything else. She responds by trashing some of David's stuff and walking out in the middle of the night to sulk.

More wacky *Real World* tension, right? Well, no. For some reason Beth, who loves being in front of the camera (*"I want to direct, and produce, and I also want to act"*) decides to become Tami's personal champion. She decides that David's refusal to stop goofing off when Tami said "No" is the equivalent of someone refusing to stop when someone says "No" in a sexual situation. Beth tells the bewildered group that David is like a rapist, and the next day the girls decide they don't feel safe with this scary black man in the house. Jon blames it on rap music (he's really a good guy, we swear).

Whatever manipulation MTV may engage in over the usual course of the show, in this case they seemed to stay out of it. Of course, this is probably complete bullshit—no doubt there were probably quite a few panicky meetings between the cast and the producers. More appetizing is the possibility that they picked David out hoping for this kind of hostile conflict. At any rate, after a house meeting, which consisted of browbeating the boys into going along, the girls kick David out of the house. He was a prick, but they turned him into a demon.

David's sad departure points up the simple reason why the *Real World* is compelling. Contrived or not, representative or not, stupid or not, genuine or not, the people on the show are still real. Not only did the tribunal put this kid out on the street, they made him into a monster for all the world to see. David is a real person, but the viewers end up judging, mocking, or identifying with him like he was a fictional character. He's just out there, trying to continue his comedy career. (David has been on *Comic Strip Live* as well as *In Living Color* and *Def Comedy Jam*—*Yo, homeboys, how many of yas are here with your bitch!? Woof-woof-woof-woof! Yo, y'all ever go down on your hos? That's crazy man! Crazy!*) Long after the other *Real World* denizens have faded into oblivion, David alone will have a place in *Ecch* history. He's not an actor, but he's saddled with the character he played on TV in a way that makes Gary Coleman's struggle look easy.

After David's exile, the gang goes about auditioning roommates and—get this—they pass on a homeless shelter manager and a Olympic track star, both black males, in favor of Glen, a white guy who plays in a grunge-rock band! Glen is a rock'n'roll visionary waiting to happen—just ask him: "I have lyrics in my head but I haven't actually written any down."

Show business definitely rules the roost in *Real World* territory. The house is perpetually littered with copies of *Variety* and *The Hollywood Reporter*—this is L.A., after all. (It's also perpetually littered with dirty dishes—these are *Ecch*sters, after all.) These kids are all interested in one thing: stardom, glorious stardom! Why else would they be here?

So we see Tami at rehearsal with her act, Reality. Reality bite. We get Glen at rehearsal with his band, Perch. Perch suck. Even more than Reality, actually. As a matter of fact, they all appear desolutely talentless, except for Jon, who's got a big country voice and fine stage presence. Over the course of the series, everybody manages to begrudgingly compliment Jon's music, though they all feel that his shit-kicker music is somehow less important than bad alternative rock or SWV rip-offs.

Most of the time, they're actively pursuing the attention of the camera. Perch come and live in the house. (Perch suck.) Dominic gets 'faced and passes out in the sand in Mexico. Aaron brings quite a few beautiful girls home. What's fascinating about the show is the "cast" tries to rationalize their participation as a growth experience, kind of like summer camp, or teen tours. As their months together wind down, they begin to regret the fact that they haven't really taken the time to get to know each other. But hey, as Tami puts it, "my life is not focused on making other people happy. My life is focused on making me happy." Tami is a perfect example of just how riveting, frustrating, and hilarious the *Real World* can be. On the one hand, she's self-centered and whiney (see above) as well as thoughtless (she gives no notice when she quits her job at an AIDS clinic) and homophobic (she's terrified that Beth Anthony might give her a friendly hug). She's also completely silly, getting her jaw wired shut to lose weight and going on *Studs*, where she attempts to cheat but loses anyway. On the other hand, her multiple instances of foolish behavior have to be balanced with the melodrama—her life as a homeless person, her abortion.

If Tami were a TV character, her life story would read like a ridiculous soap opera plot instead of the complicated, alternately silly and tragic true-life tale that it is. But the thing is, she *is* a TV character. The "reality" of the lives of the *Real World* kids cannot survive the tantalizing simulated world of television that engulfed them the minute they moved into the house. With the help of the editing, they all behave like characters, which is as it should be.

At the end of the show, Jon, always the most openminded of the bunch, says that they all learned that people can't be pegged according to stereotypes and narrow personality clichés. Perhaps Jon really did learn that during his twenty-two weeks in L.A., but what the viewer learns in twenty-two episodes is completely the opposite. For all the tearful farewells and reflective philosophizing that went on when the gang took their leave of each other, the final message of the show is, once again, no, we can't all get along.

*T*he *Real World* is the quintessential *Ecch* TV show not only because of its realization of the MTV ethos, but also because it encapsulates the essence of television's most important historical feature. Before television became so all-encompassing in the way it redefines the fabric of American life, the friendly little box's main job was to redefine the most sacred part of American life—the family. For *Ecch*, the nuclear family has achieved full meltdown, so it makes sense that the true kith and kin of the generation can be found on Nick at Nite or any other cable channel with time to fill. Familial interaction once took place gathered around the hearth; now it occurs *inside* the hearth's modern equivalent.

In the fifties, *Father Knows Best* encapsulated the Ike and Mamie Era mentality, showing elbow-patched Dad working nine to five, aproned Mom baking all day, and young Bud smoking cigars behind the garage. Of course, in real life Bud later got busted for selling reefer. (Kitten, incidentally, remains the all-time great child-actor disaster, turning tricks to pay for her heroin habit and ultimately winding up as a Jesus freak.) But Dad remained perfect, working at the hospital with that nice James Brolin and never drinking anything stronger than Sanka.

Times change, though, and in the Swingin' Sixties, monsters moved into pastoral TV suburbia. Well, *The Munsters* did, at least. Herman, Lily, Grandpa and Eddie (don't forget Spot!) were ironic, negative images of the *Leave It to Beaver* broods of the past. This family was so weird that the oddball was the square live-in relative, Marilyn. (What happened to her parents, anyway? Does Grandpa's laboratory hold the answers?) But underneath their creepy exterior, the Munsters were as "normal" as any TV tribe, the scariest thing about the series being the endless Paul Lynde guest shots.

Then, of course, there is *The Brady Bunch*, so frequently and inextricably linked with this generation that it's become boring to think about. It's pretty straightforward stuff—*Ecch* has suffered through divorce without healing, while the Bradys were all about divorce *with* healing, the perfect little family, even though we found out later that our perfect little dad may have been spending his nights cruising for rough trade with Sam the Butcher. Robert Massa of *The Village Voice* suggests that the show's true appeal lies in the extra air of sexual tension provided by accidental incest—after all, Greg and Marcia weren't really related, so it would have been okay. As a matter of fact, it sounds like a two-parter!

*The Brady Bunch* went off the air in 1974, but lived on in reruns forever after. In '91 the revival hit its boiling point with *The Real Live Brady Bunch*, which was nothing but old *Brady* episodes reenacted scene by scene and word for word by a Chicago theatrical troupe, with only mild helpings of irony. While the real Bradys went back on the air in a failed attempt at serious thirtysomething drama, the stage show went on to play to sold-out houses wherever it went.

*Ecch*'s deification of what Butt-head calls "the Bunch" has turned into a cottage industry for aging cast members. Barry Williams published a best-selling memoir and travels the continental U.S. giving paying students his patented Brady Bunch lecture. At long last removed from her consignment to Fantasy Island, Maureen McCormick made a comeback—she became a spokesperson for scumbags, got drooled over by Conan O'Brien, and played herself on *Herman's Head*.

*The Brady Bunch*, however, is diametrically opposed to *Ecch*'s favored triad of "real" family sitcoms: *Rosanne, Married with Children*, and *The Simpsons*. Not only are these three shows among the best-written series on TV, they all ostensibly document genuine, modern broods. Interestingly, the families portrayed here are all cartoons (one of them quite literally), and the realism lies in the fact that the progenitors and progeny bicker and fight constantly. Forget that Roseanne and Dan don't divorce or that Bud Bundy never goes into

Al and Peg's bedroom with a butcher knife. The simple fact is that since these decidedly unreal people argue, they are more like true American families.

**H**owever, *Ecch* families are different from those hallowed mom'n' pop clans. The ever-climbing divorce rate spawned a generation of single parent families, which in turn spawned a profusion of lame sitcoms about the difficulties of raising three sassy daughters after the wife has run off with another woman. Of course, the Harvard grads responsible for writing this dreck are influenced more by TV than the real crises in the American family. As such, shows like *Full House, Step by Step,* and *My Two Dads* are the spiritual descendants of *The Brady Bunch,* where single parents join together to raise *six* sassy kids.

For *Ecch,* family is an outdated concept. Today's youth brigade find their kith and kin in their friends, the peers that are the only ones that truly understand what they are going through. To find the stereotypical Ecch famiglia in their natural TV habitat, one need look no further than those two Fox addresses, *Beverly Hills 90210* and *Melrose Place.*

*Beverly Hills 90210* began its life as a standard-issue Fox kids drama, like *21 Jump Street* and *The New Adventures of Beans Baxter.* Network-wide, the bigwigs were shooting for the more-ignored demographics, like *Ecch* and black people. (Though one doesn't see any black people living in *90210* territory. Successful African-Americans reside in Bel Air.)

In the *90210* fantasy world, Brenda and Brandon Walsh move out to Hollywood from Deadwood, Minnesota, and find that life really is better in La-La-Land. It's not just a television cliché! It's real! On the other hand, their friends, who are not from Minnesota, lead miserable little lives. Trust funds and Corvettes can't always compensate when your parents are in rehab all the time. So with Brenda and Brandon's well-adjusted Midwestern folks acting as surrogate mom and dad, the gang lean on each other, helping each other cope with problems like date rape, midterms and what to do when Emily Valentine spikes your non-alcoholic drink with "U4IA" at a rave.

Jason (Brandon) Priestly and Luke (Dylan) Perry became instant teen idols, their moussed pompadours and happening sideburns creating a tizzy of pre-pubescent hormones. The media spent a great deal of time making Perry out to be some kind of high-haired wussy rebel icon, and the actor suffered incessant comparisons to James Dean. (Perry didn't suffer as much as Dean, though. He was a human ashtray.)

Shannen (Brenda) Doherty didn't adapt to fame well, getting into drunken fistfights on Sunset Strip, being generally abusive to everyone she came in contact with. Her behavior as a real person infected the audience perception of her character, spurring the brief "I Hate Brenda" fad. The hapless writers couldn't figure out a way to capitalize on their star's very public lunacy, and their lead character was relegated to a supporting role. Eventually, Doherty's antics—chronic lateness, disagreements with other cast members—got her fired from the show. But don't worry about the bad-tempered, breast-implanted bitch on wheels. She starred in a film with once-and-future beau Judd Nelson (with a nude scene!), and did a small layout in *Playboy*. Obviously this hellcat is one young actress to watch!

The gang finally graduated high school, moving on to the august halls of fictional California University. But *90210* is all about *Ecch* youth, the way they think, the way they act, the way they live. The cast are getting a little, shall we say, *mature* for their roles—Gabrielle Carteris must be pushing forty by now. This actually makes sense. *Ecch* is all about people in their twenties and thirties acting like teenagers. Creator Darren Star understood that the *90210* audience was growing up faster than his characters, and pube-time was over for that ever-growing demographic. These rapidly aging kiddies were through with the *Tiger Beat* puppy love fostered by *90210*. Nope, what they wanted now was hot, dirty *sex*, and lots of it. What could be done to satisfy the suddenly prurient *Ecch* viewer?

There was but one solution: spin off! The clique at Beverly Hills High were too formed by safe-sex PCism to allow for freewheeling fornicative entertainment, but *midtwenties college grads* could fuck all they wanted, with no parents or principals (principles?) to get in the way. According to broadcast standards, only "adults" can safely screw and screw and screw, without the hindrance of a preachy abortion subplot to maintain moral balance for the kids.

Undoubtedly Star felt the approaching tremors of *Ecch* beginning to assert itself into the culture. He knew that the generation weaned on television was ripe for exploitation, and there are few things in this world more exploitative than nighttime soaps. The great conceit of *Melrose Place* is that the twentysomething tenants of this supposedly lowrent complex (these college grads are still living in the dorm) suffer the same problems that *90210*'s original audience were now going through. You know, important spiritual dilemmas like how to achieve in a career, find the right combination of true love and transcendental sex and still manage to both tastefully decorate the apartment *and* work out every day? Star says he was inspired by his own twenties, "the most exciting time of my life—all expectation and fear, but also no responsibility, so you could party your brains out."

For all their stock soap characteristics, the band of bozos who populate the stucco-walled complex of *Melrose Place* are textbook examples of *Ecch* stereotypes.

### Billy:

An aspiring screenwriter in the early episodes, he's currently working at some *L.A. Style*-style magazine. Andrew Shue, who plays Billy, possesses an extraordinarily crooked mouth, perhaps due to his getting hit in the face with many soccer balls during a brief stint as a European footballer. With his snively, nasal, octave-too-high voice, Billy whines constantly, usually in tandem with his on-again, off-again roommate/girlfriend . . .

### Alison:

Herself the whiniest human being on earth, an ad exec who wears twentysomething business suits and is lousy at her job, constantly showing up late due to rape attempts, alcoholism, and sleeping with clients. She too whines a lot. Actress Courtney Thorne-Smith got an A in whining when she studied her Stanislavsky. Alison is pretty much a big idiot, doing idiotic things like, for example, while being stalked by a former boyfriend, working late, alone, with no light other than a small desk lamp. Kissing Parker Stevenson would be another good example of her chronic moronicness. She is in constant competition with her boss/nemesis . . .

### Amanda:

Portrayed by Heather Locklear. Nuff said. The character was introduced as a roadblock for Billy and Allison's romantic entanglement, and was directly responsible for the show's rise in popularity. You can't be what *People* calls a "*Dynasty* for Generation X" without a proper Queen Bitch. All the better if she was actually one of the stars of *Dynasty*. (Leave us not forget that both shows are Aaron Spelling productions.) When Billy finally chose to be with Alison, and it looked as if her usefulness was coming to an end, Amanda bought Melrose Place. Amanda is the oldest resident, and therefore the villain. She's pure *Ecch* nightmare, the evil midthirties yuppie who comes to the door to collect the rent, and possibly sleep with your boyfriend. *EEEEEEEEEK!*

### Jake:

Grant Show's character is the hunk of the show, as evidenced by the actor's *TV Guide* cover two weeks before the show even aired. A mechanic who takes off his shirt a lot, Jake is the representative of real men in a show populated by either sensitive guys or total pricks. We know he's a real man because he threw a refrigerator across the room during a fight with . . .

### Jo:

Daphne Zuniga (an actual *Ecch* film icon from her role in *The Sure Thing*) was brought in to replace actress Amy Locane after the producers realized that her Southern accent sucked. Jo's a N.Y. divorcée and freelance fashion photographer who relocated to L.A. in order to escape a deranged ex. Following her dumping of Jake after the Frigidaire incident, the only thing that keeps her on the show is the fact that Zuniga is the only nonblonde in the cast. Lives upstairs from . . .

### Jane:

Babelicious fashion designer (See Molly Ringwald in *Pretty in Pink*) and Chynna Phillips look-alike. Long-suffering. That's pretty much it. Divorced from . . .

### Michael:

A doctor, and therefore inherently a monster since the profession he chose was not in either the arts or the social sciences. He cheated on Jane with a beautiful redhead resident, who later "died" in a drunken car wreck that left the villain temporarily paralyzed . . . *and even MORE evil!*

**Matt:**

The token gay character, Matt never seems to get any, as that would be too weird for a large segment of the audience. (Though he and *90210*'s Brian Austin Green would make a faaabulous couple.) Matt formerly ran a shelter for runaways but city cutbacks caused him to find a real job, conveniently enough at the hospital with Dr. Michael.

The big difference between the denizens of Melrose Place and their younger counterparts down the strip in *90210* is that these older *Ecch*sters don't rely on each other to solve problems. In *The Real World*, Dom observes, "This ain't Melrose Place, we don't all love each other." (Obviously he hasn't been watching. And to think he's a professional TV critic!) The *Melrose Place*rs stab each other in the back and jump from sack to sack, making trouble and generating ratings. Fox's one-two punch of *90210* and *Melrose Place* has the highest *Ecch* demographic Nielsens, and yet another spinoff is in the works: *Models Inc.*, where *Ecch*-age mannequins can have life crises and soapy entanglements, but with a bonus. Bikinis! Bikinis! Bikinis! Who says you can't improve on perfection?

**R**ecently, while simultaneously watching MTV and perusing *SPIN*, we stumbled upon an interview with Neil Postman (in *SPIN*, that is—MTV was busy with a breaking story involving Tupac). We were surprised to discover that the perspicacious writer and thinker noted for his savage, skeptical critiques of television has written a bunch of things called *books*. He's much harder to understand in print than on PBS, but he's really really smart, and had a bunch of things to say about TV's effect on *Ecch*.

"... what is important here is not so much the content of the media but the experience of media itself. ... ," Postman writes. "Life, then, becomes a stylized, edited media event, and it is not inconceivable that in the 'completeness' of our immersion in media, we come to prefer medialife to reality."

To be perfectly honest, he was talking about TV's effect on "famine, suffering and violent death," but what's the diff?

Every *Ecch* filmmaker aspires to be the next Martin Scorsese, and on the surface, it would seem that at the moment Quentin Tarantino is the chosen one. How exactly do we know this? Well, for one thing, he's Italian. For another, he put Harvey Keitel in his first film. Oh yeah, and both directors share a definite taste for the visual impact of copious bloodletting.

There are further similarities: Keitel, the morally wracked antihero of *Mean Streets* makes frequent visits to a Little Italy church and prays to the Madonna. In Tarantino's debut, *Reservoir Dogs*, Keitel and his amoral antihero cronies trade lascivious repartee about Madonna.

In addition, Scorsese is known to have a home collection of videotapes and laser discs that dwarves, both qualitatively and quantitatively, the stock of your average neighborhood video store. Unless, of course, said rental joint happens to specialize in the work of Michael Powell. Tarantino, on the other hand, served his apprenticeship working as a clerk at one of those neighborhood establishments. This particular commonality is in reality a gaping difference: the difference between Martin Scorsese, cinematic artist, and Quentin Tarantino, echt-*Ecch*-film craftsman.

Scorsese is a scholar of the silver screen, using that knowledge to inform his aesthetic choices and animate his vision. Though he spent much of his youth wracked with debilitating asthma, barely venturing from his Little Italy neighborhood, the future director still led a life that brought him into contact with people whose daily concerns (*Hey, Little Marty! This vig is fuckin' killin' me!*) were more significant than whether or not their Super 8 demo was good enough to get them an internship with their friend's uncle the producer. When Little Marty attended NYU in the '60s, film school was not yet a cliché, just a genuine learning experience.

Quentin Tarantino, too, is a scholar of the movies, using that knowledge to inform . . . well, nothing! His familiarity with other people's work, indeed with the entire canvas of American popular culture, is

# Flatliners

## or

### *Auteurs sans*

### *Direction*

the sum total of his aesthetic choices and so-called "vision." Though he spent much of his youth wracked with the debilitating, humiliating name "Quentin," it didn't matter if the future director never left the house as long as the TV was plugged in. When Tarantino took his auto-didact's journey to the center of the video store shelves—in the '80s, it was *hard* to get into film school, clichéd though it may have been—he may have absorbed a few of the finer points of film technique, but mostly he filled his brain with moments, information, lines of dialogue, references. In short, the building blocks of *Ecch* cinema—minus any foundation of theme, originality or context.

*T*rue Romance was written at the height of QT's rent-boy stint, and it shows. Tarantino's script is rife with the kind of references that can only be gleaned by spending forty hours a week amongst the video store's voluminous wealth of cinema, assuming that you leave time on the weekends for collecting additional pop detritus from the comic shop, the rock club, the record store, USA, MTV and Nick at Nite. The script, sold to Hollywood before *Reservoir Dogs* hit, was not deemed important, artistically speaking. Thus it was given to the subtalented Brit commercial hack Tony Scott (director of *Top Gun, Days of Thunder, Beverley Hills Cop II*) slightly less-gifted sibling of Ridley, to turn into a potential forty-million-dollar grosser. According to Anne Thompson's annual "Grosses Gloss" in *Film Comment*, total rentals were around six.

The film opens in a neon-lit, smoke-filled bar, where our hero, Clarence (portrayed by the too old to live, too young for the part Christian Slater) is attempting to pick up a frowsy, platinum-dyed barfly by regaling her with Elvis worship. *Serious* worship: "If I had to fuck a guy, absolutely had to, I'd fuck Elvis," Christian says by way of seduction. Christian's next move is to invite her to a Sonny Chiba *triple*-feature. Even this obviously round-heeled bimbo has to reject the little weenie. If she had to fuck a guy, absolutely had to, it sure as hell wouldn't be this cob-nobbler.

So off he goes to his lowbrow film fest (*The Streetfighter, Return of the Streetfighter,* and *Sister Streetfighter*), the very picture of *Ecch couture* in his thrift-shop rockabilly garb and unwashed hair. Sitting blissfully in the third row, Clarence is surprised by Patricia Arquette's popcorn, which spills all over his head, not that you'd notice the difference between the grease in his hair and the fake butter available in the lobby. We in the audience, of course, are not surprised by this very traditional take on the concept of "meeting cute." Tarantino knows that *Ecch*sters have an extensive film vocabulary, and thus they appreciate the irony of such a Thirties meeting in a modern film.

Alabama—for that is the leopard-skinned girl's moniker—apologizes, brushing kernels out of Clarence's mop (*Yuck!*) and hopping over the seats to join him. It's clear that our boy is really hard up, because no matter how purdy a girl's vanilla-ice-cream-scoop titties are, no true film geek tolerates the interruption of movies, even if he has seen them already. The movies, that is, not the titties.

Anyway, they eventually leave the theater, and Alabama asks Clarence if he'd like to join her for "a piece of pie." (When it comes to pitching woo, Quentin is no Lord Byron). They head off to one of those old-fashioned diners, the kind that still make blue-plate specials, where they swap turn-ons and turn-offs in a booth. Huge clouds of gray smoke billow down the Detroit street. Light streams in through venetian blinds, making lines across their faces. Why? *'Cause it's a Tony Scott film!*

Clarence asks 'Bama her turn-ons and she says that she likes "Phil Spector, girl group stuff like 'He's a Rebel,' Mickey Rourke, and guys who appreciate the finer things in life, like sugar" (as Clarence dumps copious amounts of the stuff into his coffee). Welcome to Quentin Tarantino's fantasy world. It's not pretty, is it?

Clarence invites his new friend to his place of employment, a *COMICS SHOP!* ("Mostly I hang out, bullshit with customers, read comics.") Not exactly "Come weeth mee to thee Casbah," but it works. Clarence continues his mating pitch by asking if Alabama would like to see *Spider Man #1. Ooh baby! Peter Parker gets me hot!* For some reason though, he reads to her instead from a *Nick Fury, Agent of S.H.I.E.L.D.* mag, and they adjourn to his boudoir, located in the upper reaches of the store.

They boff, lit by more streetlight, then sit nekkid on the edge of the bed, facing an altar of candles and a very holy-looking Elvis bust. They take each other's hands before the King. Obviously, this is the real thing, love in the time of chlamydia.

Everything in this movie is sooo cool—from Clarence's Hong Kong kung fu posters to his window which opens up to a huge billboard where they go for the requisite postcoital cigarette scene. 'Bama, much moved by their passionate lovemaking, reveals that she's a call girl, hired by Clarence's boss as a birthday gift. Our streetwise hero isn't bothered by this. "At least you didn't have a dick," he says sweetly. *He knows all there is to know about the crying game.*

But 'Bama wants more. "I'm not what they call Florida white trash! I'm a good person!" she wails, declaring her undying love for her guy. Clarence knows a good thing when he sees it. Like his creator Tarantino, everything he knows is from popular culture, so it's not difficult for him to believe that he's such a great john that she'd gladly do him for free. Besides, she's obviously the stereotypical hooker-with-a-heart-of-gold, and apart from her profession, which is awfully darn cool in and of itself, she pretty much matches his qualifications for the ideal mate: "You like Elvis, you like Janis, you like *The Partridge Family* . . ."

"I don't like *The Partridge Family*, that was part of my act," giggles the no-longer-perfect girl.

The two go and get themselves married, and proceed to get tattooed like Johnny and Winona, then honeymoon in Clarence's pad. Clarence gets it into his roomy head (with some help, of course, from the ghost of Elvis, for that's the kind of movie this is) that in order to assert his manhood he has to kill 'Bama's pimp. That's what a character in a movie would do, and Clarence's character is based entirely on *being* a character. He's like a greasy-coiffed Möbius strip of postmodern mediocrity.

The pimp is a particularly violent guy by the name of Drexel. Off Clarence goes to P.S. 156. He walks right up to Dabney Coleman and says, "I'm going to kill you, man!" while the multicultural classroom urchins spew precocious one-liners. Then he realizes he's wandered into *Drexell's Class*. "Oops," he says to the teacher. "I am, after all, a greasy-coiffed Möbius strip of postmodern mediocrity. Sorry!"

Anyway, the pimp is a particularly violent *black* guy by the name of Drexel—a black guy played by the Caucasian Angloid Gary Oldman. Off Clarence goes, forcing the pimp's address out of Alabama, which he jots on the cover of the *TV Guide* Fall Preview ish, and heads out on his mission. Clarence arrives at the ponce pad, where his confrontation with the dreadlocked Drexel basically consists of a series of movie reference oneups. The pimp says that Clarence is like "Mr. Majestyk. Muthafuck Charles Bronson!" and questions why the young comics-shop clerk hasn't looked at the "titties" that are showing on the TV screen. Clarence explains that the movie in question is *The Mack*, a classic Blaxploitation flick, and that he's seen it, and thus the titties, seven times. *Oh yeah? I've seen it eight times!*

After a brief *nyah-nyah* duel, our hero offs the pimp, who in his death throes tumbles onto a large pile of eight-track tapes. Clarence flees, with a suitcase that he believes to be his missus' clothes. Arriving back home, Clarence announces to his one true love, "I killed him. Wanna hamburger?" Alabama starts to weep, not because she married a coldblooded killer, but because their love is so new that he doesn't realize that she detests mayonnaise on her burger. Truthfully though, 'Bama turns on the waterworks because killing her pimp was the most romantic thing anybody had ever done for her. At least since her last john bought her her implants.

Moving along to the next plot point, it turns out that Clarence grabbed the wrong suitcase (!) and the one he took is filled with cocaine (!!). The only thing to do with a Samsonite full o' blow, of course, is to go to Hollywood. So off go Clarence and Alabama to L.A. (Sounds like a movie, doesn't it?—*Clarence and Alabama Go To L.A.*)

Needless to say, the two lovebirds are being chased by the white lady's real owners, a gaggle of cartoon mafiosi, working for a cartoon *capo* with the distinctly un-Sicilian name of Blue Lou Boyle. Christopher Walken, Blue Lou's top soldier, gets to torture and kill Clarence's ex-alky dad (Dennis Hopper, in a far better performance than his sneaker snortin' Nike commercials) in his hunt for the rat bastards who have stolen his boss's merchandise.

Clarence and Alabama make their way west, and there they meet up with Clarence's aspiring actor pal, Dick Ritchie. (He's currently up for a part on *The New T. J. Hooker*—"Peter Breck's already been cast.") Using his impressive connections as a C-list TV actor, Ritchie hooks them up with a flunky for a Joel Silver–type producer.

The mafia dudes eventually track down the kids and a particularly violent sequence occurs where Alabama gets the living shit beaten out of her by a cold-blooded Detroit thug. She kills him, of course, and Clarence takes her out to a vacant lot by LAX to remove the shards of shower door glass from her bloodied but still pouty bottom lip (the second most romantic thing he ever did for her). There they talk about their big plans for when the dope is sold. They can travel with their ill-gotten gains. "I always wanted to see what TV in other countries looked like," Clarence says, definitely at his most *Ecch. Wow, Sabado Gigante is everywhere!*

Eventually, they decide on Cancún, because, as Alabama puts it, "It sounds like a movie: *Clarence and Alabama Go to Cancún.*"

But first they have to get rid of their cache of coke. A meet is arranged with the Joel Silver–type producer (who likes to refer to the coke as "Dr. Zhivago"), and a series of plot contrivances too contrived to mention leads to the big bloody final showdown between the mobsters, the Joel Silver-type producer's mercenary bodyguards, and the L.A.P.D. (or is it the L.A. County Sheriff's Department? Jurisdiction sure is confusing in the City of Angels).

Anyway, everybody dies, with the exception of Dick Ritchie, Alabama, and Clarence, who gets shot through the eye, but survives. (Apparently, Tarantino's script called for the death of his hero, but the Hollywood heads prevailed.) The final moment of this two-hour journey to the dark heart of the American Dream finds our Teenage Bonnie and Klepto Clyde on the beach, in Cancún, where Clarence (wearing an eyepatch like Nick Fury—*ooh, foreshadowing!*) frolics in the sand with their toddler. Alabama's voice-over informs us that, yes, the rug rat's name is Elvis, and that her love for Clarence is eternal. Why? Because the words "You're so cool. You're so cool" keep reverberating between her ears. *Que?*

*True Romance* is so relentlessly *Ecch* it's ridiculous. The flotsam of pop culture is everywhere in this film, from the ubiquitous movie posters on every wall and the Elvis camp (horseshoe rings, purple Caddys, big sunglasses and hell, the goddamn ghost of the goddamn King) to the leopard-skin kitsch that adorns literally every scene. The postmodern ideal is in full bloom here, but this isn't an art film. (You will never see the words "art" and "a film by Tony Scott" in the same sentence, not counting this one, of course.) No, this is an homage to the B-crap that *Ecch* worships, finding the irony and genius in previous generations' exploitational dross. Tarantino operates in the universe, where old movies, good or bad, become the only real American history.

This is not necessarily a bad thing as one of the many elements in a movie, but here it replaces everything that made those films matter in the first place. All is reference—character, plot, location, and set decoration are merely vehicles for Tarantino's litany of things that are cool. *True Romance* is like a transcript of the time Quentin was on *The $10,000 Pyramid:* Thunderbirds Are Go!; Chesterfields; Yoo-

Hoo; candy necklaces; Charles Whitman; *Palm Springs Weekend; Highway 301—Uh... Things that had no redeeming social value in their own time, but have somehow become relevant? No? Um... er... things that are cool?*

The stuff of great filmmakers used to take form on studio backlots, where aspiring *auteurs* refilled highball glasses for crazy directors with bullhorns and German accents. Later, film schools came into the picture, and would-be artists toiled in the basement of some archaic building that used to house the Greek Studies program, learning the art of the narrative by painstakingly cutting 16mm shorts about existentialism and ex-girlfriends. If they were lucky, Haig Manoogian saw something in their work, and took them under his wing.

Things have changed though, and in *L'Age d'Ecch*, the vast knowledge and skills required to create great art can be found at any mall or shopping center. Quentin Tarantino is just one of many *Ecch* filmmakers who learned everything he needed to know about the cinema from the local video store.

Ah, the video store. Certainly one of the greatest inventions of the late twentieth century, the home rental shop has turned every *Ecch* flat into a campus retrospective theatre, only better. At home you can be engrossed and moved by *The Bicycle Thief,* and still order out for pizza!

Tarantino, of course, didn't just couch-potato his way to the director's chair. He *worked* at a video store, and you know what that means. When the hot new director's cut-letterboxed edition of *Bob le Flambeur* is released, the vid-clerk is in the power position to take the flick home on the first night! The other cool thing about this archetypal *Ecch*Job is that it affords the driven young *artiste* plenty of counter-time to read Syd Field and write screenplays.

Aside from the ever-growing *oeuvre* of Mr. Tarantino (... *Dogs* and ... *Romance* were followed by Oliver Stone's *Natural Born Killers* and the Tarantino-directed *Pulp Fiction*—hey, his movies aren't original, so why should his titles be?) video store employment is responsible for one of the truly great *Ecch* films, *Heathers.* Screenwriter Daniel Waters, the wageslave in question, spent his hours at the video store *writing* instead of merely quoting. Rather than falling back on, say a scene where everyone sits around the lunch room talking about *Gilligan's Island,* or a Big Sound Track Moment featuring R.E.M. (for currency) and Blondie (for nostalgia), Waters invented his own references, his own slang, even his own fake pop group in Big Fun, makers of the fake hit "Teenage Suicide (Don't Do It)."

It is significant that *Heathers* was little seen in its time but now, through the miracle of video, rightfully revered. Any movie with a cast of Winona Ryder, Christian Slater, and Shannen Doherty would be considered important, *Ecch*—wise. But the cast, with Ryder giving one of her best performances and Slater and Doherty pre-tiresome and repellent, is only a minor factor in *Heather's* artistic success. Waters and director Michael Lehmann set for themselves the bizarre and unusual goal of making a good movie with something to say and a sly way of saying it.

*Heathers* has something that is to be found in many of *Ecch's* favorite pop culture signposts, but not among *Ecch* itself—imagination. Hell, as long as the pop culture signposts have it, why should new creators add anything of their own? Such are the intellectual consequences of growing up in the video age, where media is the only reality and what's more, the line between movies and television has totally collapsed. This is a truism that stretches from the boardrooms of the major studios, where video sales and TV rights have become just as important as theatrical performances, to the actual filmmaking process. Waters and Lehmann were beaten down by the Way Things Are very quickly—since *Heathers,* they are responsible, together and apart, for such fine flicks as *The Adventures of Ford Fairlane, Hudson Hawk,* and *Batman Returns.*

The obvious proof of TV's wholesale victory over cinema is as plain as the names of *Ecch's* great *auteurs.* The important directors of the time—people whose films have been nominated for *Academy Awards,* for God's sake!—are filmmakers that the world knows best by the names Opie, Laverne, and Meathead. Flash forward to the year 2000, and picture the Best Director nominees at the Oscars: Bob Saget, Sinbad, Jerry Seinfeld, and Shannen Doherty (plus James Ivory, of course). Well, maybe not Shannen Doherty—the Oscars rarely nominate strong women in the director category.

But while it provided Ron Howard with a job where it's *de rigeur* to wear a baseball hat, thereby saving him from severe tonsorial embarrassment, TV basically destroyed contemporary movies on the formal and stylistic battlefield. Bad enough that there are lots of movies by film-school grads whose entire visions were based on the previous achievements of other movies. Today's *Ecch* filmmakers, whether a king of cheeky obscure references like Tarantino or a former music-video director like Russell Mulcahy, have taken this process one horrible step further. Hollywood is riddled with directors who are wholly products of not only film school, but early careers spent in TV, music videos and advertising. Films by people like Adrian Lyne and the two Scott boys, Ridley and Tony, are all style, yet beyond the cool lighting and glittery production design, their imagery says not a damn thing.

We even have a filmmaker who used to be a production designer, *D.C. Cab* director Joel Schumacher. While not always an *Ecch* filmmaker in his chosen topics, Schumacher has managed to turn out a couple of dandies during his curious career, including *Flatliners*, a Bratpack (Julia, Keifer, etc.) film where medical students find out what it's like to be dead. Very little Method Acting on that one, boy.

He also made *The Lost Boys*, a film that epitomizes the MTV rock video style of filmmaking, complete with red lights, super-fast edits, a bad rock sound track, motorcycles, gauzy lenses, wind, strobes, and a cast that includes Jason Patric, Keifer Sutherland, both of the Coreys, Jami Gertz, and Alex-ander "Bill" Winter. It's the kind of movie that would have been a perfectly acceptable "B" picture in the '30s, but instead it was a big commercial hit that is cherished by thousands of idiots. Schumacher directed it as if he were still doing blow.

*Ecch* kids interested in making movies could turn out to be even worse for the wear because they are products of film school, TV, music videos, advertising, *and* the awful movies made by the previous students of these things. Of course, *all* the members of Generation *Ecch* are interested in making movies, or making it in some other area of the Bizness. This is a generation that has more to say about last week's grosses than the quality of a film's direction. Today's film students can tell you what it'll cost to get Warren Beatty as your lead, but they don't know who John Reed is. ("Former coach of the New York Knicks" is *not* the correct answer. Though Willis's name was on a few Worker's Party mailing lists.)

It's a most curious paradox that *Ecch* is the generation of technology, of visual rather than written art, yet very few directors manage to do anything original with all this innate visual acuity. The films of Lyne, Schumacher, etc., are little more than scene after scene of snazzy footage to go with the inevitable sound track video.

Not that anyone is really paying attention. As the generation of video rentals, *Ecch* thinks it's okay to talk to the person next to us during the movies. Hell, thanks to *Mystery Science Theater 3000,* a work of great genius but not one to be taken as a public behavioral model, *Ecch* also thinks it's okay to talk to the movie screen during the movies.

Finally, *Ecch* is the generation that knows of no other type of hit movie but the blockbuster. Post *Jaws* and *Star Wars,* movies were measured by their size and spectacularness (and profitability) rather than their art. Thus the early '70s gave us films like *The Godfather, Nashville,* and *Shampoo,* all fairly big commercial hits. But post-Spielberg and Lucas, the aesthetically sound commercial success is rarer than a Van Damme movie without the butt shot.

**S**uch is the state of *Ecch* filmmaking in the '90s. But there's more to *Ecch* film than just the way they look and the things they steal. There's also the subject matter.

A culture can always be measured by the stories it tells, whether it's Greek mythology or the Old Testament, Aristophanes or Homer, Shakespeare or Marlowe, Groening or Trudeau. The folklore of olden times can be broken down into the two basic categories of tragedy and comedy. The literature of today's boomers and senior citizens can be broken down into the two basic categories of Michael Crichton and John Grisham.

*Ecch* film is a little tougher. There are in fact several distinct sub-genres in the *Ecch* filmic universe. Each have considerable overlap to the other categories—familiar plot twists transplanted from film to film, bands used from sound track to sound track, the presence of Emilio Estevez or Sean Penn more times than would seem necessary.

But then, if Penn achieves nothing else in his career, you've got to give him this—he bagged Madonna (okay, so maybe that's not so unique) and he is, along with writer Cameron Crowe, the originator of a most important *Ecch* cinema icon: the teen stoner, much-loved center of The Stoner Film. Though a real debt is owed to Cheech and Chong, *Fast Times at Ridgemont High*'s Jeff Spiccoli was the father of them all: Bill and Ted, Wayne and Garth, *Dazed and Confused*'s Slater, even Beavis and Butt-head.

Spiccoli is unique because he's one of the very few stoners who is verifiably a real toker. Otherwise, the drug use of these stupidity-glorifying heroes is completely implied. For that matter, so is almost everything else about the stoner: they love rock 'n' roll, but so much of the music they listen to, in the words of (and with the exception of) Beavis and Butt-head, sucks: the crap-metal that proliferates on the *Bill and Ted* sound track, the dreadful Hendrix and Sweet covers offered up by *Wayne's World*. They're all male id set loose on the screen, living to leer at and lust for girls, but it's all theoretical, crushed by the weight of male fear and male bonding. In their sequel, Bill and Ted manage to get two women—*Our girlfriends are most chaste, dude*—pregnant, yet it's impossible to imagine them having sex, and the filmmakers were aware enough of this fact that they had to give them really bad fake beards to emphasize their virility.

Significantly, after years of non-pot-smoking potheads on the screen, *Slacker* director Rick Linklater came out with his excellent (like, we mean, *excellent!*) *Dazed and Confused*, a movie in which pot smoking and libido are not only portrayed but encouraged. *Ecch* being a much more weed-friendly generation than its predecessors, it was okay to make a movie with pot in it again.

Cutting close to the stoner movie with its themes of wasted alienation and social transgression is the second important *Ecch* film type, known only as the "S. E. Hinton genre." *Stay golden, Johnny!* Actually, there's never been a particularly great, or even particularly poignant, movie made in this genre. But the American teen and the American film community were affected by them nonetheless. For one thing, with *The Outsiders* and *Rumble Fish*, Francis Ford Coppola took himself from the precipice of filmmaking failure . . . and flung himself even further over. For another, in these two films alone *Ecch* audiences were able to savor the performances of Matt Dillon, Ralph Macchio, Patrick Swayze, Rob Lowe, C. Thomas Howell, Emilio Estevez, Tom Cruise, Mickey Rourke, Vincent Spano, Nicolas Cage, Christopher Penn, and, years before *Godfather III*, Sofia Coppola. Hinton's books also began the filmmaking career of young Emilio—after writing the script of *That Was Then, This Is Now*, he moved behind the camera with such masterpieces as *Wisdom* and *Men at Work.*

More conventional portrayals of *Ecch* society—i.e., people who don't say "dude!" a lot or get into gangfights—can be found in the other two genres. The *Ecch* jock movie takes its cue from either *Rocky* or *The Bad News Bears,* with *The Karate Kid* being the most obvious example, though serious *Ecch* scholars should not overlook *Visionquest* (Matthew Modine as a geeky wrestler) and *Gleaming the Cube* (a post-*Tucker,* pre-*Heathers* Christian Slater as a geeky skate-punk).

The prep school movie, a category that safely covers any film featuring boys in underwear in close quarters with other boys in underwear, has been a launching pad for such teen idols as Cruise and Penn (*Taps*), Ethan Hawke and future serial killer Robert Sean Leonard (*Dead Poets Society*) and lesser regarded slabs of beefcake like Sean Astin (*Toy Soldiers*) and Brendan, "Funny, he doesn't look Jewish" Fraser (*School Ties*). In addition, Charlie Sheen's most notable film, *Platoon,* is really just another military school yarn, with Tom Berenger instead of Kurtwood Smith and icky, bloody jungles instead of pastoral New England snowscapes.

By no means do these categories cover the entire *Ecch* film landscape. But as far as mainstream Hollywood films go, those are the basic parameters. The thing is though, whether the kids are getting stoned under the bleachers or running around naked in the winter shouting "Carpe Diem!," all *Ecch* films are essentially high school movies. This is as true of *Porky's,* about a bunch of horny teenagers trying to get laid, as it is of *Singles,* about a bunch of horny post-grads trying to get love.

**A**nd when it comes to the high school movie, there's only one filmmaker who truly matters. His influence is recognizable on virtually every cultural artifact that passes for *Ecch* creativity. As Ingmar Bergman, the poet laureate of windy cinema, is to chess-playing existential Swedish knights, so John Hughes, the poet laureate of the Windy City, is to *Ecch.* The portly, bespectacled *auteur* is—more than Spielberg, more than Lynch, more than Tarantino—the most significant filmmaker of the *Ecch* era. His works not only define the generation, they're damn near the sperm that created it.

A formerly gifted *National Lampoon* hack (author of the classic "My Penis"), Hughes made his Hollywood entrée with a bunch of megascripts, including *Mr. Mom* and *National Lampoon's Vacation*, movies that were marked by cheap laughs and roles for Chevy Chase and Anthony Michael Hall. But it was *Sixteen Candles* that truly heralded the arrival of this film chronicler for the Next Generation. The heartwarming story of a suburban girl's romantic traumas, with a backdrop of insane family life and mischievous high school hijinks, *Sixteen Candles* was a genuinely inspired little teen comedy. It also introduced the world to Molly Ringwald (the Bibi Andersson of Hughesian *ciné*).

*Sixteen Candles'* particularly teen-sympathetic brand of realism made it a formative film for the generation that would come to be *Ecch*. For his next effort, Hughes upped the stakes further, with a flick that was intensely relevant to *Ecch* when it was first released and remains incredibly pertinent to and revealing of the generation today.

The words "... and these children that you spit on" is the first image of Hughes's *magnum opus* of teen angst, *The Breakfast Club*. The line, of course, is David Bowie's, but the sentiment is Hughes all the way. At the time he was totally devoted to fighting the good fight for the downtrodden American teenager. As the film begins, this epigraph (from "Changes," by the way), is shattered by an unseen rock or something—a practically meaningless shot that wants to tell us that these children will no longer be spit on, and all of our illusions about youth will soon be broken.

The breaking screen then reveals lovely Shermer High, a suburban bastion of higher learning and intensely stratified social activity. Less than ten seconds into the movie Hughes provides us with a second rock lyric quote, in the form of graffiti that reads "I Don't Like Mondays." This hip Boomtown Rats reference could be taken literally, but more likely it's supposed to be viewed as something with much deeper meaning—the story behind the song is about a woman in California who shot up a schoolyard. Hughes is such a nihilist.

"In the simplest terms and the most convenient definitions," to quote a key line of dialogue, *The Breakfast Club* is the story of "a brain, an athlete, a basket case, a princess, and a criminal. That's the way we saw each other—we were brainwashed." Yes, it's only because of narrowminded teachers and parents that the rich kids don't hang out with the white trash.

These unfriendly class warriors have come together for an all-day detention session, where they are asked to write your basic self-exploring "who am I?" essay for the evil social studies teacher, wonderfully played by Paul Gleason. Before they arrive, we are treated to a brief glimpse of each character's personal parental pain—Molly the princess's spoiling, distant and near-divorced upper-crusters; Emilio the jock's domineering daddy; Anthony Michael Brain's adoring, expectant family; and basket case Ally Sheedy's unacknowledging mother, who floors the gas on the Seville when her daughter ventures an attempt at communication.

Judd "the Criminal" Nelson arrives alone, because he doesn't need anybody, man, and besides, his parents are irresponsible shits who give him cases of beer for Christmas and show affection with cigarette burns. Judd is the demon of this little group, the antagonist figure who prods all the others into anger, action and introspection. Molly and Emilio find him particularly distasteful. "You don't even count," wrestler boy says, while Judd fumes, in a transparent bid to get his nostrils nominated for an Academy Award. "You may as well not even exist at this school." When that little jab doesn't draw blood, Emilio falls back on more familiar jock discourse, calling him a burner and a faggot.

Judd also eats his own spit and lights his shoes on fire for fun—*Fire! Fire!*—an act of daring that gets Molly Ringwald's repressed little loins all wet and toasty. He smokes pot and sings rock 'n' roll and destroys books, making fun of Molière and rearranging the card catalog. He talks back to the teacher, earning himself month after month of extra detention time just to keep up his rebellious stance. In short, as an alienated victim of fag-bashing, with his green army coat, flannel shirt and sullen, permanently flared nostrils, Judd the Thug is the grunge rocker of the future, though he resembles Mudhoney's Mark Arm much more than the archetypal Kurt Cobain.

Besides Judd, the other member of the club who is most *Ecch* is Ally Sheedy, the mop-headed, black-garbed, nail-biting psycho who kills time by cutting off the circulation of her fingers with a strand of her hair. Early in the film, her character gets so little dialogue that the part could have been played by Marlee Matlin. But eventually she opens up, giving everyone a glimpse into her problems, her soul, her pocketbook. She's a mess, the kind of person who throws away her olive loaf and replaces it with a Cap'n Crunch–and–sugar sandwich (on Wonder Bread, natch). But she's also a prodigiously gifted artist who decorates her pencil-sketched landscapes with snowy dandruff from her very own crown.

The early part of the movie is mostly consumed with bickering, though Hughes is careful to drop in little hints of the deep personal connections that will form between these seemingly different souls later on. Ally musters enough energy to shout out, "Ha!!" Molly puts Anthony Michael Hall in his place yet again, calling him "a neomaxi zoom dweebie." Judd tries to hound Molly into bulimia by implying that she's fat, then quizzes her about her sexuality. "Do you want me to puke?" she responds, but those pouty lips are saying something other than the words they form. He's sexually harassing her, and she looooooooooves it. Later, he leers, "Being bad feels pretty good, huh?" *Ooh, Judd, you dog.*

The whole construction of the film is immensely clever for the way it manipulates little teenage minds by appearing to speak directly to and for them. These are minds that ask for little more from art than escape, or, if you have to get deep about these things, reflections of their own petty problems and deepest shallow feelings of depression and ennui. The whole thing is very dramatic and theatrical, slapstick Christopher Durang one minute, bizarre Edward Albee the next. One scene comes off a lot like something from a lost Beckett play: Judd does a little one-man dramatization of Anthony's prissy happy little family, then launches into a bravura performance of his own shitty home life. This in turn prompts the big sound track rock music to come on—in the school library. With this noise as a spark, Judd finally explodes from the pressure of his pain, with a scream that would come to define so many others of his generation long after the high school years had passed: *FUCK YOU! FUCK YOU!*

All the bickering subsides when the little group of detainees is forced to unite in the face of authority. First they band together to protect Judd when he shuts the door of the room against the teacher's wishes. Prisoners of an academic war, they pass the time whistling the song from *The Bridge on the River Kwai*, though chances are they only know it as the "Comet—it makes you vomit" song.

After lunch, they decide to go on a little adventure, mainly because Judd has some weed in his locker, and this bunch is going to need to get wasted to advance Hughes's empathetic feel-good philosophy later in the movie. *Should we smoke pot? I dunno. It'll dissolve the petty, narrow-minded social prejudices and bring us together. We can dance. There'll be cool music on the sound track.*

Then, with a giggle from Anthony Michael Hall and a big cough from Molly, the confessions and craziness begin. It turns out that Molly and Emilio are deeply unhappy behind their "I'm so popular" facade. The loud music that Judd cued a few scenes before starts up again, and Emilio seems to revert to his punky *Repo Man* persona again, jumping around and screaming—screaming so loud, in fact, that one of the glass doors shatters. Along, of course, with the characters' last remaining preconceptions about one another.

The stage is set for bonding when Ally steals Anthony's wallet. She offers to display the contents of her purse, but the boys decline. Her frail ego further battered, she defiantly dumps the thing on the library couch. Her bag is filled with enough stuff to decorate an *Ecch* kid's room, a precautionary loading-up of supplies because "you never know when you may have to jam," Ally explains. She wants to leave home, and the future is a road atlas of unlimited possibility: "I can go to Israel, Africa, Afghanistan, the country, the mountains, the ocean." Perhaps she's curious to find out what TV in other countries is like.

Straight arrows Emilio and Tony Mike remain skeptical of Ally's rebellious talk. They've always done what their parents told them— Emilio landed in detention because *he taped a guy's butt* to please his father (who the hell is his father? Señor Menendez? *Knees!* Actually, his father is Señor *Estevez.* But we digress . . .)—yet they're simmering with resentment about it. Delivering a tragic soliloquy worthy of an O'Neill play, AMH reveals the horrible pressures of GPAs and SATs and IQs that he has to live with every day. We finally find out that the reason *he* got detention is because he had a gun in his locker. Having destroyed his 4.0 by failing shop—if only he had met Judd Nelson earlier he might have gotten some tutorial—he decided to off himself with a flare gun.

"Is your home life so unsatisfying?" Emilio says to Ally, and then AMH steps up (*drum roll, please*) with the big philosophical summation of *The Breakfast Club:* **Everyone's home life is unsatisfying—if it wasn't people would live with their parents forever.** This little revelation somehow makes it possible for Emilio to get closer to Ally, a final bit of foreshadowing for the inevitable coupling to come later.

"What's wrong?" he asks her, trading in his surly wrestler personality for a more sensitive demeanor, one more befitting say, of a fencer or debater: "Is it bad? Real bad?"

"They ignore me," is the reply.

"Yeah," Emilio offers, biting his lip, perhaps thinking of all those years competing for father-love with Charlie.

"My God, are we going to be like our parents?" one of them wonders a little later. "It's unavoidable" is the hard truth given in response to that question. "When you grow up, your heart dies." Yeah, but in your attempts to relive your precious youth, you get to make stupid movies that gross *millions*.

In case the audience is unaware that everyone has finally come together, there's another big musical number, choreographed to some song called "We Are Not Alone" that never achieved the hot hit status of "Don't You (Forget About Me)." All the characters dance and jump around and hug, moving through the world of the library's bizarre playscape. It's like the Living Theater. You keep waiting for Judith Malina to come out.

Meanwhile, over in the world of adults, Hughes is busy wrapping up the film's thematic and structural loose ends. We've already been introduced to a heroic, working-class janitor type, a fellow who's seen it all and knows about truth and youth and happiness. "Look at John Bender in five years," Gleason says to the custodian, the disdain dripping off his voice like bile. *Yeah, he'll be signed to Geffen, on the cover of every magazine and touring around Europe.* Judd's character, that is. Judd himself had no such success.

"Each year, these kids get more and more arrogant," the embittered social-studies teacher continues. "When we get old, these kids are going to be running the country." Hey, he sounds just like he's writing a generational exposé for *Time* magazine. "When I get older, these kids are going to take care of me."

"I wouldn't count on it," the janitor counters. Damn right. We're trying as hard as we can to cut off your Social Security benefits and NEA retirement pension, you youth-suppressing, fascistic white male authority figure!

*The Breakfast Club*, though, was written and released well before young people truly understood the evil of the white male authority figure—indeed, it can be seen as partially responsible for *Ecch* awakening in that regard. But Hughes was unforgivably remiss as far as multiculturalism goes. These are all suburban white kids, for god's sake. If *The Breakfast Club* were made today, Judd Nelson's part would be played by Tupac, and Anthony Michael Hall's by B. D. Wong. Ally Sheedy's character would be a lesbian, and the Emilio Estevez character wouldn't exist.

What finally bonds everyone together in Hughes-land is this line of dialogue: "We're all pretty bizarre—some of us are just better at hiding it." This is actually the opposite of the message Hughes's script actually suggests. In promoting his "we're all depressed human beings" ideology he strips the characters of their individuality. They are united in blandness and in having common traumas—teachers that suck, parents that just don't understand, the social pressures that make high school such a trying period in one's young life.

Hughes then tacks on an ending that further overstates his case while making absolutely no sense dramatically, except as pure Hollywood happy-ending convention. Molly gives Ally Sheedy a makeover, turning her into a glowing, pretty little preppy, ready to share soda pops and finger fucks with suddenly interested jock Emilio. For her part, Molly finally acts on those naughty feelings of attraction/repulsion toward Smilin' Judd. She ventures off to Paul Gleason's office (where Judd has been confined) and puts the moves on him. They look longingly at each other and kiss, then Judd bids her farewell. *Stay alive! No matter what occurs, I will find you!* Freeze frame on Judd, fist in the air, walking away from the school on the football field, of all places, triumphant in scoring some blue-blood nookie. Soon he would join Ally in the preppy makeover department, playing her husband in *St. Elmo's Fire.* Molly's career would continue for a while, and for some reason Emilio still gets work, while Anthony Michael Hall grew up to be Judd Nelson, a geek transformed by the magic of hormones (or steroids).

"What we found out is each of us is a jock, a princess," etc., are the final lines of the movie, uttered by AMH under the pretense of serving as the group's collective assigned essay. We're all people! This message strikes a chord in young hearts because all teenagers are hungry for connection, and all of them continually sacrifice their individuality in order to make those connections during the high school years. They pretend to be jocks, or princesses, or brains, etc., etc. But what *The Breakfast Club*'s audience doesn't realize is that Hughes creates exactly the same situation—what we're left with, instead of individuals, are generic proto-Hughesian adolescents, embryonic versions of *Ecch*, the generation that trades in their individuality to be grunge, or rave, or feminist or pro-pot.

Unfortunately for the art of American film, John Hughes still had a lot more to say about class struggle in the high schools of suburban America. *The Breakfast Club* was the end of John Hughes as an artist, comedic, philosophical, or otherwise—*Weird Science, Planes, Trains and Automobiles*, and *The Great Outdoors* were among his next films. But as a producer, Hughes and his protégé director Howie Deutch came up with the odious *Pretty in Pink* as well as its less significant doppelganger *Some Kind of Wonderful*.

Opening quite literally with a shot of the wrong side of the tracks, home to motherless Molly Ringwald and her drunken, unemployed, played–by–Harry Dean Stanton father, *Pretty in Pink* is a truly execrable film, the kind of movie that even the stupidest of *Ecch* kids looks back on with an amazed "I can't believe I used to like that." Essentially a Deanna Durbin melodrama, but with alternative rock on the sound track and Andrew McCarthy instead of Bob Cummings, *Pretty in Pink* casts a lazy eye on the trials and tribulations that occur when a pathetic poor girl who sews her own clothes (this is pre grunge and thrift-store chic, remember) falls in love with a sensitive boy in a Beemer. It's your basic *Romeo and Juliet/West Side Story* situation. There's no Mercutio, but Jon Cryer's new-wave geek boy Duckie is rather mercurial, while James Spader, as McCarthy's snobbish best friend, dresses like Tom Wolfe and talks as if he's in a dentist chair.

Deutch/Hughes gives us the usual accoutrements of young rich suburban life: the Saabs and Porsches and motorcycles, the Nik Kershaw covers on the soundtrack, the nonexistent cool punk record store in the middle of Wilmette, the vapidly beautiful blond girl cavorting around plush mansions in bras and panties. There's only one remotely vivid moment in the film: the scene in which Andrew and Molly spend a romantic evening in the stable and stab a bunch of horses in the eye. Then a bunch of people in bamboo horseheads come out and dance around naked for a while. (No, wait a minute, that was *Equus*. Or was it *Fresh Horses*?) The best performances are given by Annie Potts, doing a Wendy O. Williams imitation, and Andrew Dice

Clay, who plays a bouncer character known as "the Diceman" (probably so he wouldn't miss his cues).

Even though Molly is dirt poor, she drives a cool car. With her glasses on, she resembles no one so much as Dustin Hoffman in *Tootsie*. When Andrew McCarthy walks into the record store to buy a Steve Lawrence record (a *Steve Lawrence* record? What does he think this is, *True Romance*?), giving her one of those crinkly, doe-eyed, melting looks that only Andrew McCarthy can give (it's his *Method*), it's L-U-V. It's also trouble for poor Jon Cryer, who's carrying a torch for Molly that's bigger than Andrew's dimples.

But there's no way it can work—the social pressures high-school cliques exert are just too powerful. James "Mumblyboy" Spader, who's secretly in love with Molly, apparently because she sees through his dandy act, tells his pal Andy, "If you've got a hard-on for trash, don't take care of it around us." Oooh. He thinks Andy is only doing this to piss off his parents. Andrew doesn't care for this piece of advice, and tells Spader to fuck off. Spader's reaction? He says, "Mmmsgheios hmmmhhskejmmmf fmgrsdgd."

Eventually, though, Andy gives in, blowing off the big prom date that Molly made her very own dress for. She goes anyway, to let them know "they didn't break me." Jon Cryer is there, also alone, and it looks as though dramatic justice will be served—in a clichéd and predictable fashion, but served nonetheless. Cryer says he's "the most interesting date of the generation!" Sadly, he might be right.

However, as with the ending of *The Breakfast Club*, there's still another twist to come. Andy shows up, brokenhearted and disgusted with himself, and pledges his troth. Jon Cryer is so moved by this romantic epiphany that he renounces his crush on Molly so that the two lovers can be together. Then a very young Kristy Swanson (*Mmmmm!*) asks him to dance. Everybody's happy. Once again we learn that love is bigger than class, especially if you can get the Psychedelic Furs to do a bad remake of a once perfectly fine song on the sound track.

**P**retty in Pink was pretty much the end of Hughes as an *Ecch* filmmaker. He wrote and produced dreck like *Career Opportunities*,

*Curly Sue,* and *Only the Lonely,* with the rather successful *Home Alone* sandwiched in between. John Hughes's influence on today's five-to-twelve-year-olds will be even greater than his influence on *Ecch.* He also made *She's Having a Baby,* an attempt to bring his characters into the world of adulthood.

But as it turned out, John Hughes was not going to be the person to do that. The all grown-up, final Hughes-style *Ecch*ploration of kids in the '80s came, fittingly, from one of the filmmakers whose efforts have so tarnished the nature of modern cinema, stylistically as well as narratively. Joel Schumacher's great masterpiece, *St. Elmo's Fire,* came a few years before *The Lost Boys.*

*St. Elmo's Fire* is a yuppie melodrama that's sort of a bridge film for *Ecch* between the high-school memories of John Hughes and the college angst of *Less Than Zero.* Cowritten by Schumacher, the film earns its *Ecch* wings with its cast alone—Rob Lowe, Judd Nelson, Ally Sheedy, Demi Moore, Andrew McCarthy, Emilio Estevez, and Mare Winningham. (Okay, so she doesn't count.)

It's the kind of movie in which Judd Nelson's neo-Republican character wears a "Fear and Loathing" shirt. In which Demi Moore tells Andrew McCarthy that "gay became very chic in the seventies." Andrew, of course, is the sensitive-boy soul of the movie—he's secretly in love with Ally Sheedy—keeps a coffin in his room, and has confessional conversations with prostitutes. Judd Nelson is the devil, while Rob Lowe and Demi Moore are also serious *Ecch* archetypes, as an immature musician who wishes all of life was "Out of Hand" and a fucked-up drugged-up tramp, respectively. Demi has it all figured out, though: She's going to "fuck her boss, move up, write a best-seller and get her own talk show. This is the eighties. Get caught in a sex scandal and retire in massive disgrace. Do a black mink ad." Hey, it sounds like a plan.

Sampled dialogue from *St. Elmo's Fire:* "I just wish everything could be like we used to be." "It's our time on the edge." "I never thought I'd be so tired at twenty-two." "I don't just even know who to be anymore." Yes, this is a movie about confused youngsters who refuse to grow up. But eventually, they do. They patch up all their differences and, instead of going to St. Elmo's Fire, past site of all their friendship and debauchery, they opt for brunch at Houlihan's instead. They're adults now.

*   *   *

In the fall of 1993, actress/comedienne Janeane Garafolo went out of her way to tell David Letterman that her upcoming film, the Ben Stiller-directed *Reality Bites*, was not a Generation X film. She said that people were going to call it a Generation X film, but it wasn't.

When the movie, which stars Winona Ryder and Ethan Hawke in addition to Stiller and Garafolo, came out in February of '94, it turned out that Garafolo was very right and very wrong. Right, because a quick survey of first-month press on *Reality Bites*—*SPIN, GQ, Rolling Stone, The New York Times, Details*—did not turn up a single article without the words "twentysomething" or "Generation X." Wrong, because the pigeonhole was completely justifiable. *Reality Bites* is a perfect combination of the John Hughes-style high school romance (moved up a few years, but high-schooly just the same) and the Quentin Tarantino-style reference fest. Everything about *Reality Bites*—from the script and the acting to the direction and sound track—is rendered in complete *Ecch* fashion.

At some point, saner heads might have prevailed. When Hawke first saw the script, he told *SPIN* his reaction was "I really don't know why you need to make a movie about a bunch of white kids complaining. They have absolutely nothing to complain about besides their own mediocrity." Eventually, though, Hawke decided that "it was okay to complain about your own mediocrity" and took the part. How very . . . *mediocre* of him.

*Reality Bites* opens with a half-inarticulate, half-sanctimonious speech from Winona's college valedictorian character Leilaina. She talks about "repairing the damage we inherited" and says the answer to all the big questions is "I don't know." Leilaina is making a documentary about her friends, essentially an excuse for Stiller to break the fourth wall and go all postmodern by making the film look like . . . that's right, a *television show.*

If someone wanted to make a case for the stupidity of a generation, Leilaina would be a pretty good place to start—as the film unwinds, we find that she cannot give a dictionary definition of "irony," which seems unlikely no matter how dumb she is, and is also unable to add eighty-five and forty-five, even on the third try. What the film never mentions, but seems to imply, is that Leilaina was the valedictorian of her class at the *community* college.

At its heart, *Reality Bites* is just a cute little predictable romantic comedy. Winona has to choose between the amicable but yuppiefied TV exec, played by Stiller, or the sensitive, sullen grunge poet, played by Hawke. Any sane women would have to disqualify Hawke solely on the basis of his oil-slick 'do, but in this case we're dealing with someone who runs her hair through Dave Pirner's dreadlocks every night. (Pirner, in fact, joins fellow rock hunk Evan Dando as two of the film's many cameo performers).

With a likeable cast, decent jokes and able direction, this movie could have been one of the really good *Ecch* films. But unsurprisingly, twenty-three-year-old screenwriter Helen Childish . . . erm, Childress . . . didn't trust her own abilities, and had to gussy up her story with the usual seventies pop culture quotes, preempting any other themes, characters, or emotional histories with the predictable shared pop culture contexts. Why create a character when you can just saddle someone with a job at the Gap, a *Charlie's Angels* lunchbox, and a list of the sixty-six different men she's slept with? As if there's some sort of correlation!

The problem, though, is not so much Childress's as it is the generation. Well, maybe it is. She was, after all, hired by Michael Shamberg, producer of *The Big Chill*, to replicate the homogenized hipitude of Larry Kasdan's feel-good fave. (If only one of *these* characters would off themselves.)

*Ecch* has no other life except as media creatures, which means that *Ecch* characters have no other features except for media memories. The honor role from *Reality Bites* is impressive, shameless, and horrifying: Favorite episodes of *Diff'rent Strokes, Good Times,* and *One Day at a Time* (what, no *Alice*?), faux-rhapsodic moments over Squeeze and the Knack, quotes from the old *Schoolhouse Rock* episodes, a *Planet of the Apes* doll, posters of Boston and Kiss record covers, *Saturday Night Fever* music, philosophizing about Big Gulps and an obligatory Peter Frampton scene that goes further than most: Stiller's character not only reminisces about *Frampton Comes Alive* (a scene that can also be viewed in *Wayne's World II*), he actually uses "Baby I Love Your Way" as his make-out moodsetter—in 1994! In addition, Ethan Hawke's character gets his own special roster of personality-defining signposts—because he's a sensitive, sullen grunge poet, he's above things like sitcoms and disco. Instead, he reads Heidegger, recites Gregory Corso while strumming his guitar, and covers old Violent Femmes songs with his band, Perch (no, they're actually called Hey, That's My Bike!).

It's ridiculous that Stiller and the actors associated with the film deny its *Ecch* qualities; it's even more pathetic that they blame that label on "the media," because Childress doesn't hesitate to portray every cliched, media-defined example of social and economic *Ecch* angst—the post-graduate economic uncertainty, the hippy parents, the divorce fallout, the unhealthy obsessions with old sitcoms. Douglas Coupland and *Time* magazine should sue!

In the end, the character who comes off like a sage in *Reality Bites* is Joe Don Baker, playing Winona's father. Sure, he's only sprouting Childress's cartoonish idea of what the "authority figures" say about the generation—"you have no work ethic! Use some ingenuity!" But anyone who's ever seen *Walking Tall* should know that when Joe Don Baker says something, you'd damn well better listen.

**T**hese days, to criticize *Ecch* film is to criticize pretty much all Hollywood films. The non-*Ecch* output of the major movie studios isn't much better, and as frenetic little *Ecch*sters snap up those jobs as D-girls and associate producers and screenwriters, things can only get worse. The last bastion, then, of the serious film buff, is supposed to be in the art house, where foreign and independent films are free to be great without the distraction of commercial considerations.

In the age of *Ecch,* the American independent film is said to have undergone a great renaissance, beginning, perhaps, with Joel and Ethan Coen's *Blood Simple,* all the way up to *Reservoir Dogs,* with important *Ecch* films like *Blue Velvet, Metropolitan,* and *Slacker* in between. Those are the good ones.

*Slacker* in particular has suffered greatly from its coincidental synergy with the *Ecch* phenomenon. The people who have latched onto the buzzword, or even the film itself, aren't necessarily getting it. Far from glorifying the idea of slack, the film portrays just as many bullshit artists and losers as it does cultural iconocasts and social margin walkers. While director Richard Linklater was certainly guilty of getting caught in the media's *Ecch* slipstream while out promoting his film, the movie itself does not belong on any bandwagon. Even the book that came out in conjunction with it is refreshingly devoid of any "How to be a Slacker" charts or generational generalizing.

Movies like *Slacker* and *Metropolitan* (a virtual masterpiece that, in a weird way, articulates much of the *Ecch* dilemma as it applies to upperclass New York WASPS) aside, the strain of *Ecch* running through American independent and "art" films is not too pretty. Post-*Blood Simple* and *Raising Arizona*, the Coen Brothers, in their own wry, hyperactive way, have become the highbrow intellectual flag-bearers for the all-style school of *Ecch* filmmaking. Unlike Hollywood's fabulist hacks, the Coens are smart, so they can't be accused of style over substance. Instead, they're all style and all substance without feeling or meaning. What their overworked brains have produced are films (*Miller's Crossing*, and, especially *Barton Fink*) that are nothing but mindgames, cool tracking shots and movie homages, with characters that are bare abstractions and never-ending sequences that say nothing but "look how clever we are!" What's more, the plot of their recent *The Hudsucker Proxy* turns on the invention of the Hula Hoop. Good thing it was a period piece, or it might have been mood rings and pet rocks. (Incidentally, do you know why it's called *The Hudsucker Proxy?* 'Cause it sucks!)

If the Hollywood film is often sunk by lack of artistic ambition, the "art film" is often ruined by too much of it. In their pursuit of the experimental, filmmakers like the Coens or Hal Hartley frequently end up losing sight of emotions and narrative. While it's slightly less odious for a film to get lost in formal innovations instead of old sitcom references, the result is the same: empty, aimless moviemaking for empty, aimless audiences. Besides, in many ways the Coens and Hartley are no different from the likes of Tarantino—they just make their references to William Faulkner and Jean-Luc Godard instead of William Castle and John Woo.

If the bulk of American independent film takes more chances than Hollywood material, its success rate isn't much better. What's more, the themes and stories of these so-called cutting edge movies can often be reduced to genericisms as easily as a buddy picture or fish-out-of-water comedy. If you're inspired by Martin Scorsese and *Bon-*

*nie and Clyde,* you make the quirky crime-spree indie film. If Altman and Henry Jaglom is more your thing, you make the small multicharacter-study indie film. And if you dig Cassavetes, you probably go for a little of both.

Good or bad, more adventurous or not, the indie film carries a very strong stench of *Ecch.* The worst offender might be Gus Van Sant, who is responsible for the amazing *Drugstore Cowboy* but also directed one of the most overrated art films, *My Own Private Idaho.*

A combination of *Cruising* and *Henry IV,* the film tells the story of a narcoleptic gay hustler (River Phoenix) and his rich friend (Keanu Reeves). River plays the grunge type, unshaven, in a flannel shirt and a knit wool hat, taking his first willful, stumbling steps on the road to life. Keanu is more like the boomer hippy, the guy who betrays his friends and throws away life in the underground to go hang out at St. Elmo's Fire after he gets his inheritance. See, *My Own Private Idaho* really is based on *Henry IV,* which means that Keanu grows up to become Kenneth Branagh. (You were expecting us to say Olivier, perhaps? Hell, even Branagh is stretching it—the guy speaks in iambic pentameter like he was still playing opposite Alex Winter!) But Keanu is not just a hippy—he's the future of *Ecch.* He'll hang out with unshaven gay guys in flannel shirts for a while to piss off his parents, but eventually he'll toe the line.

On the surface, *MOPI* (pronounced "mopey") seems like a difficult film, the kind designed to deflect all potential criticism with a dismissive "oh, well you just didn't understand it." It's filled with flashbacks, surrealism and, for the sex scenes only, still-framed, kinda sorta stop-motion sequences that engrave the encounters as pure affectation and emotionless physicality, even the scenes that are supposed to be tender.

But despite its incoherent "experimental" structure and voluminous Shakespearean references, the basic themes of *MOPI* stand out like someone wearing gray at a rave. It's a movie about (lack of) love, and (lack of) family, and (missing out on) the American Dream. We know this, because every time River falls face-first on the pavement he thinks about his mommy, plus Van Sant uses "America the Beautiful" over and over again on the sound track.

River is *so* lost, and *so* sad, that the contrast between this and his hustling is just too obvious. When the boys recount some of their harsher chicken-hawking tales, Madonna's "Cherish" plays in the background—*this represents pop music's idealized notion of romantic love, in contrast to the hustling.* When River joins Keanu on a trick for a rich lady, she's old enough to be a mother figure, and makes them dance to old dance hall music before things get started—*this represents everyone's idealized notion of family and romantic love, in contrast to the hustling.* When we meet River's sole known family member (his brother actually turns out to be his father—what is this? *The Jack Nicholson Story?*), we find that the guy's job is painting Kmart-quality portraits of other families which he keeps for himself if they don't get bought—*this represents everyone's idealized notion of*... and so on, and so on. The whole thing is awkward and obvious and sentimental in the arty context of transgression that the film provides.

We also know the movie is about narcolepsy because it opens with a shot of the dictionary definition of the word. It's important that future viewers of *My Own Private Idaho* see this shot, lest they think the film is a documentary about the death of River Phoenix. There's a particularly eerie scene in the middle of the film, where River's character is sitting in that weird German's hotel room watching an episode of *The Simpsons.* It's one of the Halloween episodes—*an episode that was rebroadcast the very Halloween that River Phoenix died! Doh!*

**Y**es, if there's one event in the film world that means more to *Ecch* than anything else, it has to be the untimely death of River Phoenix. The young actor was seized from the jaws of life on a bleak Halloween night—actually, after midnight, the morning of Halloween—while hanging out with Butthole Surfer Gibby Haynes and Red Hot Chili Pepper Flea at Johnny Depp's nightclub, the Viper Room.

*Entertainment Weekly* printed a picture of his death site with the caption "Generation X marks the spot." This tragic story has been rehashed so many times that if you don't know it, once again you're in danger of losing your *Ecch* membership card. For the sake of brevity, this book will stick to only the most important details from the most reputable sources.

The *National Enquirer* reported that River came running outside the club crying, "Help me, I've done a speedball! I'm gonna die, dude." The paper also said that he injected the speedball, which turned out to be untrue. River preferred to take his pleasures orally—say, some wok-fried tofu and bean curd with a little liquid morphine on the side.

But hey, the *Enquirer* still had the scoop. A friend is also quoted quoting River as saying, "Life's too short not to live it up. I don't want to die from old age in a nursing home. I'll be the best looking guy in the morgue." Actually, Raul Rivera, a twenty-two-year-old former model and forensic medicine intern at Cedars-Sinai, is said to be quite a spectacular physical specimen—and he has a heartbeat.

One of the other tabs said that River referred to speedballs as "John Belushis." *Help me! I've done a John Belushi!* Yes you have, our little dear departed friend, but it could have been worse—you could have done a Dan Aykroyd, staying alive long enough to make twice as many bad movies and develop a really really huge butt.

Specifically, the coroner ruled that it was accidental death involving an acute ingestion of both cocaine and morphine—at lethal levels. He also had marijuana, Valium, and an over-the-counter cold medicine in his system. Yeah, that combination of junk and pseudoephedrine (that would be Sudafed, but we don't know that for sure—he might buy generic) gets you every time. We're kidding, but producer and experienced druggie Julia Phillips told *EW* that every junkie knows to stay away from cold medication.

The coroner responsible for these findings was Lakshmanan Sathyavagiswaran, though we prefer to think of him or her as Quincy. (*No, no—Lakshmanan Sathyavagiswaran as the coroner's assistant Sam. Jack Klugman as the coroner.*) Whatever you call him, it's gonna be hard for him to get as good a book deal as Thomas Noguchi with that name.

(*Editor's Note: Hi, Dave Dunton here. I'm the editor of* Generation Ecch! *Don't you feel sorry for me? You should. I would like to denounce the above paragraph, which is, at best, an unnecessary bit of xenophobic nonsense, and at worst, racist. We apologize to anyone who might take offense, especially my family physician of fifteen years, Dr. Rameesh Krishnan.*)

Quincy, of course, was famous for that episode in which he discovered how bad punk rock was 'cause it killed some girl. Clearly, there's no question that River Phoenix was also a victim of the punk rock lifestyle. Hangin' out with guys like Flea and Gibby will kill ya for sure, especially when you've spent your whole life living on communes. River the vegetarian boy just couldn't hang with the real men. In the disdainful words of Primal Scream guitarist Andrew Innes, "Lightweight . . ."

**W**hat was terrible about the death of River Phoenix, perhaps even more terrible than the tragedy itself, was the media's coverage of the incident. Over and over again we were told of River's vegetarianism and his commune lifestyle. Occasionally, we were reminded that his parents were actually wacky cultists with the Children of God for many years. *Hey, maan, we're all Children of God.*

Over and over again we were told how River was named for the River of Life in the Herman Hesse novel *Siddhartha.* Yeah, so why wasn't he named "River of Life" Phoenix? Shouldn't his parents have been more specific? He could be named after the Swanee for all we know. And where did the other kids get their names?

Well, since you asked, Leaf was named for a piece of Double-Bubble his dad found while pacing outside the Venezuelan hut during the kid's birth, and Rainbow (who prefers being called Rain) was named after Ritchie Blackmore and Joe Lynn Turner's excellent hard rock band. Dad had the cover of *Rainbow Rising*—you know, the cool one with the fist coming out of the water holding a rainbow—painted on the back of his denim jacket.

The worst coverage of the tragedy came from the Gray Lady, not from Styles, but from an editorial that could have given Hilton Kramer fodder for months. "The Young Prove Mortal Again," the headline read on November 2, as the powers that be at the paper paused to contemplate a cultural moment that totally overshadowed Fellini's passing (though he did get a page-one obit).

"Every generation faces moments when the myth of its own immortality is shattered," the editorial opined. "Somebody young and beautiful dies, somebody who, like them, was going to live forever." It compares him immediately to James Dean, Jimi Hendrix, Jim Morrison and Janis Joplin. That's all it took, really—River is already bigger in death than he was in life.

The editorial continued: "The passing is particularly sad because, to many in his generation, River Phoenix had something beyond the bratty appeal of a Christian Slater or a Johnny Depp—something thoughtful, caught in the same conundrums. They had looked forward to growing up with him. Now that's not going to happen." Aww. So basically, the *Times* editorial board is saying that it wouldn't have been a tragedy if Christian Slater had died. Actually, it's hard for us to disagree with that sentiment. Now if it had been Brad Pitt, the *Times* really would have been crushed—he was in *A River Runs Through It,* and that Howell Raines, he *loves* fly-fishing.

Johnny Depp, on the other hand, is a real talent who hasn't been recognized as such compared to his blonder, blander pal River. River may have knocked people out in *Stand by Me, The Mosquito Coast,* and *My Own Private Idaho,* but he was also in films like *I Love You to Death, A Night in the Life of Jimmy Reardon,* and *Running on Empty,* a film for which he was nominated for an Oscar, though his work under director Sidney Lumet wasn't that much better than Timothy Hutton's in *Q&A* or Melanie Griffith's in *A Stranger Among Us.* However, at no point in the film did he say, "If you touch my dick I'll kill you," or fall brazenly in love with a hot young Hasidic boy.

Depp has never made a bad choice or a bad movie after doing what he had to do to get his career going with *21 Jump Street.* He's no Richard Grieco or Luke Perry. We smell conspiracy. Maybe Johnny wanted to get rid of the competition. This was obviously one of those artistic feuds, like Vidal/Mailer, Davis/Crawford and Lapham/Morris, gone horribly awry.

*Entertainment Weekly* reported that in the last couple of years the formerly straight-arrow River had changed. He went to a wedding without putting on a tux. Peter Bogdanovich, director of River's final film, was worried about the crowd he was running with. As if hanging out with him and Dorothy Stratten's little sister was a good thing. As if a career move like *The Thing Called Love* was a good thing. Poor guy—his last movie wasn't released in most American cities, and it had Travis Tritt in it. Then, as if that wasn't bad enough, his last commercially released film was a western from the director of *Far North. Silent Tongue* director Sam Shepard also happens to be one of America's greatest playwrights, but according to *Premiere,* Riv was unaware of his Pulitzer Prize–winning dramaturgy.

One person suggested that it was that awful Gus Van Sant crowd that changed him during *My Own Private Idaho*. He began hanging out with druggies to better understand his character. Just another young actor having problems with the Method.

*EW* helpfully followed up the tragedy with a big story on *drugs and young hollywood*. It revealed to a breathless world that young people who live in Los Angeles and work in the entertainment industry hang out in clubs and DO DRUGS! Oh, the humanity! Yes, it's one of "Hollywood's open secrets," *EW* whispered—"drug abuse by the PC generation."

The great thing about the piece, though, is the aforementioned photo, complete with the graffiti that has gone up (along with the cover charge) at the Viper Room since the incident: *"River was real and ALWAYS stood for truth (peace sign)." "River—What's Up? Remember the Rainbow? Was wondering where you went. Always be in my heart. . . ." "When a flood of evil comes, everything we grow to fear—Aeschylus." "River Phoenix/Rising from the ash/Your sun sets/To rise again! Peace."*

Among the postmortem poetry spawned by Phoenix's kicking, the most mawkish comes from L.A. songwriter Grant Lee Phillips (of Grant Lee Buffalo). "You were like my own James Byron Dean/*Private Idaho* was my *East of Eden.*"

But the last best word on the subject came from Moms Phoenix, who goes by the first name of Heart. River, she explained, "fell victim to a scene that was way beyond his usual experience and control." But she does not blame her progeny for his little detour on the road to Hollywood hell. No, she said, "it is my prayer that River's leaving in this way will focus the attention of the world on how painfully the spirits of his generation are being worn down." *Aaaah, now we're at the heart of things.* All of *Ecch* is a River waiting to dry up.

"Drug abuse is a symptom of an unfeeling, materialistic, success-oriented world where the feelings and creativity of young people are not seen as important," she continued. Uh-huh. Maybe Mom should have had a little Heart-to-River chat about this subject *before* he embarked on a career as a Hollywood actor and would-be rock star. Maybe the other kids should stop acting.

The whole thing is just like the end of *My Own Private Idaho*. You're on a road in the middle of somewhere, fucked up on drugs and starved for love. Have a nice Day! Mommeeeeee! Mommeeeeee!

# Ecch-Men

## or

### With Great

### Power Comes

### Great

### Responsibility

Since his arrival on Earth in 1939, Superman has survived battles with Nazis, Bizarros, Lex Luthor and Mr. Mxyztplk. But not even the last son of Krypton could withstand the menace of . . . *GENERATION ECCH.*

Yes, the generation that elevated comic books to "graphic novels" and shelled out fourteen bucks to see two movies with a neurotic Batman relegated to a supporting role, a generation whose bloodlust was unquenched by the death of Robin, KILLED Superman!

Actually, the heinous deed wasn't committed by *GenEcch* per se. The killing of Kal-El came at the hands of Doomsday, a really ugly escapee from an Intergalactic Insane Asylum. Well, he *was* an escapee from an Intergalactic Insane Asylum, but before Chapter 1 of the 242-part miniseries even hit the streets, those kooks from the National Federation of Nutbars, Loons and Crazy People—um, excuse us, we mean the Coalition of Consumer Self Advocates, a Rhode Island-based organization 250 loons strong—pitched a fit. They felt that it would reflect badly on the nonalien, nonsuperpowered mentally ill if one of their own did something wacky like that.

The folks at DC then toyed with the idea of making him a Jewish character named Judas Iscariot, but that didn't fly either.

Anyway, Doomsday finally emerged as your garden-variety apocalyptic supervillain. He's actually quite mad, but nobody ever points this out—you wouldn't want to offend anybody with razor-sharp bones protruding from their head.

Doomsday levels most of Metropolis, then administers the killing blow to our beloved *Übermensch*. Supey dies in the arms of his fiancée, Lois Lane, who, over the years, has not only learned his secret identity but also become a kick-ass Linda Hamilton–type babe along the way.

The comic-book crucifixion of Clark Kent signifies nothing less than the collapse of Truth, Justice and the American Way. Elvis aside, Siegel & Shuster's invincible creation was our last god. He protected us from various villains, both real and imagined, for much of the American Century. Previous generations were comforted by his omnipresent benevolence, knowing that nothing too bad could happen with Superman around. His death was inconceivable—*Kill Superman!? No way!* No matter how many different colors of Kryptonite his writers invented, Superman always prevailed.

But for *Generation Ecch*, his perfection is intimidating, disenfranchising. Those of us who don't have X-ray vision or a Fortress of Solitude are left out. He's a classic symbol of what Robert Hughes calls the "patriarchal penis people"—even though he's an illegal alien.

On the other hand, maybe his demise was just a ploy to sell a whole mess of Superman comic books.

**A**nd what a mess it was! Superman's funeral took place over nine issues of comic books, all available in multiple packages: in polybags, as trading cards, with die-cut foil-embossed covers, on bonus posters—everything but a bloody swatch of red-and-blue costume. The two-dimensional vigil was attended by more high-powered celebrities than a Marianne Williamson retreat. The media covered this breaking news story with a flurry of Op-Eds and obits, *as if it had really happened.*

Then, faster than you could say, "Faster Than a Speeding Bullet,"

Superman was resurrected. Only now, the world's greatest hero had become four multicultural superdudes—a gorgeous mosaic of invulnerability. *No way!* And here everyone thought that Time Warner subsidiary DC would discontinue its four Superman titles. (Four! What a coincidence!)

The four Supermans were created through some impossibly convoluted bioenergy process involving cloning, cybernetics, leftover fragments of the planet Krypton and some gobbledygook about "the matrix." Frankly, we haven't really been able to figure it out ourselves. (Note to comic-book geeks and DC editors: Save your letters—we don't really care that much.)

All right, so there were four Supermans. First up was the Eradicator, an "immaterial wraith" who pilfered the "thirty years of bioconverted solar energy" from Superman's corpse.

Next was the first black Superman—that is, if you don't count Shaft (*John* Shaft. *Damn right!*). No, he was John Henry Irons, aka the Man of Steel, an ordinary steelworker whose life was saved by the one true Superman. Steel might not have been "the black private dick that's a sex machine to all the chicks" (. . . *Shaft!*), but he was one hell of a tinkerer. Inspired by his hero's death, he went down to the basement and, with nothing but a toolbox, a roll of aluminum foil and some old-fashioned comic-book ingenuity, built himself a suit of armor, replete with high-tech laser blasters and turbopowered boot rockets. Of course, the gleaming silver shell made him look, well . . . white, thereby diminishing the Afrocentricity of the character.

Superman #3 came from a truly rare minority group—Kryptonian cyborgs. Half man, half machine, Supercyborg possessed part of the true Superman's consciousness, though he had suffered some memory loss, due, as one brilliant scientist explains, to "severe trauma—death, and apparently some kind of rebirth. Trauma victims often exhibit such problems."

Finally, there was Superman #4, a teenage clone who had all of Superman's powers but none of his original personality. He sports a leather jacket, shades and a punk-rock haircut, and gets uppity when you call him Superboy.

(Okay, so maybe they're not as multicultural as the original DC press leaks implied, even if there was a larger role for Supergirl while cousin Kal "rested.")

After a mere three months of this crap, the real Superman returned, teaming up with a few of his successors to vanquish Supercyborg, who, as it turns out, was big-time evil. The Eradicator sacrificed himself to save Superman, who regained his life force in the process. He also got a hip head of shaggy blue hair—it's so difficult to get a good trim when you're dead (regular scissors never worked on those invulnerable indigo locks anyway).

Superman was back, his demise nothing more than a way to revitalize a tired old series, paving the way for further exploitation in the more lucrative world of television. Time Warner's precious corporate commodity was reinterpreted yet again, this time as the sensitive hunk on the ABC series *supersomething* . . . erm . . . *Lois and Clark: The New Adventures of Superman*. As always, death is a good career move.

T he Bible says there comes a time to put away childish things. For *Ecch*sters, this has never really applied. Sure, children have always loved comics, from *Richie Rich* and *Archie* to *Superman* and *The Incredible Hulk*. But like most prepubescent romances, the affair eventually ends. Teenagers traditionally move on to more enlightening pursuits, like literature, sports, sex or drugs. Then there are mortgage payments, health insurance and all that other grown-up stuff. Previous generations just didn't have time to keep up with the adventures of the Mighty Thor.

*GenEcch*, though, has continued to consume comic books long after adolescence. Whether it's the goofy twenty-six-year-old geek hoarding multiple copies of the new *Batman* or the pretentious twenty-six-year-old geek writing long, ponderous fan letters about the archetypal elements of *The Sandman*, comics have an older audience than ever before.

For *Ecch*, the average funny book offers all the depth and acuity of television without the distractingly strenuous mental challenge posed by real books. Why paint a picture in your mind when somebody's already done it on paper?

Comics are a reliable fantasy world, open for visitation on a weekly, biweekly and monthly basis, and so much more colorful and exciting than the real world. You could spend your time with friends fretting over the deficit, or you could debate important matters like "Could Aquaman take Wolverine in a fair fight?" and "How come Human Torch's costume doesn't burn up when he flames on?" (The answers, by the way, are "No" and "Unstable molecules.")

With a half-life roughly comparable to that of the *Ecch* attention span, comics are as addictive as drugs, soap operas and Sonic the Hedgehog. They leave you breathless and impatient before you've even finished them, eager to blow your cash on another dose right away. Immediate gratification! "I gotta know what happens to the X-Men!"

**They fuck you up, your mum and dad.**
**They may not mean to, but they do.**
**They fill you with the faults they had**
**And add some extra, just for you.**
— Philip Larkin

Perhaps the late British poet had Marvel's *The Uncanny X-Men* in mind when he composed this immortal verse. You see, X-Men are teenage *mutants*, which in Marvel Universe lingo means that they possess atomically twisted DNA that gives them really cool superpowers but makes it difficult for them to blend into normal society. The fact that their inability to fit in stems from flawed genetics makes their plight distinctly *Ecch: It's their parents' fault!*

The best-selling series of all time, *X-Men* is the defining comic book of the *Ecch* years. "Gifted" outcasts who form a surrogate family, the X-Men not only fight evil but make mistakes, solve each other's problems, and try to make the world a more accepting place for kids burdened with acne or enormous feathered wings. It's a lot like *90210*, only with brightly colored costumes and a great deal of violence.

The warped children of a radioactive world, these misfits of science unite at "the School for Gifted Youngsters," located in the rolling hills of upscale Westchester County, New York (home to *all* the best private schools), and run by one Professor Charles Xavier, a wheelchair-bound telepathic-genius type. Professor X, as he is affectionately known, recruited "his X-Men" to battle baddies and learn how to cope with the slings and arrows of a society that doesn't welcome mind-reading teens.

Way back in the sixties the original X-Men were all white males, with the exception of Marvel Girl, who was there primarily because young boys have always liked to look at girls in skintight costumes. This band of outsiders represented the youth culture's emerging feelings of separation from a world they never made. Like hippies, the X-Men resisted society's norms while adhering to some semblance of conformity within their own ranks—the X-Men's uniform blue-and-yellow attire equaled the hippies' uniform costume of long hair, love beads and dirty dungarees. Whether it's hippies or *Ecch*, the X-Men seem like perfect symbols of adolescents who see themselves as special but feel isolated, misunderstood. On the other hand, sometimes a prehensile tail is just a prehensile tail.

The updated X-Men, the ones who captured the brains of millions, are a more multicultural mélange of mutants. The revivification of the series came when Professor X gathered new freaks from around the world: Nightcrawler, a West German acrobat who can teleport himself at will; Colossus, a big Russian dude who transforms his skin into invulnerable armor; Storm, an African princess with the power to control the weather; and the most beloved X-character, Wolverine, a short Canadian thug with adamantium claws. (Notice that the X-Men practice affirmative action in the same way most major companies do: They hire a *black woman*.)

For the most part, this postnuclear family gets along pretty well. There are the standard disagreements that go with any soap-opera clan. The only time things get really ugly is on Sunday, when they fight over who gets to read Styles of the *Times* first.

The X-world became so lucrative for Marvel that they did what any wise pop-culture producer does in the age of *Ecch*: Spin-off! Spin-off! Spin-off! There was such an X-acerbating X-cess of X-Men that one thirty-two-page comic could not contain them all—new groups like X-Factor, X-Force and Excalibur (the English branch, natch) were formed, each with its own individual comic mag.

All of today's X-persons struggle with discrimination in a way that their forebears never had to. During the Reagan years, the powers-that-be of the Marvel Universe codified hatred with the Mutant Control Act, which established three classes of people:

**"H," for Baseline Human, clean of mutant genes, allowed to breed**
**"A," for Anomalous Human, a normal person possessing mutant genetic potential . . . forbidden to breed**
**"M," for Mutant, the bottom of the heap, made pariahs and outcasts . . . hunted down, and with a few rare exceptions, KILLED WITHOUT MERCY**

Missing from the code were the classifications:

**"I," for Idiot, clean of mutant genes, spends way too much money on X-Men comics, would like to breed but cannot find female partner**
**"C," for Chris Claremont, a normal person possessing mutant imagination . . . Marvel Comics writer who came up with all this stuff, extremely wealthy, should be KILLED WITHOUT MERCY**

The X-Men were typical of the way Smilin' Stan Lee's Marvel reimagined the comics universe in the early sixties. Lee and his Bullpen developed a Cold War–influenced roster of garish gamma-ray-charged doctors and scientists locked in mortal combat with freaky aliens, scary monsters and weird-looking mole-men.

While this sounds ridiculous, Marvel stories were actually quite groundbreaking when they took over young America's waking dreams. The recurring devices of cosmic matter and technology gone amok were transparent metaphors for the Atomic Era. Within that decidedly fantastic modernist framework, the Marvel style of art, pioneered by such people as Jack Kirby, Steve Ditko and John Romita, took the brightly colored flamboyance of superheroes and grounded it in a realism not seen before. The stories took place in the real world, in cities like New York rather than fictional metropolises like "Gotham City." When their multicolored Dr. Dentons came off, the Marvel heroes faced the mundane problems of real people.

For nascent *Ecch*sters passing the time of their adolescence turning the pages of Marvel, nobody's problems were more real than those of Peter Parker, aka the Amazing Spider-Man. Once Peter was the geekiest kid in school, the dweeb, the nerd, the four-eyes in the sweater vest. An orphan, Petey was raised by his elderly aunt May and uncle Ben, but their doting adoration couldn't salve the sting of the daily wedgies, pink bellies and book poppings. Even his happening job as a freelance photographer for the *Daily Bugle* wasn't enough to make him cool.

This budding Louis Pasteur spent all of his free time in the chemistry lab, and it was there one fateful afternoon that his life would change forever. He might have discovered the cure for cancer or the formula for LSD that day, but *la forza del destino* (that's *die Macht des Schicksals* in German) intervened in the form of a bite from an irradiated arachnid. It seems somebody in the chem lab was screwing around with uranium, as scientists were wont to do in those days before they had heard of lead protection—though you would think that the paint jobs of New York schools in the sixties would have been sufficient.

"Ouch" was Peter's first reaction. Suddenly, he didn't feel so well, and he decided to go home for a big old bowl of his uncle Ben's rice. Absentminded-professor type that he was, Peter almost got run down on the way home. *"I'm walkin' here!"* Peter shouted, then leapt out of the deadly auto's path . . . and found himself stuck to the wall three stories up. A moment's encounter with a radioactive spider and Petey had gone from wallflower to wallcrawler.

Being a chemist, Peter immediately fashioned a pair of "webshooters," from which he could project strands of sticky, indestructible proto-jism. He was finally becoming a man—Spider-Man, that is. He stitched up a fancy costume, and he was ready to do what any teenager who suddenly discovered himself with superpowers would do—use them to get respect, money and girls. So he went on TV to become a big star. That'll teach those kids at school. *I'll show them! I'll show everybody!*

While at the studio, Spidey encountered a robbery but selfishly refused to intervene. Arriving home he discovered that his dear uncle Ben had been killed by an intruder. Spidey decided to use his powers for vengeance and seek out the killer of his surrogate dad, eventually trapping the willful murderer in an abandoned warehouse. Spidey nabbed his man, but not without great trauma—he discovered that the bad guy was the very same robber he had let pass back at the studio. From that day forward, Spider-Man would only use his powers for good. With great power comes great responsibility.

With Uncle Ben dead, Peter was left in a single-parent family, forced to mature because he was the man of the house now. To the kids at school, he was still the same old geeky Petey, but Spidey's powers had given him pride, and he didn't care what other people thought anymore. Plus, his Spider-sense enabled him to know in advance when Flash Thompson and the other jocks were approaching to yank his underpants up to his ears.

In the nineties, Peter Parker has become the very picture of a thoroughly modern *Ecch* webslinger. He's been a grad student for almost thirty years, though it should be noted that comic-book years are a lot like dog years. He's still a freelance photographer, struggling to make ends meet from picture to picture, though he does have unparalleled access to action-packed Spidey snaps. Mostly, he lives off the earnings of his fabulous babe actress/model wife, Mary Jane Watson-Parker. They moved recently, after a protracted and difficult search for a Soho loft with a skylight for Petey's nocturnal missions. It's a lot like Jay McInerney's *Bright Lights, Big City*— Petey has grown up, but he's not really a grown-up. He has all the trappings of responsibility, but at night he gets dressed up and goes out swinging.

In *GenEcch*, we are all Peter Parker. Put yourself in his place, think very carefully, search the depths of your soul and ask yourself—If I were bitten by a radioactive spider, would I be:

**A) a superhero**
**or**
**B) a supervillain?**

If you answered "B," you are the average honest young adult, strapped for cash in a postrecession economy and desperate for a way out. If you answered "A," you must be *Ecch* to the core, eager to help others and make the world a better place. Good luck, puny little do-gooders!

*comics... FEH!*

**B**y carrying their obsession with funny books into what we'll call, for lack of a better word, "adulthood," *Ecch* required comic books that were, for lack of a better word, "adult." *Ecch* is the first generation to take comics seriously as art, elevating them to the same aesthetic plane as painting, literature, cinema and television.

There have actually been "adult" comic books for some time, from the underground hippy anarchy of *Zap* to the highbrow postmodernism of *Raw*. Harvey Pekar has regaled the world with his autobiographical *American Splendor* since the seventies, while Dave Sim's infinite saga *Cerebus* began more than a decade ago.

It wasn't until the eighties, however, that cool comix for literate *Ecch*sters really materialized. The underground scene has produced what amounts to one of the finest novels of the late twentieth century, Los Bros. Hernandez's *Love and Rockets*. (Okay, so it's not *The Sun Also Rises*. But it ain't *The Bridges of Madison County* either.) With his history of the impoverished Latin American country Palomar, Bro Gilbert has produced a rich, serious magic-realist chronicle. Pretty impressive for a comic book, eh? But as wonderful as Gilbert's work is, it isn't exactly *Ecch*. That's where Bro Jaime comes in.

Jaime's stories are like *Archie* comics for kids who have outgrown their Stride Rites: Punked up, pop-culture savvy and transplanted from idyllic Riverdale to the harsher but more happening climes of East L.A. Cool barrio chicks Maggie and Hopey careen around the margins of society, obsessing over romantic relationships, be they with boys, girls, or each other, going to see and/or playing in bands, gaining and losing weight, cadging off eccentric millionaires and following the fortunes of their favorite female professional wrestlers. Jaime's sly, amicable storytelling gifts and ingeniously stark pen-and-ink drawings are thoroughly insinuating—he makes Maggie, Hopey and the gang seem like your friends. Reading *Love and Rockets* is like a phone call from an old roommate, bringing you up to date on the hijinks and heartbreaks of various pals.

*Love and Rockets* was the first burst in a veritable explosion of independently produced *Ecch* comics. Often autobiographical, they are usually presented in black-and-white, the idea being that it is somehow more realistic than the glaring ROY G BIV of superhero books. This is actually strange, because if you think about it, real life is in color. It's also been said that superhero comics are like dreams—except dreams are in black and white. Following that logic, the realistic comic books should be more like dreams. Except they're not. Color it all very confusing.

Actually, black-and-white art emphasizes meaning over form—it's less distracting than color, drawing the reader into the story on a more personal level. Oh yeah, and it's cheaper.

Comics like Chester Brown's pornographically surreal *Yummy Fur*, Daniel Clowes's fifties retro *Eightball* and Julie Doucet's savagely frank *Dirty Plotte* all play big with the college-educated *Ecch* crowd. The most popular guy these days is Peter Bagge, a writer/artist who uses an in-your-face, Big Daddy Roth/*Hot Rod* magazine–influenced style of caricature to document the day-to-day life of one Buddy Bradley, a misanthropic *Ecch*ster who abandoned his ironic sitcom family, the Bradleys, to star in his own book, appropriately titled *Hate*. Coincidentally, he moved to Seattle just when the words "Sub Pop" and "grunge" were permeating the nation's consciousness. Bagge writes about people, as writer/cartoonist J. D. King says, "whose sad lives are a Bermuda Triangle defined by the comics shop, the porno shop and the used-record shop." *Hate* is a viciously funny slacker satire, the usual obscure references mixed with Buddy's quests for beer, neurotic women and mint copies of Harvey Kurtzman comics. With a perfectly *Ecch* combination of adoration and contempt, for both his characters and his audience, Bagge mocks the emptiness of these rock-club losers and human pop-culture receptacles.

Of course, indie-comics fans are guilty of the same highbrow elitism and intellectual pretensions as indie-rock fans. The die-hard *Hate* reader views *Batman* followers with the same disdain a Sebadoh fanatic reserves for Pearl Jam devotees.

**B**ut the majority of grown-up *Ecch* readers look at these provocative tomes and say, "Hey! Those aren't comic books! Comic books have superheroes and color and stuff! What is this, like, *art* or something?"

Fortunately, DC Comics was there to provide hip, iconic/ironic stories about guys with secret identities in bulletproof long underwear. By the early eighties, the venerable home of the Justice League of America had long since become second to Marvel in fans' hearts and wallets. DC was considered megawimpy, still cranking out the same old adventures of white-bread heroes like Superman and Green Lantern. Marvel had the X-Men and Spidey; DC readers were stuck with the continuing exploits of lame-os like Element Lad, Hawkman, and Superman's Pal Jimmy Olsen.

The man who made DC Comics cool again was writer/artist Frank Miller, with his revisionist *Götterdämmerung der* Batman, *The Dark Knight Returns*. By introducing self-doubt, moral ambiguity and ultraviolence, Miller redefined Batman as the borderline psychopath he always was. Think about it: Here's a millionaire philanthropist who spends his nights dressed as a bat, prowling the streets of Gotham beating the shit out of people. His parents are dead, he lives in a cave and his only significant relationships are with young boys and old English men.

In creating the first superhero comic with adult pretensions, Miller brought those elements to the surface. He also did something that is ordinarily unthinkable in the world of comics—he let the hero age, reimagining Batman as a bitter old man in a world of media overload and roving violence. *The Dark Knight* brought Batman back to the pop-culture playing field while opening up a whole new market of older fans.

Miller's work was influenced by the postapocalyptic sci-fi mayhem of *Judge Dredd*, one of the most popular titles of Great Britain's more cutting-edge comics scene. Sensing a trend, DC began hiring anyone with an imagination and a British accent, starting with Alan Moore, the godfather of the Brit Pack.

Moore and artist Dave Gibbons gave the world *Watchmen*, the first book to truly earn the honorific "graphic novel." The term had already been applied to *The Dark Knight Returns*, but unlike Miller, Moore created an original universe apart from the DC context, with his own fully realized group of faded heroes. *Watchmen* was essentially a deconstruction of comic-book meanings and conventions, a metacomic, if you will. Moore acknowledges the inherent ridiculousness of the genre, then proceeds to make it matter again.

Following in Moore's footsteps were such writers and artists as Neil Gaiman, Jamie Delano, Dave McKean, Peter Milligan, Grant Morrison and Brendan McCarthy. Books like *Shade the Changing Man* and *Hellblazer* are geared toward the segment of the adult comics audience that still grooves on the unreality of trad super-hero stuff but requires something less obvious, something smarter and more original. These books have been described collectively as "dark fantasy," which basically translates to more horror, less Hobbits. The best of the bunch is Neil Gaiman's *The Sandman*, a witches' brew of such elements as Shakespeare, Classical Lit 101, J. R. R. Tolkien, serial killers and everyone's favorite superhero, archetypal analyst Carl Jung. DC had such success with these books that in 1993 they created a new imprint, Vertigo, to specifically handle the weirder, tougher, smarter strain of stories.

*Watchman*, *The Dark Knight Returns* and the Vertigo titles have garnered reams of publicity, prompting many people to pay attention to the possibilities of comics again. Miller in particular completely transformed DC's treatment of Batman—the darkness of *The Dark Knight* permeated the regular Batman stories, as well as Tim Burton's black-hearted blockbuster films. Ultimately, though, the superhero world was unaffected by Miller, Moore et al. There's more merchandise to sell, and there are more kids to outfit with complete sets of limited-edition comics, action figures, trading cards, pewter statuettes and T-shirts. Once again, Batman is just another crappy comic book. Goofy superhero comics remain goofy superhero comics.

**A**nd goofy comic books mean goofy ploys by comic publishers, in an effort to sell goofy guys more goofy stuff. Comics are another way of separating the men from the boys by the size of their toys—a fifty-year-old man buys original comics art at Sotheby's bi-annual auction, a prosperous yuppie is ten issues away from filling out his pricey collection of Jack Kirby back issues, while *Ecch* kids are buying five copies of *everything* new, certain that in five or ten years' time the collection will be worth a fortune. So why bother getting a job till then? The only problem is the collections are never worth what they are supposed to be, for when a publisher prints more than a million ultraspecial "limited-edition" collectibles, anyone who wants one can get it—even now, many of the supposedly precious "Death of Superman" stories are available at cover price. Besides, the true collector is never willing to actually part with his precious possessions.

But he's always willing to buy more. The market is now driven more by characters that can sell merchandise than by the books themselves. It became so lucrative that *X-Men* and *Spider-Man* artists like Rob Liefeld and Todd McFarlane realized they were missing out on the big bucks because they didn't own the characters that their labor helped make so profitable. So they formed their own company, Image Comics, where they could have the creative freedom to perpetrate shoddy rip-offs of *X-Men* and *Spider-Man* without sharing the money with Marvel. This move also gave them the much-needed creative freedom to write their own stories, because frankly, working with professional writers was hampering their vision. So what we're left with is a fresh batch of badly written generic superhero crap, without even the heritage and nostalgia factor of the Marvel characters. Unsurprisingly, Image immediately established itself as a veritable license to print money for its artist owners, its sales figures dwarfing even Marvel and DC's at times.

**B**ack in the fifties a fellow named Dr. Fredric Wertham denounced comics as immoral and intellectually destructive. In his book *Seduction of the Innocent*, he fretted that comics would send kids spiraling into irresponsibility, hedonism and stupidity. Now it seems as if he was right, though the issue of causality is still pretty fuzzy.

But even Doc Wertham couldn't predict that comic books would be part of people's lives well into adulthood. Not that there's anything wrong with comics—whether it's Art Spiegelman's brilliant Holocaust memoir *Maus*, Kyle Baker's loopy *Ecch* chronicle *Why I Hate Saturn* or something just plain dopey like *X-Men*, comics are just words and pictures, an aesthetic tradition that goes all the way back to cave paintings and Tijuana bibles.

Besides, these days, the relationship of people to the printed word is so skimpy that naysayers should get down on their knees and thank the deity of their choice if they see *Ecch* kids reading comix. Hey, at least we're reading.

## *Ecchcelsior!*

With Great Power Comes Great Responsibility

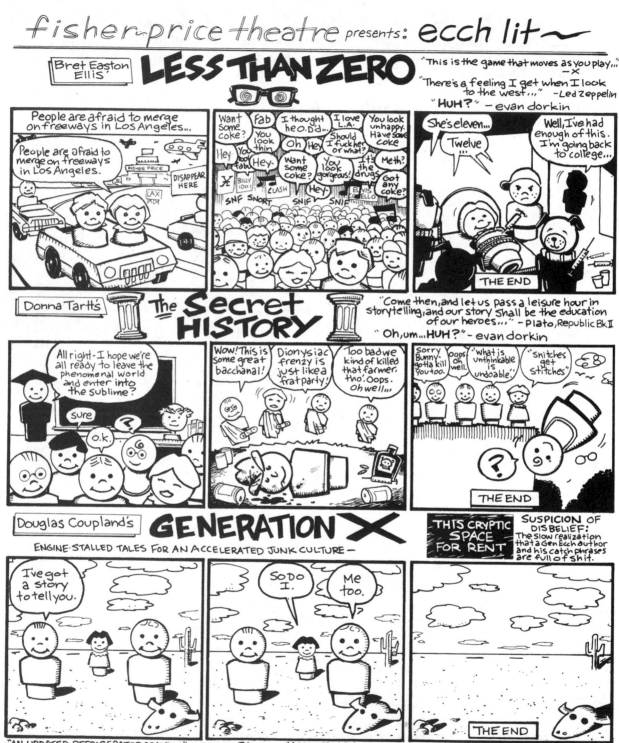

**W**hoever first said "You can't judge a book by its cover" never surveyed the appalling literary *oeuvre* of *GenEcch*. Take, for instance, *Fast Sofa* by Bruce Craven (please!), possibly the least distinguished example of today's literature for the postliterate.

The book's cover is by Los Angeles artist Robert Williams, best known for the banned "alien-rape" sleeve of Guns N' Roses' *Appetite for Destruction*. As if to say, *This ain't fiction, man, this is rock'n'roll!*, said cover is stamped with the PARENTAL ADVISORY: EXPLICIT LYRICS seal, as well as a confounding command to PLAY THIS NOVEL LOUD!, which is very hard to do without moving your lips.

As if that weren't *ROCK'N'ROLL!* enough, this odious and overblown chunk of a novel is packaged as an eight-by-eight square—sort of an oversize CD. Or a scaled-down record—the book provides its own sound track with a two-song flexidisc by past-its-prime punk band the Flesh Eaters.

In interviews, Craven has attempted to hop the hip musical movement of the moment, dubbing himself and his so-called peers "the grunge pack." Our investigation has yet to turn up anyone else associated with this vague clique. What's Craven on about? Were Chris Cornell and Kurt Cobain collaborating on a current-day *Candide?*

One of the trademarks of this genre is the compulsory photo of the author gazing at potential buyers in all his hunky glory. *Ecch* writers are required to be as photogenic as movie stars, resulting in a series of back covers resembling a wall at the second-rate Chinese restaurant around the corner from any acting school.

Ever the poseur, Craven shuns the young-and-beautiful-literati look. Rather, he mugs saucily for an ersatz James Dean shot, tall and leathered in front of an X-rated video store, one hand placed smugly in hip pocket and the other shielding his balding babyface. If the photo looks something like an idealized, appropriately "dangerous" self-image of a Columbia Business School journal editor, well . . . guess what Craven's day job is. The author bio further establishes Craven's hipster bona fides by informing us of his status as a nationally ranked ultimate Frisbee player, as well as his stewardship of a poetry magazine with the oh-so-California moniker of *Big Wednesday.*

There *are* words between the covers of *Fast Sofa*, and they're just as inspiring. The book is a manufactured Mad Lib for this generation, a series of *Ecch*-referential conversations about *Gilligan's Island*, SST Records, junk food, heavy metal, game shows and *X-Men*, tied together by the internal meanderings of one Rick Jeffers. Rick is a "heroic" loser who lives for easy sex, hard music, cheap pornography and expensive tequila. *AW-RIGHT!*

With *faux* attitude dripping off him like yesterday's bongwater, Rick ditches his long-suffering girlfriend to go on a profound and heartfelt quest for the Holy Quail—porno queen Ginger Quail, that is, she of the buff bod and fine cocaine supply. His chase takes him on what must be the shortest literary road trip ever, from Los Angeles to Palm Springs. It's not exactly an odyssey of Homeric proportions.

Along the way he hooks up with Jules Langdon, a repressed, nerdy middle-aged ornithology freak. In the great tradition of *On the Road*, *Easy Rider* and *Thelma and Louise*, they bicker, get their asses kicked, blow some stuff up and learn a little bit about life from each other. All this on a trip that normally takes around three hours!

Rick teaches Jules how to drive a car, and the four-eyed birdboy promptly kills himself in a car wreck. As for Rick . . . well, he doesn't really learn anything, but by journey's end, he begins to come to terms with the schmuck that he is. He's getting in touch with his inner asshole.

Rick is a shallow person, but he's also shallowly characterized. Craven's attempts at emotional complexity are expositional rather than dramatic, giving them all the impact of a Robert James Waller song. As Dorothy Parker once said of some long-forgotten novel, this is a book for the ages—the ages of six to eight. Sadly, *Fast Sofa*'s target audience is between the ages of sixteen to twenty-eight.

The social circumstances of the characters aren't articulated in any meaningful way beyond the pop-culture namechecking. "Nazareth was the wood. The Flesh Eaters were the nails. And Motörhead *was* the hammer," Rick's best buddy, Jack, insists, in a typical *Fast Sofa* passage. Rick disagrees. "If anything," he replies, "Ted Nugent was the wood. X *were* the nails. And the Butthole Surfers *are* the hammer.

Maybe Motörhead can be some kind of hyperfine wood finish!" Why bother reading this conversation in a novel when we *Ecch*sters spend far too much time having it ourselves?

With *Fast Sofa*, Craven documents the denizens of *Ecch* culture without making a real statement about them. Unless, of course, his statement is "THESE PEOPLE ARE IDIOTS"—in which case he's a genius.

In fact, if "These people are idiots" is the statement, all *Ecch* fiction is downright masterful.

*Bright Lights, Big City:* a dreary New York pseudointellectual gets dumped by his fashion-model wife, goes to clubs, does heaps of blow with his jerky friends, listens to Talking Heads, has some sex and searches for meaning. *Idiots!*

*Less Than Zero:* a dreary L.A. college student comes home for Christmas, goes to clubs, does heaps of blow with his jerky friends, listens to Talking Heads, has some sex and searches for meaning. *Idiots!*

*Generation X:* a bunch of dreary, unemployed pseudointellectuals don't go to clubs, don't do heaps of blow with their jerky friends, don't listen to Talking Heads and don't have any sex. But boy, do they ever search for meaning. *Idiots!*

*Ecch* lit's influences are not life experience, or even other literature, but rather television, money, rock'n'roll, drugs and ambivalent/ambiguous sex. All of which are fine things, but despite the introspection accorded to such trivial pursuits, the absence of any sharp insight or affecting emotions makes these books little more than underexposed Polaroids of unpleasant people. We get portraits of solipsism, blankness and reticence that are themselves solipsistic, blank and reticent, providing more information about record collections than glimpses into the human condition.

Hey, kids! Test your knowledge of useless cultural information! See if you can identify your favorite *Ecch* novels from their portentous, microcosmic opening lines!

**A.** "Back in the late 1970s, when I was fifteen years old, I spent every penny I then had in the bank to fly across the continent in a 747 jet to Brandon, Manitoba, deep in the Canadian prairies, to witness a total eclipse of the sun."

**B.** "I'm like, I don't believe this shit."

**C.** "ABANDON ALL HOPE YE WHO ENTER HERE is scrawled in blood red lettering on the side of the Chemical Bank near the corner of Eleventh and First and is in print large enough to be seen from the backseat of the cab as it lurches forward in the traffic leaving Wall Street and just as Timothy Price notices the words a bus pulls up, the advertisement for *Les Misérables* on its side blocking his view, but Price who is with Pierce & Pierce and twenty-six doesn't seem to care because he tells the driver he will give him five dollars to turn up the radio, 'Be My Baby' on WYNN, and the driver, black, not American, does so."

**D.** "Something clicked midway through *Pleasure Quest*."

**E.** "and it's a story that might bore you but you don't have to listen, she told me, because she always knew it was going to be like that, and it was, she thinks, her first year, or, actually weekend, really a Friday, in September, at Camden, and this was three or four years ago, and she got so drunk that she ended up in bed, lost her virginity (late, she was eighteen) in Lorna Slavin's room, because she was a Freshman and had a roommate and Lorna was, she remembers, a Senior or a Junior and usually sometimes at her boyfriend's place off-campus, to who she thought was a Sophomore Ceramics major but who was actually either some guy from N.Y.U., a film student, and up in New Hampshire just for The Dressed To Get Screwed party, or a townie."

**F.** "The snow in the mountains was melting and Bunny had been dead for several weeks before we came to understand the gravity of our situation."

**G.** "You are not the kind of guy who would be at a place like this at this time of the morning."

**H.** "People are afraid to merge on freeways in Los Angeles."

**I.** "My mother, Jasmine, woke up this morning to find the word D-I-V-O-R-C-E written in mirror writing on her forehead with a big black felt pen."

**J.** "If you really want to hear about it, the first thing you'll probably want to know is where I was born, and what my lousy childhood was like, and how my parents were occupied and all before they had me, and all that David Copperfield kind of crap, but I don't feel like going into it, if you want to know the truth."

If you answered

A—*Generation X:* Douglas Coupland
B—*Story of My Life:* Jay McInerney
C—*American Psycho:* Bret Easton Ellis
D—*Fast Sofa:* Bruce Craven
E—*The Rules of Attraction:* Bret Easton Ellis
F—*The Secret History:* Donna Tartt
G—*Bright Lights, Big City:* Jay McInerney
H—*Less Than Zero:* Bret Easton Ellis
I—*Shampoo Planet:* Douglas Coupland

then you've obviously got way too much free time on your hands. If you're looking for a prize, put down this book and send a postcard to *Jeopardy!*

**Y**ou may have noticed there is one quote left. It's from a little classic called *The Catcher in the Rye*, written more than forty years ago, a few years after the Big One (that would be World War II for you non–history buffs). While the literary glorification of shallow young adults dates as far back as the Bible (Jacob screwing Esau out of wealth and power; Joseph's meteoric ascent in the Egyptian social scene), the story of Holden Caulfield is the yardstick against which all other alienated-youth fiction is measured. It's also the only book grown-up reviewers of the genre seem to be familiar with. A sampling:

> **"Catcher in the Rye for the M.B.A. set."**—*Playboy* on *Bright Lights, Big City*
> **"An updated Catcher in the Rye."**—the *Los Angeles Times* on *Less Than Zero*
> **"A modern-day Catcher in the Rye."**—Louise Bernikow, *Cosmopolitan*, on *Generation X*

And, best of all:

> **"Having called Coupland's first book a Catcher in the Rye for our time, I repeat myself. . . ."**—Louise Bernikow, *Cosmopolitan*, on *Shampoo Planet*

Hey, Louise, did you get paid twice for that? And by the way, folks, it's called *THE Catcher in the Rye*.

Amazingly, no one has ever said *Story of My Life* is "like *Catcher in the Rye* with a chick" or *American Psycho* is "*Catcher in the Rye* if Holden got a job on Wall Street, bought some expensive clothes and killed women." We would, however, like to offer up this blurb of our own:

> **"*Fast Sofa* is kind of like *The Catcher in the Rye,* only it sucks."**—Jason Cohen and Michael Krugman, authors of *Generation Ecch!*

Feel free to use it on the next book, Bruce.

For *Ecch, The Catcher in the Rye* is to fiction as *The Brady Bunch* is to drama. It's one of two books that even the most aliterate members of the generation have read (the other being *The Cat in the Hat*).

Holden Caulfield may be American literature's first punk rocker. With his red hunting hat and bad attitude, he walks the streets of New York bemoaning how everything is "crumby" and "phony." Like any sixteen-year-old, he's a contrarian: "I hate the movies like poison but I get a bang imitating them," "I'm quite illiterate, but I read a lot," "Last year I made a rule that I was going to quit horsing around with girls that, deep down, gave me a pain in the ass. I broke it, though, the same week I made it—the same *night,* as a matter of fact. I spent the whole night necking with a terrible phony named Anne Louise Sherman."

His little brother is dead, his parents are "touchy as hell" and he has no idea what he wants to do with his life—today, tomorrow or next year. It's a virtual blueprint for *Ecch* fiction, though references to Ring Lardner and the Lunts have been replaced by David Byrne and Richard Dawson.

It's quite possible that nobody should have bothered writing another teen angst story after *The Catcher.* J. D. Salinger is a *real* writer. As bad as the modern authors might be, the bullcrit comparisons to Salinger hurt them even more. Fifty years later *The Catcher in the Rye* remains startlingly original, a work of rich detail, genuine feeling and distinctive voice. *Ecch* writers, saddled with literary laryngitis, turn Holden Caulfield's primal scream into silent but deadly farts of unwarranted self-pity, trendy postmodernism and emotional indigestion.

It's also interesting to note that the current paperback edition of *The Catcher in the Rye*, after years as a small, plain red book (not unlike *The Sayings of Chairman Mao*), is a small, plain, white book, retailing for under five dollars. There are neither quotes nor an author photo on the back. You might say that all the art is *inside* the book.

In an age when magazine features and talk-show appearances turn authors into not-so-popular pop stars, J. D. Salinger's status as the AntiCeleb makes him cooler than ever. While most *Ecch* authors turn up regularly in the society pages, playing softball in the Hamptons with Wilfrid Sheed or posing with model-slash-actresses at nightclubs, J. D. Salinger has never had Bellinis at Nell's nor a late supper at Nan Kempner's.

Incidentally, the authors of this book have come into possession of a letter from Salinger denouncing *Ecch* writers as half-brained plagiarists. Unfortunately, for legal reasons, we are unable to publish it. Sorry.

**A** few years after *The Catcher in the Rye*, British writer Colin MacInnes wrote *Absolute Beginners*, a brilliant youth-culture novel that, unfortunately, is best known in America as the basis for the lame David Bowie musical with the really really long opening shot. MacInnes suggests that, as a result of postwar prosperity, the generation that came of age in those years were the first teenagers. Their disposable income gave rise to disposable culture. This being the years before rock'n'roll, these *ur*-teens dug that crazy bebop while tooling around swingin' London on their Vespas.

America, of course, had its own hepcats. *Generation Ecch* is frequently compared to the Beat generation. As with *Ecch*, the establishment saw the Beats as pretentious, self-indulgent and stupid, with no respect for authority.

True rebels who were genuinely alienated from society, the Beats were trying to escape the Ike-and-Mamie mentality. *Ecch* authors, equating complacency and sloth with revolution, may think of their work as antiestablishment, but for all his talk-show appearances, does anyone really think *Ecch* spokesmodel Doug Coupland is anything other than a thirty-two-year-old Canadian with a receding hairline and a bitchin' condo?

Like *Bright Lights, Big City* or *Less Than Zero*, *On the Road* was vilified in its time, most memorably by Truman Capote, who said, "That's not writing, that's typing." The difference is, this time the critics are right. Let's face it, Tad Allagash is no Dean Moriarty. At least the Beats read poetry while they did their drugs. *Ecch* watches Nick at Nite.

Most Beat literature has yellowed with age. *On the Road* is Kerouac's only real written legacy—know anybody that's read *Dr. Sax* recently? Only Kerouac, Ginsberg and Burroughs (who hung out, but was never really a Beat writer) endure at all. Whatever its quality, the work of John Clellon Holmes, Gregory Corso and Lawrence Ferlinghetti is largely forgotten. It seems likely that the bulk of *Ecch* fiction will go the same route. Actually, some of it already has.

The Beats lived how they wanted and wrote how they lived, chasing after the best jazz, the best high, their best friends' wives, and conduits for the muse of wanderlust and adventure. It's almost as if they had a creative-writing teacher following them around the country, shouting "Write What You Know! Write What You Know!" over the din of the motorcycle backfires and animal sex-cries.

Take away the motorcycles and the sex and you've got the greatest influence on *Ecch* novelists—the creative-writing class. Our story begins in Iowa, the land of tipping cows and Tom Arnold. A group of successful short-story writers/failed novelists decided that fiction writing could be taught, just like history, physics or macramé.

The Iowa Writers School, as the University of Iowa's program is commonly known, has certainly produced a large handful of iconoclastic, important writers. When the talent and temperament are already there, a little training never hurts. But training and teaching can also be the enemy of inspiration and originality. Remember that kindergarten teacher who wouldn't let you draw shapes with anything but straight lines? There you were, trying to invent abstract expressionism all by yourself at the age of five, and Mrs. Krabappel was stifling your vision. Now you're a lawyer (sob!).

Like law school, creative-writing school has become a monolithic, ideology-driven assembly line. There is a "correct" way to write fiction, and if you learn it properly, you might be able to mask your meager talent and get an A. The Iowa program is most closely associated with minimalism, the kind of writing exemplified by Raymond Carver and Ann Beattie but practiced by scores of inferior minds. They write morose, self-absorbed little stories full of vapid suburban details and soap-opera family situations that turn on a single moment or emotion. Tom Wolfe calls it "Kmart Realism."

Unless you're Joyce Carol Oates, who writes a couple dozen novels a year, it's impossible to make a living writing literary fiction, so most Iowa grads are also creative-writing teachers. There are now hundreds of writing programs on campuses all over the country. It's no exaggeration to say that every single one of them has a faculty member who is either an Iowa grad or a former student of one. The American literary community no longer consists of people who go off to foreign lands to fight fascism, run for mayor of New York City or wear white suits twelve months a year. It's a happy little professional fraternity of tweedy people whose major concerns are faculty parties and placing the occasional story in *The New Yorker* (publish or perish, babe). What would Jean Genet say?

When a soulful seventeen-year-old shows up for his first day of creative-writing class, he is taught two things right off the bat— "Don't Ever Write a Short Story That Ends with the Main Character Killing Himself" and "Write What You Know." There would probably be a lot less bad fiction out there if young writers would just ignore the first part of that advice while following the second.

The "Write What You Know" problem is already glaringly obvious in the work of the teachers, who tend to write stories about, oh, say . . . a short-story writer! Who teaches at a university! And his Honda Accord needs a new transmission, and his father died seven years ago and it's still troubling him, and both the alimony checks are due and things haven't been so good with the third wife, who wears Anne Klein skirts and works part-time at the hospital. The redhead in the 9:00 A.M. workshop is really a promising writer, isn't she? Cute, too. Her youth, her innocent intelligence, the way she reminds him of his second wife when *she* was in the creative-writing class! He needs a drink. He needs a life! Or an imagination! What's on TV tonight?!

**S**uch an approach to literature is even more horrific in the hands of a twenty-year-old. Or, for that matter, a thirty-year-old. Jay McInerney learned his craft directly from Raymond Carver, but he comes from a flighty upper-middle-class world that's as far away from his mentor's as Jacqueline Susann's. "Jay McInerney was born in Hartford, Connecticut, and has lived in London; Vancouver, British Columbia; western Massachusetts; Tokyo; and New York," the author biography inside *Bright Lights, Big City* reads. "A graduate of Williams College, he has held fellowships from Princeton and Syracuse universities."

McInerney is the prototypical college-trained, postminimalist writer. He was young, he was beautiful and he knew all the right people—or rather, he knew Carver and editors Morgan Entrekin and Gary Fisketjon, who knew even more of the right people, like George Plimpton and Gordon "Captain Fiction" Lish.

*Bright Lights, Big City* was one of the first books to bear the color-coded spine, art-deco lettering and lush cover art that are the marks of a Vintage Contemporary, the literary equivalent of Garanimals. You see, it was too much work for eighties readers to actually choose a book based on the reputation of the author or the subject of the work. With Vintage Contemporaries, they could just pick a book that looked like the last one they read.

It was a brilliant marketing ploy, and many a good book was reprinted as a VC. But there was nothing good about the climate that led to the creation of Vintage Contemporaries (and the subsequent overpriced-trade-paperback boom). Still, it was always fun to look at the shelves of a mideighties dorm room or yuppie efficiency, one filled with Shakespeare, Descartes and *Jude the Obscure*, the other with nothing but pretty little trade paperbacks, all lined up in one smartly appointed uniform row.

"You hunt up your slippers and read the spines of the books in the shelves," the protagonist of *Bright Lights* says, during a doomed attempt to stay in for the night. "A random sampling of titles induces vertigo: *As I Lay Dying, Under the Volcano, Anna Karenina, Being and Time, The Brothers Karamazov.* You must have had an ambitious youth. Of course, many of these spines have never been cracked. You have been saving them up."

**B**right Lights, Big City reeks of autobiography. Not just of Jay McInerney, but all of his peers. Not for nothing is the hero nameless, the book told entirely in the second person. Here's a guy we—oh, excuse us, we mean "you"—can identify with.

In the book, our nameless hero, henceforth referred to as "Michael J. Fox," has been dumped by his fashion-model wife and is working as a fact checker at a *New Yorker*-like journal (back in the good old days, when Mr. Shawn was still there). He spends most of his time at parties and in nightclubs, inhaling "Bolivian Marching Powder," hitting on women and constantly talking about his friend and cultural signpost, Tad Allagash.

Curiously, Michael J. doesn't seem to be enjoying himself. The Bolivian Marching Powder is making his nose bleed. He has a morbid fascination with the *New York Post*, equating his lifestyle with that of the "Coma Baby," the unborn child of a pregnant car-wreck victim, waiting to be born while its mother lies unconscious. As it turns out, the root of his problems is less his dissatisfaction with his job or his wife's desertion, but the fact that his mommy died. A year ago, no less. This crucial bit of information is withheld until five pages before the end.

Following the "Write What You Know" axiom, this is what we learn about Jay McInerney from *Bright Lights:* He went to a lot of chic restaurants and discos. And he really, really wanted to be a writer. "You have always wanted to be a writer.... Then your night life started getting more interesting and complicated, and climbing out of bed became harder and harder. You were gathering experience for a novel. You went to parties with writers, cultivated a writerly persona. You wanted to be Dylan Thomas without the paunch, F. Scott Fitzgerald without the crack-up. You wanted to skip over the dull grind of actual creation.... You wanted to go out.... People were happy to meet you and to invite you to their parties. So much was going on. Of course, mentally, you were always taking notes. Saving it all up. Waiting for the day when you would sit down and write your masterpiece."

You wanted to write *Bright Lights, Big City*. You would not be the last.

**F**or *Bright Lights, Big City* was merely the beginning. Like Dr. Frankenstein, Jay McInerney, with the cooperation of his editors, the media and a couple hundred thousand literary lapdogs, created a monster. But for all the Tama Janowitzes (or should that be Tom A.) and Jill Eisenstadts and Michael Chabons that followed, there was but one Dark Prince of *Ecch* Lit, Bret Easton Ellis. "What Jay McInerney did for New York in his *Bright Lights, Big City*, this novel does for Los Angeles," declared no less an authority than *People*, the common man's *New York Review of Books*, of *Less Than Zero*.

Ellis's debut was the first true *Ecch* novel, shifting the focus of the genre from earnest young professionals to soulless young punks. This chronicle of a passel of spoiled L.A. brats is told in the supposedly innovative form of short, videolike bursts of emotionally inert prose. This new style of typing should be Ellis's most significant achievement, but according to popular legend, the brevity of the "chapters" was the brainchild of Ellis's Bennington College professor, "journalist" Joe McGinniss, to whom the book is dedicated. Apparently, Bret the Creative-Writing Student's original manuscript was actually quite a bit more than zero, twice the length of the novel we all know and despise. It was the wise McGinniss who suggested the byte-size structure.

To be fair, the format did say something about its author and intended audience. Unfortunately, that something was "Gee, my attention span sure is minuscule." This MTVesque brand of fiction would permeate the novels of *Ecch* for some time.

Young master Ellis uses the lazy, referential approach that Carver and the like have used to "define" place in the modern era. Song lyrics by L.A.'s punk heroes X and cock-rock gods Led Zeppelin serve as the novel's epigraphs. The Zep quote ("There's a feeling I get when I look to the West . . .") is from "Stairway to Heaven," perhaps the most overwrought, overblown, and overplayed song in all of rock history. The difference is, in rock'n'roll, overwrought and overblown are GOOD things.

Ellis seems to have never been taught the powers of subtlety, and his weighty symbols have all the impact of a sock full of mush. From the opening kvetch about Los Angelenos' fear of merging to the constant referral to a billboard that says, "Disappear Here," *Less Than Zero* is chockablock with overly simplistic metaphors that are meant to convey emotions the stick-figure characters cannot express.

The best known of these would be the Elvis Costello poster (which Ellis tells us is a "promotional" poster, since his hero, Clay, is so in with the in crowd) that hangs over the hangdog hero's bed:

"Elvis looks past me, with his wry, ironic smile on his lips, staring out the window. The word 'Trust' hovering over his head, and his sunglasses, one lens red, the other blue, pushed down past the ridge of his nose so that you can see his eyes, which are slightly off center. The eyes don't look at me, though. They only look at whoever's standing by the window, but I'm too tired to get up and stand by the window."

The image is almost entirely swiped, in both tone and composition, from a scene in *Fast Times at Ridgemont High*. Still, this is one of the few passages in the book that truly evokes character. Unfortunately, ELVIS COSTELLO IS NOT A CHARACTER IN THE NOVEL!

The niblets that make up *Less Than Zero* tell the tale of Clay, a first-year student at New Hampshire's prestigious Camden College, who returns to his hometown of Los Angeles for Christmas break. Clay (aptly named considering he has all the personality of one of the California Raisins) is not what you'd call a happy young fellow. Rather, he is the most angst-ridden teenager to ever grace the pages of a brightly colored trade paperback. The populace of *Less Than Zero* are so blank that the only thing that actually seems to affect them (aside from the smorgasbord of smack, coke and Valium) is MTV, and even that is just something to stare at. Like the drugs, it serves as neural wallpaper.

Clay's movie-producer dad is separated from his all-used-up mom, his high-school girlfriend doesn't understand him anymore and his best friend is turning tricks with fat guys in cowboy hats to work off a substantial drug debt. Clay's plight is meant to mirror the emptiness of L.A. rich kids, and to that effect, *Less Than Zero* is remarkably accurate. But it does nothing more than document the whims and

Even Less Than Zero

pains of *Ecch,* and you don't get the feeling that Ellis has any distance from, or even more intelligence than, his subject. *Less Than Zero* might have been fine as an overlong Joan Didion essay in *The New Yorker,* the kind of journalistic exploration of a youth culture devoid of sense or sensibility that appears every time there's a generational shift. You know, like the one you're reading right now.

Not a single character here possesses one iota of, well . . . character. Clay and his amoral friends suck off their parents' teat and spend most of their time getting fucked up on various controlled substances while they attend parties with people they hate, see movies that they can't recall ten minutes afterward and have sex with whoever's handy at the time. Sounds like fun so far, right? But these kids experience everything through a wall of self-pity and self-hatred, without ever expressing an impassioned opinion or feeling. Neither Ellis nor his characters betray any awareness that there are harder things in life than tooling up and down the Sunset Strip feeling sorry for yourself. Just ask the twelve-year-old girl who gets raped at the end of the book.

The only thing that ever made Clay happy was his time spent as a youth with his grandparents in Palm Springs, back when his family was still a nuclear unit. Italicized flashbacks flash throughout the novel, simplistic images of the only peace Clay has known. Wouldn't you know it, though, Clay's loss of innocence hinges upon the fact that—yep, you guessed it—his *bubbe* died.

By novels' end, Clay has outgrown his friends. He's ready to put childish things behind him. Somehow his four-week vacation affected him in a way that his whole life never had. He was so much younger then—he's older than that now.

"There was a song I heard when I was in Los Angeles by a local group," Clay tells us in the final "video" of *Less Than Zero* (incidentally, the group is called X, and Clay refers to them by name frequently in other parts of the book). "The song was called 'Los Angeles' and the words and images were so harsh and bitter that the song would reverberate in my mind for days. The images, I later found out, were personal and no one I knew shared them. The images I had were of people being driven mad by living in the city. Images of parents who were so hungry and unfulfilled that they ate their own children. Images of people, teenagers my own age, looking up from the asphalt and being blinded by the sun. These images stayed with me even after

I left the city. Images so violent and malicious that they seemed to be my only point of reference for a long time afterwards. After I left."

After Clay left, he went back to college, where he becomes just one of many characters in Ellis's second novel, *The Rules of Attraction*. In an apparent attempt to prove that East Coast college kids can be just as irritating as West Coast party boys, Ellis takes on the point of view of what seems to be the entire Camden College student body. The only real difference between the jerks and morons of *Less Than Zero* and the jerks and morons of *The Rules of Attraction* is that *The Rules of Attraction* has more of them.

Ordinarily this kind of rondelet could come off as experimental, but all the students speak in the same affectless yet melodramatic tone. Which is probably the point, but why should we care? "I thought about trying out for that Shepard play, but then thought, why bother, when I'm already stuck in one: My life," one character decides. Yes, she's a theater major. Her dorm room is overflowing with carrots and stolen toasters.

Most of the action involves drunkenly remembering all the boys and girls they've slept with, and then drunkenly attempting to find the few left over that they haven't. It's a truly awful, virtually unreadable book, unless, of course, the premise is "These people are idiots!" However, in this book, unlike *Less Than Zero*, that might well be the point. Ellis seems to know how ridiculous these characters are. To actually care about these talking junior-high diary entries is impossible, so Ellis treats them with lightness and hilarity, pulling off some good bits of high comedy in the process. Courses have names like "Kafka/Kundera: The Hidden Connection" (*Kundera has a secretary named Franz and Kafka had a secretary named Milan. Makes you think! Also, both their names start with a "K" and end with an "A." Class dismissed!*) and "Ethnic Chamber Drama." The voluminous sexual encounters ought to be painful, but they play out like slapstick.

The characters, unreliable narrators all, obsess over their intellect and their happiness, but they barely mean it. "I'm in a good mood anyway, mostly because Vittorio, my poetry teacher, says I show a lot of promise," one woman enthuses. "[P]lus Judy and I might buy some Ecstasy tonight."

Ellis also breaks the big suicide rule, offing one character and letting another attempt it. "I changed once more, turned off the Smiths tape and was on the verge of leaving when Raymond burst into my room," Paul, one of the kinda sorta gay characters, tells us. "His face was white and he was panting and he told me, 'Harry tried to kill himself.' . . . I had a feeling all day that there would be something that would screw this night up."

In the fascinating metaphorical moment that follows, a doctor examines Harry and finds he has no pulse, even though he's walking and talking and breathing, just like a real live person. Get it?

The Great McInerney was also interested in the psychosexual machinations of young people. A year after the publication of Ellis's *The Rules of Attraction*, McInerney unveiled, in hardcover, no less, the difficult second novel (though his pre-*Bright Lights* tome, *Ransom*—a book whose final line describes its Eastern-philosophizing hero's decapitation—was published in the interim). In *Story of My Life*, McInerney joins the world of truly *Ecch* lit.

He does so with one of those writing-school tricks, that of writing from the point of view of the opposite sex. Alison Poole is a rich New York twentysomething who goes through the usual rigmarole of Uptown drugs and sex. The author gets under her skin by showing her doing girly stuff, i.e., playing Truth or Dare, worrying about pregnancy and going to auditions.

Turns out her casual lifestyle is a result of, yes, the death of someone close to her—Alison's daddy poisoned her horsey for the insurance money.

Then, in 1991, just when you thought it was safe to go back to the bookstore, Bret Easton Ellis made his fictional entrée into the New York Nights scene that he knows so well. *American Psycho* is the epic saga of one Patrick Bateman, stockbroker, clotheshorse and all-around twisted fuck. Ellis tells his story using an endless litany of arcane designer names, be they of pricey *nouvelle cuisine* or *haute couture*.

Ostensibly, *American Psycho* dissects the banality of consumer culture, equating it with the banality of barbaric murder. This is a black-comic novel that attempts to display the effects of a culture dominated by greed, detachment and sensationalized brutality. *"There are too many fucking movies to choose from,"* Bateman despairs, as he haunts the video stores in search of inspiration, which he finds in the porno section and Brian De Palma's *Body Double*.

As if killing women wasn't enough to make Bateman a monster, his CD collection clinches it. Ellis follows Bateman's lovingly detailed, excessively grotesque killings with lovingly detailed analyses of excessively grotesque eighties pop stars, like post–Peter Gabriel Genesis and—Eek!—Huey Lewis and the News. Our narrator actually takes pride in admitting he owns two copies of Bruce Willis's *Return of Bruno*.

The public (read: media) reaction to the novel only serves to underscore Ellis's premise. It could almost be a scene in the book. Imagine our dapper young psycho settling in to watch his "Panasonic thirty-one-inch set with a direct-view screen and stereo sound." He sees an enormous hubbub regarding a book, of all things. *Woman are being tortured and mutilated in this awful novel*, the liberal establishment shrieks. *This is so horrible IT SHOULDN'T BE PUBLISHED!*

Imagine Bateman's reaction as he hears that Simon & Schuster (America's *finest* publisher) has decided not to publish the book. What would he think as he witnessed the furor that attended *American Psycho*'s subsequent publication as a Vintage Contemporary? Would he find it amusing that, as a result of the media *fatwa*, it's likely that the real loonies out there, who might have never even heard of the book, were introduced to it? Would Patrick Bateman grasp the incredible irony?

*American Psycho* was seen as exploitative simply because its author is seen as an asshole. Misogyny has long been a staple in American fiction, notably in other books by talented assholes: cf. Dreiser's *An American Tragedy* and Mailer's *An American Dream* (you might say that killing women is all-American). As in those books, Bateman's treatment of women is not meant to titillate, but to signify an unfortunate condition of society.

Ellis's book is blatant and obvious satire, not a cheap newsstand Nazi-porn paperback. As it happens, *American Psycho* finds Ellis entering the world of adults, and, appropriately, his writing has matured considerably. For the first time in his career, Ellis uses a fleshed-out (literally) character with a genuinely compelling voice. If you thought the reprehensible characters in *Zero* and *Rules* were scary, here's somebody who *really* represents the collapse of American mores.

As is his habit, Ellis uses characters from his other books in *American Psycho*. Sean Bateman from *The Rules of Attraction* is Patrick's brother, and Vanden, a minor character in both previous novels, stops by for dinner. Ellis even uses characters from other people's books: Bateman works at Pierce & Pierce, Sherman McCoy's firm in *The Bonfire of the Vanities*, and at one point there's an encounter with the inimitable Alison Poole. No, he doesn't kill her. Sorry!

*American Psycho* is hardly a masterpiece. It may not even be an artistic success. But it is an ambitious attempt in a way that Ellis's other books are not. Certainly it has been misread at least as much as it's gone unread. If nothing else, Ellis has become a killer comedian. There are samples of his morbid humor in the other novels, but here he's full-blown funny. In one of the book's many amusing moments, we discover that Bateman lives in the same high-rise as Tom Cruise, whom he encounters on the elevator. "I thought you were very fine in *Bartender*," Patrick tells the box-office heartthrob. No, he doesn't kill him either. Sorry!

Bateman smokes cigars with his stockbroker cronies and sups on "gravlax potpie with green tomatillo sauce" and "monkfish and squid ceviche with golden caviar." In a chapter called "Tries to Cook and Eat Girl," he tries to turn one of his victims into gourmet fare. Of course, we realize that's not funny. But, "after an hour of digging, I detach her spinal cord and decide to Federal Express the thing without cleaning it, wrapped in tissue, under a different name, to Leona Helmsley [*Editor's note: Hey, what are you guys trying to do, get me in trouble here?*] . . . then I rest by watching a tape of last week's new CBS sitcom, *Murphy Brown*." Now c'mon, *that's* funny!

**F**rom *The Rules of Attraction:*

**"But who *doesn't* go to The Dressed To Get Screwed party, besides that weird Classics group (and they're probably**

Yes, as a matter of fact, that's exactly what the classics majors were doing. They were doing it in a book called *The Secret History,* which Bret Easton Ellis glimpsed as a work-in-progress while he was toiling away on *Rules.*

Donna Tartt's eight-years-in-the-making debut is supposed to be about ideas, philosophies, morals—everything the literary *Ecch* pack lacks. With her photos appropriately lit and retouched in an effort to glam her up (though one astonishingly schnozzy profile shot did slip through), Tartt has been portrayed as more than just the smart-trendy-attractive novelist of the moment. Hard to believe, considering she attended the same school as Ellis, to whom the book is dedicated. He also helped get it published, but didn't provide a back-cover blurb, which indicates either respect for the idea of conflict of interest (a first in blurb-land) or the fact that the praise of Tartt's fellow Mississippian John Grisham makes for a far more attractive quote.

Tartt is in fact a smarter, more elegant writer than any of her contemporaries. But the book isn't anything more than an occasionally witty highbrow potboiler that is frighteningly reminiscent of Lois Duncan's young-adult thriller *Killing Mr. Griffin.*

The book focuses on an exclusive group of Greek scholars whose study consists of much more than simply poring over the subtleties of the *Iliad* or weighing the merits of two different obscure *Oresteia* translations (though they spend plenty of time on such matters). These Klassics Kids, who include among their number a homosexual and a set of pale (almost albino) incestuous twins, also listen to grave philosophical lectures from their enigmatic professor Julian. "All truly civilized people . . . have civilized themselves through the willful repression of the old, animal self. . . . [I]t's a temptation for any intelligent person . . . to try to murder the primitive, emotive, appetitive self. But that is a mistake."

Instilled with this empathy for things Dionysian (they are college kids, after all), four members of the group, after weeks of intense preparation, put on an actual bacchanal. Wines and poisons are consumed, togas are worn, a "certain carnal element" is present, hallucinatory ecstasy is achieved and—whoops!—a farmer is accidentally killed when the revelry spills over onto his land.

But they can live with that. "I mean, this man was not *Voltaire* we killed," one of them rationalizes. "But still. It's a shame. I feel bad about it."

The difference between Tartt and her good pal Bret isn't that marked. Ellis's characters do drugs and kill for thrills because of angst, depression and alienation. Tartt's characters do exactly the same thing, cast as victims of their own arrogance, moral relativism and intellectual superiority. Her references to classical history and philosophy mask the superficiality of her ideas and the superciliousness of her characters.

But unlike Ellis, Tart ignores Professor Julian's advice, killing off that wonderful primitive emotional appetite by refusing to actually write about the kinky sex and mannered violence. You don't even get the cheap thrills. Thanks, Donna. Thanks for nothing.

**T**he most *Ecch*cruciating novelist of them all has to be the smug Canadian whose book made "Generation X" the catchall catchphrase that it is today. If Douglas Coupland is the "voice of a generation," then Kerouac's cadaver is in perpetual rotation.

*Generation X* is the story of three disaffected and sensitive children of the eighties who forswear the trappings of conventional society—the profit motive, the meaningless labor, "the odor of copy machines, Wite-Out, the smell of bond paper"—and choose to live on the margins. And where would that be? you might ask. The Bowery? Compton? Haight-Ashbury? Seattle?

Nope: Palm Springs, California. Dag, Claire, and Andy have taken up residence in quaint little bungalows, yearning for a truer, purer life of big skies, big cacti and big retirement communities. Kinda like the time Val Kilmer and the other Doors ventured out into the desert just east of L.A., except Dag, Claire and Andy don't do drugs, don't play rock'n'roll and don't really have sex either. Perhaps that's because they don't have a ghostly Indian shaman to guide them through their spiritual journey.

As Andy puts it, "We know that this is why the three of us left our lives behind us and came to the desert—to tell stories and to make our own lives worthwhile tales in the process." These, then, are the "tales for an accelerated culture" referred to in the novel's subtitle.

Trouble is, the fables that spring from Coupland's diminutive imagination move at a snail's pace, and don't come close to making his characters' "lives worthwhile." We are graced with kitsch-ridden morality plays or retrofuturistic parables about fantasy lands like Texlahoma, the place where it's always 1974 (so *that* explains Ross Perot's haircut). These piddling little homilies serve to explain, ad infinitum and over and over again, what exactly is so disenchanting about mainstream American life. Dougie places the blame squarely on processed cheese.

The blame that's left over—and in *Generation X* there's plenty to go around—is reserved for Mom and Dad. *Generation X*'s second chapter bears the title "Our Parents Had More," and on the third page of the book Dag vandalizes a Cutlass Supreme bearing the bumper sticker WE'RE SPENDING OUR CHILDREN'S INHERRITANCE [sic]. "I want to throttle them for blithely handing over the world to us like so much skid-marked underwear," Andy remarks, further perpetuating the *Ecch* complaint about pissed-away prosperity.

As expressions of *Ecch* anger over its wasted economic future, these moments are merely clichéd, but what's most absurd is that the characters are driven as much by greed as anything else. Dag, Andy and Claire were looking forward to spending their inheritance, and the only reason they've dropped out from society is that the market is down and the price of Beemers is up. They don't believe in the American dream now, but they will if they get the chance to buy into it. Maybe holding on to their jobs would have helped them toward their materialistic goals.

One wrecked auto is not enough for Dag/Doug—one of the book's pivotal moments is when the Dagster blows up an Aston-Martin with an ASK ME ABOUT MY GRANDCHILDREN bumper sticker. Hey, it's Clay from *Less Than Zero*'s grammy and grampy—we thought they were dead! Why *do* so many of these *Ecch* books take side trips to Palm Springs, anyway? Maybe Rick Jeffers will come back and teach all three of these flibbertigibbets how to drive!

Despite the distrust and outright hatred *Generation X*'s triad feels for the idea of "family," it is, as usual, the absence of mother love that turns out to be the root cause of their troubles. The three of them have formed one of those newfangled nuclear units among themselves, but it too proves to be dissatisfying. At the end of the book Andy finds himself in a lemon grove observing a "cocaine white egret," when suddenly he's engulfed by a gaggle of retarded teenagers. "I was dog-piled by an instant family, in their adoring, healing, uncritical embrace, each member wanting to show their affection more than the other. . . . [T]his crush of love was unlike anything I had ever known." He's home at last, surrounded by his fellow idiots, swimming in a warm hug of drool.

One of the many reasons why *Generation X* is such a bad novel is that it wasn't conceived as fiction—Coupland's publishers originally commissioned him to pen a *Preppie Handbook*–style *Ecch* guide. Before he even wrote the first page Coupland decided that such a book was unworthy of his extraordinary talent.

Nonetheless, the book's *Ecch*cyclopedia roots are visible in the only vaguely redeeming portion of *Generation X,* those pithy pseudo-dictionary entries that appear in the book's margins. Here Dougie uses a made-up lexicon to describe genuine *Ecch* phenomena. The best-known example would be "McJob"—"A low-pay, low-prestige, low-dignity, low-benefit, no-future job in the service sector." Thus, a stultifyingly bad book becomes margin-ally interesting.

Still, the McDefinitions can't redeem the marginal quality of the narrative itself. What the hell are these things doing in a novel anyway? For that matter, what the hell are all these other things—a series of sociological statistics, a bunch of Jenny Holzerish slogans-*cum*-illustrations and chapter titles like "Quit Your Job" "Dead at 30 Buried at 70" and "Eat Your Parents" (that's the chapter in which Patrick Bateman vacations in Palm Springs)—doing in this "serious" work of fiction?

Even worse is how happily Coupland allowed the media publicity machine to transform him from a man of letters—presumably how he sees himself, with or without good cause—into an *Ecch* spokesperson. Though occasionally squeamish about his Marlin Fitzwater status—in one of the newsweekly stories he claimed that, as a "thirtysomething," he had nothing to do with the debate—Coupland managed to warm up and become a walking, talking, jug-eared *Ecch* cliché. He wrote think-pieces for the *New York Times* Op-Ed page, and in a multitude of interviews he namechecked *The Brady Bunch,* whined about Social Security and made damn sure that everyone around him was wearing clothes from the Gap. Yep, the days of Upton Sinclair and John Dos Passos are long gone—*this* is what it means to be a social critic/novelist these days.

There is one important fact worth noting in relation to *Generation X* that even true haters of the book cannot deny, an anomaly that's nothing short of miraculous: Somehow, 250,000 *Ecch*sters actually shelled out ducats for a *book*.

The same, however, cannot be said for Coupland's second effort, *Shampoo Planet*. An actual hardcover novel, it failed for exactly that reason. While every attempt was made to replicate the gimmickry of *Generation X* (two different jacket designs, a jokey "Table of the Elements" on the inside covers, an ironic photo of the suspendered-and-necktied author grasping some *objet d'art* that looks like a twenty-second-century toilet), its concept failed to be the *geist* of the *zeit* that its predecessor was.

Not that the would-be *littérateur* didn't try—the generational sub-set under scrutiny in *Shampoo Planet* is the so-called Global Teens, the younger half of *Ecch*, born of flower children but influenced by the aggressively capitalist age they grew up in. They are referred to briefly in *Generation X*, and *Shampoo Planet*'s main character, Tyler, has the same name as Andy's little brother from the first book. Shades of Bret Easton Ellis!

There's little point in discussing this insignificant instant re-minder any further, especially when you consider these two simple questions:

**1.** Do you know anybody who read *Shampoo Planet*?

**2.** Have you ever seen a news article, glossy magazine cover or *Dateline NBC* story on the phenomenon of "Global Teens"?

Besides, the loaded situation of hippie progenitors/preyuppie prog-eny has already been explored in the annals of American culture in far superior fashion. So just skip the book, grab that remote and spend twenty-two minutes watching *Family Ties*!

* * *

**U**ndoubtedly cognizant of the reasons for *Shampoo Planet*'s failure—after all, it couldn't have been the *quality* of the book, seeing how the best-selling one sucked too—Coupland and his publishers put the gimmick machine into overdrive for his *Life After God*. Where *Generation X* pioneered the now omnipresent oversize paperback (*Ahem!*), *Life After God* is like a half-baked Shrinky Dink hardcover, scaled down to better reflect the size of its author's talent—at a mere 6¼ by 4¼ inches, it's small enough to fit inside the average Gap jeans back pocket.

*Life After God*, a section of which is dedicated to Michael Stipe (presumably because of "Losing My Religion," a song that isn't really about religion), asks the musical questions "How do we cope with loneliness? How do we handle anxieties about ourselves and the world? *How do we enter the secret world which exists just underneath the surface of our own world?*" Billed as "an illustrated collection of stories and parables for modern times," it's an *Ecch* cross between *Dianetics* and *Jonathan Livingston Seagull*. It's a hardcover *Happiness Is a Warm Puppy*.

Much of the action—as it were—takes place in the California desert areas familiar from *Generation X*. The stories also share a similarity in tone with their predecessor, minus much of the irony but with a whole lot more junk food. This is supposed to be a book about introspection, so Coupland loads up on quirky, meaningful moments (encountering a wizened drifter, the narrator tries "to give our situation a comfortable guy-like dignity, like two models chatting in a J. Crew catalogue") and poignant societal snapshots (a child, upon being told that its parents are divorcing, hides in the attic for two days). Most innovatively, there's a lot of wandering and a lot of driving, not so much for any Kerouacian reasons, but because of the mindless quiet that comes with the long open road: "A fast moving car is the only place where you're legally allowed to not deal with your problems. It's enforced meditation and this is good." *C'mon, man, turn up the stereo.*

Best of all, following in the footsteps of *Generation X*'s graphic goofiness, the book boasts "original illustrations by the author." *I'm not just a writer and an MTV Bumper Boy—I'm an artist!* Page after page contains Coupland's *The Little Prince*-style renderings of two birds flying in the air (two pen lines with little blots at the end, that is), the desert (two lines for road and a little skull) and a can of microwave Beefaroni and a McDonald's apple pie. Incredibly, the drawings are also completely literal about the scenes they portray. It's as if the audience for Coupland's work is so idiotic that it needs the picture of the apple pie as well as the prose description of it.

Coupland's work documents the emptiness so familiar from the work of his bratty predecessors, but in his world the emptiness has become so profound that it's lacking in even the good stuff. At least books like *Bright Lights, Big City, Less Than Zero* and even, God help us, *Fast Sofa* offer a certain vicarious joy in the excessive follies of their morally bankrupt, drug-taking, moneymaking, sport-fucking characters/symbols. But *Generation X* is such a negligible book that one has to believe it's something like *A Brief History of Time* or *Foucault's Pendulum* for *Ecch*, a temporarily hip book to be glanced at but not actually read.

What links all the *Ecch* authors (aside from artistic mediocrity) is their consistent attempts to portray a generation to itself without any special insight, aesthetic integrity or provocative narrative. The tone and attitude of these books do more than simply hold a mirror up to *Ecch*—they *are Ecch*, with all the generation's worst characteristics expressed as literary form, style and content. Just because one is writing a story about a pop-culture-crazed world doesn't mean it's sufficient to make pop-culture references the sum of one's imagining of that world. Just because nothing seems to happen in real *Ecch* lives doesn't mean nothing can happen in a novel about those lives.

The idea of literature by and for the postliterate generation is inherently oxymoronic, and frequently just plain moronic as well. Literary critic John Aldridge, the curmudgeonly, self-appointed enemy of all young novelists, puts it best: "They depict a spiritually empty world that is attractive to readers who are themselves spritually empty, and so in reading them experience a faint twinge of self-recognition. . . . A book about people who cannot think or feel had better provide some clue as to the reason they cannot think or feel."

*The following are a few selections from the novel* Ecch-topia. *Alan Smithee's best-selling debut, published in the spring of 2003, was hailed by Nobel laureate Donna Tartt Ellis as "a thirtysomething* Catcher in the Rye . . . *Smithee captures the restless spirit and tragic ennui of a generation that refuses to grow up," while John Grisham said, "I'd give my Pulitzer to write a book this good." The older critical establishment was equally impressed. Herbert Mitgang of* The New York Times-Post *said, "Smithee succeeds in portraying the current life of the kind of people who populated Sir Douglas Coupland's immortal* Generation X." *Screen rights have been optioned by Academy Award–winning filmmaker Sara Gilbert.*

*From Chapter One*

### Max

". . . these people are idiots!"

I walk through the vestibule, handing my Armani overcoat to the butler hired to give this shindig a little class. I'm wearing a Donna Karan leather toga fastened with Sub Pop for Men fourteen-karat-gold safety pins. Phillip, who refused to forgo his usual monkey suit even though I told him he would look even stupider than the rest of us, is already starting in.

"I don't know why you made me come here. You know I hate this shit," he says. "I try to stay away from all things Greek, except for coffee, salad and Costas Mandylor."

"Yeah, and that's only 'cause he's yours," I say. What I want to say is "That's not the only thing you like Greek," but I think it better not to bring that subject up.

Phillip is my agent. He complains at every party I take him to, but by the end of the night he's usually made four deals and four dates, generally with the same people. I stopped fucking him after my seventh work sold for a whole bunch of yen. It gave me an excuse to switch to girls for a while. "Philip, you always act like this and then you have a good time in spite of yourself," I say, looking away from him for a moment to grab an olive stuffed with goat's heart from the hors d'oeuvres tray. "Just ease up."

"Everything I do I do in spite of myself," my agent says. "Which way to the bar?"

Phillip walks off in search of libation and I survey the scene, wondering who will offer me sex or drugs or money just to be seen spending time with me. This party always brings out the phony in me. It's our Thirteenth Annual Bacchanal, a gathering of all my friends from those Camden College days. It's something of a college reunion, except that me, Trish, Magnolia and Trip see each other all the time, and we're the only people from the Classical Studies program left other than our professor, who is now the U.S. ambassador to Crete, happy at last, but unable to jet into L.A. for the bash.

So everybody's in a toga, and, I'm chagrined to discover, I'm not the only one brilliant enough to not wear white. As with the previous twelve, I've lent Trip the first virtual-reality painting I ever did, *Good Mourning America Becomes Oresteia*, based on a piece I did at Camden after our first bacchanal.

I say hello to Dag, Trish's friend from Halifax, who is chatting with that weird rock'n'roll guy whose name I can never remember, Nick or something-or-other.

"You know Jeffers, don't you?" Dag says in that affected voice that he puts on at parties.

"Sure," I say, offering my hand, even though I have my suspicions about Dick's personal hygiene.

He doesn't shake my hand, which I find more offensive than the smell of the ancient flannel shirt that he's wearing tied around his waist. "We were just discussing the orgasm," he says, and I get the feeling that I've interrupted something.

"Natural or chemical?" I ask, already bored.

"Jeffers was saying how the natural orgasm is no longer valid," Dag says, "and I was thinking how far we, as a society, have progressed sexually since I was a boy."

"Speaking from my own experience," I say, looking around for someone who can rescue me from these two, "no drug has ever given me as much pleasure as this hand." I make a point of gesturing with the hand that Mick rejected.

"Masturbation wears thin after your twenties," Jeffers replies dismissively. "The technically enhanced ejaculation is a far more powerful experience than that which can be obtained with a partner, let alone a porno film."

I recall something about this character and a porno actress, but don't say anything. Not only is he a pretentious jerk, but there's something vaguely criminal about him that would best be avoided. I see Maggie heading out to the balcony and decide that even her company would be an improvement.

"Well, Dick," I say, tossing back what's left of my highball, "whacking off is something I'd rather skip this evening, so if you'll excuse me."

I turn, quite rudely, actually, from them, and as I walk toward the French doors that lead outside, I hear him say, "That's *Rick.*"

"*Prick* would be more accurate," I mutter, but he doesn't hear me. I grab another ouzo punch from a Mexican maid who is wearing the ankle chains of an Athenian slave, and go out into the hot night air.

"Howza going, Magpie?" I say cheerfully, knowing how much playful nicknames irk her. She looks over her shoulder at me, and turns away toward the ocean.

"Max," she says, clearly hoping that I'll go away. Even though we've slept together two, maybe three, times, Maggie always acts like we hardly know each other. I guess that's because she doesn't want Stefan to find out about those nights. Stefan, of course, isn't here.

I take a much-needed blunt out of the pocket I had stitched into the inside of my toga, and light it with a large red candle that is melting all over the piano that Trip keeps out here for his late-night melancholy spells. "Want a hit?" I choke, offering her the big joint.

### Magnolia

It was a dark and stormy nightmare. I've always wanted to say that, particularly for no reason at all. Another party talking to people I know and don't like, while scrupulously avoiding the people I don't know and do like. I only like people I don't know. This is especially true of men. I try to remember how many people in the room I slept with before I was even a sophomore. And how many I slept with again once we were all in L.A. It can't be done. That's the only good thing about these anniversary bacchanals; we don't all end up on the floor licking lamb's blood from each other's orifices like we did in college. It's also not as cold.

I've always hated *Good Mourning America Becomes Orestia.* Who am I kidding, I hate all of Max's work. He came in a minute ago in a leather Toga, even though it's 105 out there. *Whatsamatter, Max, silk sheets at the cleaners?* The A/C feels great against my perspiration, but the oxygenators always make me dizzy, even a little high. Which is as high as I get, so, like, what's wrong with it? As long as I never sink so low as to end up looking at Robin Parfitt when I wake up in the morning. I don't do that anymore either. It might be a good wake-up call for Stefan, though. He'd probably complain that there wasn't enough room in the bed is all.

"Sugar Magnolia," I hear somebody behind me say. Of course it's Trip. It seems like all of my friends call me something other than Maggie. Trip is the only person I know who has a real job. The opportunities for Greek Studies majors were always limited, even after the great Millennial Economic Merger, which finally ended the Ten Years' Recession by establishing the yen as worldwide currency. Back in the nineties, when the whole world seemed down on our generation, Trip wrote an article in the *Camden Review,* "Generation Chi," tee-hee, attacking his peers' hedonism and apathy while laying all the blame at the feet of our parents, something we all do exceedingly well. He dropped out of school six months later to do market research for J. Walter Thompson.

"Hi, Trip. Congratulations on another smashing bash."

"Thanks, honey," Trip says, "even though you don't mean it. Have you seen Trish around?"

"Not yet. She's probably trolling around for one of our ex-boyfriends. This is a rare chance for her to get one to herself." Except for Stefan, Trish and I have slept with all the same boys. In high school, this phenomenon is very common, because there are usually only two girls in a five- or six-person clique. Of course, in college the boys figured out how to expand the pool of available sex partners by including each other. It was part of the curriculum.

"I've got this new model—I'm using him in all the new White House ads—that I want her to meet."

"Aw, c'mon, Trip, I think we've all outgrown model sport-fucking."

"No, no, I want her to cast—"

"Hey now!" Trish screams, joining the circle, leaping onto Trip's shoulders. Trip promptly falls to the floor and Trish's toga comes partly undone. I can see the scars where her piercings used to be.

*From Chapter Three*

## Max

BLEET

BLEET

BLEET

I wake to the evil siren emitted by my new, top-of-the-line Sony holophone. "Christ," I say, reaching over the night table and smacking down the "project" button. The noise stops and the air around the holo seems to sparkle. Within a second, Trish appears, completely lifelike, except I can see through her into my bathroom, where someone appears to be taking a shower.

"How're you feeling, sport?" Trish says, laughing.

"Who's in my bathroom?" I answer. I close my eyes and fall back on the bed.

"Do you remember anything from, uh, the party?"

"I seem to recall arriving with a heart full of self-pity and a soul craving mead, which I assume from this headache was quenched in abundance."

"Yes," Trish says. "Yes, you definitely were in full Falstaff mode."

My thumbs and forefinger probe my temple.

"Who'd I fuck, Trish?"

"Wasn't me, sport."

"No, that'd be unforgettable, *mon ami*. The question then remains, who is currently in my shower?"

"Max, the party was three days ago."

"It's Robin, isn't it?"

"Well, you two did seem friendly."

"Shit. I don't need this," I say. "Did you say three days?"

"It's Tuesday, Max."

"Morning?"

"Yes. I've got to tell you something, and I don't know how you're going to take it."

"Later, hon. I've got a slot on the Tube at two, and there's a most unpleasant confrontation approaching."

"It's serious, Max. I need—"

"Call you tonight bye." I hang up.

I lay back down and pull the silk sheets over my head. *What the hell have I been doing?* I try to call up any image of the past seventy-two hours. *The bed stinks of sex,* I realize, feeling my face redden with shame. *You can't hide from this, Max. There's no way to get out.*

The shower stops flowing and I peek over the covers to see Robin's perfect back and ass. Robin is unaware of being watched and towels all cracks and crevices. Long hair pulled back, gleaming wet, pink skin from the hot water. I feel myself getting hard. *I'm in hell, aren't I?...*

*From Chapter Seven*

*Driving along the coast you are sure that your father is only doing this because he doesn't have time for you. You understand that his latest picture is in trouble but you don't care. If he loved you he would find a few hours to spend with you. This little trip is only a bribe, a way for Dad to get rid of you without guilt.*

*"What kid wouldn't want to spend the night with him?" you heard him say to Mommy as he picked you up for his weekly visitation. You were throwing one of what your mother called "your famous tantrums" because, even at ten years old, you knew why your father had set the meeting up.*

*"Look, Jerry," your mother had replied, "the kid just wants to be with you, though for the life of me I can't understand why. I think he likes to look at your little stripper girlfriends walking around the pool half naked."*

*"Don't start that shit, Estelle," your father said, and you could see his face turning that red color that you used to think was his normal complexion. "That happened once, okay? I told Roxy to always wear a top around the kid, and besides, you don't care about him seeing some tits, for Chrissake, you care about* me *seeing some tits."*

*Your mother started to scream. "You fucker! How dare you come into my house and make like you love him! He knows, Jerry, he knows! Why do you think he's so upset?"*

*Curled up in the corner you tried to catch your breath. If Mommy didn't have a date for the weekend you would be able to stay home.*

*"There are a million goddamn kids who would give their right arm to go to Michael's house. I'm giving him a memory that will last him his whole life!" your father said, grabbing you by the neck of your Journey T-shirt. "C'mon, pal, let's get the hell out of here."*

*You tried to pull away but he was holding on tight, his huge fist all white knuckles around your collar. Mommy had already turned her back to the two of you, saying, "Just don't bring him back here till Sunday," and you could tell that she was crying.*

*From Chapter Eleven*

### Magnolia

"Maggie!" Stefan calls from the living room. "C'mon, it's about to start!"

"One sec, hon," I say, tossing the sushi's to-go container in the recycler. I arrange the maguro and the umimasu on a large platter. *How can I tell Stef about Trish? He's so excited about Max I could walk in there with panties on my head and he'd ask me to pass the wasabi. Tonight just isn't the time or place.*

I take the two Cutters out of the fridge. *Yessir, Magnolia old girl, procrastination is definitely the way to go. It's not like he's suspicious or anything.* I hear Stefan: "Hurry up, Mag, it's on!"

*Men are so predictable. Our relationship is crashing against the rocks and all Stef cares about is the Tube.* Taking the sushi in one hand and the two bottles of near beer in the other, I push open the swinging kitchen door with a hip, just in time to hear the familiar theme song and irritating Harvard accent of the announcer.

"... It's *The Amy Fisher Show!* Tonight, Amy's guests will be *Playboy*'s twin Playmates of the Year, Ashley and Mary-Kate Olsen; the hot new musical group the kids are wild over, Standpipe; and controversial artist Max Holbrook. All that, plus funnyman Jake Johanssen. Now, please give it up for America's sweetheart, the one and only AMY!"

"Thanks, Conan, that's quite a lineup. And believe me, folks, I know from lineups."

"Ha-ha, lineups! Ha-ha!"

"Shut up, Conan, or I'll shoot you in the head a couple of times. See how you laugh with only one side of the face."

"Ha-ha, shoot me in the head! Ha-ha."

"Oy! So, what's going on in the hemisphere today? The World Series ended last night, and for the third year in a row, the Florida Marlins took the championship. Their manager, Darryl Strawberry, says that no one can dispute the fact that his club is the best team in baseball since the '94 Mets. Well, Darryl, I know all of the '94 Mets, if you know what I mean, and let me tell—"

"WE INTERRUPT THIS PROGRAM FOR A SPECIAL NEWS BULLETIN. FROM NBC NEWS IN LOS ANGELES, HERE'S DENNIS MILLER."

"Good evening. We have just received word from the White House in Beverly Hills that President Schwarzenegger has been shot. . ."

I have been trying to pick a piece of seaweed out of my back teeth with my tongue, and I nearly choke. After that, nothing. It was news and it happened and there will be more news and I can clap or something but for the new nightmare that will come tomorrow. I want to talk to Trish. We could put on each other's scent patches and circle the room in a fatal, futile defiant dance, chanting, with (ironic, of course) joy, "PRESIDENT QUAYLE, PRESIDENT QUAYLE."

Trish is probably more concerned about Max getting bumped from his network-television debut because of some stupid newsbreak (which is how he would put it. Max hasn't voted since the Clinton impeachment).

"Shhhhhh!" Stefan shoots at me, without looking away from the screen.

"I didn't say anything." No response. "What's going on?" I say. Stefan is still okay about responding to direct address. We might have never hooked up otherwise.

"They don't know. Dennis hasn't really said anything yet. He was having lunch with Maria and Senator Barkley at the Planet Hollywood Mess."

"In the White House?"

"Yeah, that's all they've said. Shhhhhh!"

Okay, I decide, guess I better look at the screen after all. I've always had an ambivalent relationship with the television. I've always had an ambivalent relationship with everything and everyone. The only thing I've ever been convinced of is I should have stayed at the Cannery in Alaska, even if that creepy Jewish doctor wouldn't stop following me around. He had a thing for girls named Maggie.

"We have word from the White House," Dennis is saying on the television. "Apparently the gunman is a disgruntled postal worker who was trying to impress NBC television personality Amy Fisher. He had been working at the Planet Hollywood Mess for several months. The Secret Service has not revealed his name, or any information about the president's condition, but it has been reported that the gunman fired nine rounds of automatic shells. He was able to circumvent White House security by loading a vintage Uzi the president himself used in his classic film *Last Action Hero*."

Back in that summer when dinosaurs ruled the earth, I remember seeing *Last Action Hero* with my high-school boyfriend, Rip. Well, I was in high school. He was a drug dealer, three credits short of a philosophy degree at USC. That wasn't why I went out with him, though—it was the Jeep. We drove from Century City to Culver City to Universal City, trying to get tickets to *Jurassic Park*. Unsuccessfully. Afterward we walked around the neon-lit parking complex and Rip lit two English cigarettes. He muttered something about Pirandello and Woody Allen and I nodded, thinking, *You're so cool, you're so cool.* Rip had his thumbs dangling from the pockets of his Dockers and for a moment I had an urge to unzip his fly. Then I remembered what I had read in that book about subliminals, that guys looped their thumbs like that to make you notice their crotch, subconsciously. I felt manipulated. Rip OD'ed the next day.

It wasn't until I saw it again when I was twenty-five that I really fathomed the depths of Jack Slater's absurdist dilemma. I had a boyfriend—yep, another one—whose master's thesis was "A Postmodernist Deconstruction of the Dialectical Parameters of Hegemonic Perpetuation of the Reluctant Father Figure Paradigm in *Kindergarten Cop, Terminator 2* and *Last Action Hero*." I pretended to read it. But since that time I've thought about Jack Slater a lot. That feeling of uncertainty, of mistrusting your own existence. *Am I real, or just a character in a movie? What world is this?* That's why

I voted for Schwarzenegger last time, even though I had a lot of trouble backing a Democratic ticket. You can't pick your relatives, I guess, and Joe Kennedy is not a man to say "No" to anyway.

"Holy fucking shit," Stefan says evenly.

"Huh?" I utter.

"Shhhhh! Dennis just said he was glad the president died. What the fuck?"

". . . and you know what else? I always liked Bruce Willis better," the anchorman is saying. A couple of guys in uniforms are standing behind him, and then one grabs Dennis by his hair. "Well, folks, I guess you know what this means . . . I am out of here!" The screen gets all fuzzy and some test patterns appear, and then all of a sudden we're back on *The Amy Fisher Show*.

"Ladies and gentlemen," Amy is saying, "what you just saw was the latest virtual-reality piece by celebrated Los Angeles artist Max Holbrook. He'll be back to talk about it after these messages."

Stefan is grinning. I am too, a little, but I'm annoyed. Max is always the one to get attention. From the TV audience, from Rip, from Stefan. Even Trish. I run out of the room to the kitchen phone, desperate to catch her for a second before the commercial break ends.

*From Chapter Fourteen*

*"You're gonna die up there."*

*You are on his bed, watching* The Exorcist, *which your mother forbid you from seeing when it was on HBO. When you tell him this, he says not to worry, it will be our little secret.*

*The movie isn't scary at all, and the two of you just roll around the enormous bed, giggling at the dirty words. You start wrestling, tickling each other, and all of a sudden he says that that he is getting sleepy and it's time to turn out the lights.*

*You ask where your bed is, and he says that there's enough room there for the two of you, why don't you sleep here with him? You're uncomfortable with this—your father has never let you sleep in the big bed with Mommy, and you have never shared a bed with anyone. He senses your hesitation and tells you that he'll sleep on one side and you can sleep on the other.*

*He's been so nice to you all day, showing you his llama, teaching you how to dance. He even let you wear his glove. So you say okay* and go into the bathroom to put on your PJs. When you come out, he is under the covers. He tells you to come over to his side and give him a kiss goodnight. You notice that he isn't wearing pajamas. This strikes you as being a little weird, but you don't say anything.

You get into your side of the bed and remember to thank him for the nice day. The fight you had with your father when he left you here is forgotten, and you are glad that you're here instead of at your father's, where your bedroom is all the way on the other side of the house from where he and Roxy sleep. Thinking that you will have to apologize to your father, you start to fall asleep.

As you reach the point where asleep and awake meet, you hear Michael say something about playing a game. . . .

"**S**omething serious is happening with the stuff that no one calls marijuana anymore. . . . These days, it's hemp, cannabis, or just plain pot, and from music to fashion to social consciousness, its culture is reconfiguring itself. . . ."

Yes, a sweet cloud of spicy *sativa* smoke was wafting across the nation, and needless to say, the Styles of the *Times* was there. The Sunday section's cover story, "Repotted" (March 7, 1993), revealed to the masses that, *goodness gracious*, those krazy kids were smoking pot again. If you think about it, this makes perfect sense. For *Ecch*, the only sane response to a world with no art, no jobs, no economic future and no family is to stay at home and get stoned out of its fucking gourd!

Recreational drug abuse was squelched for *Ecch* early on, largely because of crack (the AIDS of drugs), which was demonized by the media as worse than child abuse, or communism. *Ecch*'s coming-of-age was a time when the only socially acceptable vices were greed and patriotism. *Just Say No*, we were incessantly told by such reputable figures as Mr. T and William Bennett. That, combined with the frightening visage of Nancy Reagan, unquestionably scared off potential young dopers.

Freewheeling sex was out, blow sucked and driving drunk was totally uncool. Forbidden these fruits, *Ecch* grew up with a nostalgic view of drugs—yet another thing the boomers enjoyed in the Swinging Sixties that was denied to their unfortunate spawn.

But if anything, the antidrug fever of the eighties only contributed to today's reefer revival. Let's face it, people are gonna get high. Little wonder, then, that when getting toasty faced made its big comeback, the popular choice was that ol' debbil weed. For *Ecch*, pot is safe drugs, illegal, yet suddenly more socially acceptable than cigarettes.

The times have changed so drastically that Cheech Marin has gone from lovable *Michuacan*-addled *cholo* to Cheech the School Bus Driver, a benevolent and bilingual kiddie entertainer, for Chrissakes.

Hell, it's so environmentally correct that even Raffi could take a toke if he was so inclined, without tainting his good name.

Just a few years back, Douglas Ginsburg was deemed to be irrevocably unqualified for the highest court in the land due to his dabbling in doobage. But now it's accepted that anybody aged fifty or younger has at one time or another "experimented" with nature's friendliest hallucinogen. Vice-President Al Gore freely admits that he and the wife partook. *Yeah, back in college me and Tipper used to get whacked and screw to* Weasels Ripped My Flesh. Poor Bill Clinton took a thrashing from journalists and late-night talk-show hosts not because he toked, but for that "I didn't inhale" business. (We believe him—he's got allergies. It said so in the *Times*).

Once again, America is standing up for jay! It's the only possible explanation for the emergence of such culinary monstrosities as fudge-covered Oreos, Little Caesars Crazy Bread, S'mores Pop-Tarts, and Berry Berry Kix. (*What a great new concept in marketing! Breakfast cereal fortified with the great taste of an eighteenth-century disease! What's next, Leprosy Lucky Charms? Multigrain Smallpox Chex? Cap'n Crunch with Cinnamon and Scurvy?*)

Of course, on the downside, some studies have shown that regular dopers suffer brain-cell destruction, lung cancer, short-term memory damage . . .

um . . . . . . . . brain-cell destruction . . . . . . . . . Er . . .

*oh yeah* . . . and a serious (s)lack of motivation. Of course *Ecch* likes to indulge in a taste of the boo. It perfectly mirrors the generation. Not only that, it's, like, a plant (*It's natural, maan*), it's relatively cheap (*Yeah, where you scoring, dude?*), and, as drugs go, it's pretty darned benign (*It's natural, maan*).

\*     \*     \*

The bhang boom has manifested itself in that most *Ecch*ian of ways: as a stoopid fashion trend. Dope-sucking was once a private matter, something you did where the police couldn't see you. In the days of beats and bebop hepcats, smoking tea was perceived by the public as depraved behavior akin to heroin use. During the sixties, people were smoking pot more frequently but the Man said Mary Jane was a "gateway drug" that would lead to hard stuff, like *LSD*. By the seventies, doing grass was common, but guys with gold pot-leaf lapel pins and coke-spoon necklaces were the object of ridicule. *Ecch*, however, loves to advertise its personal totems on its person, all shabbily dressed walking billboards for Guess? or Stimpy or Sonic Youth. Adorning your personage with the seven fingers is like a big green badge of cool.

The icon of the sweet leaf began to sprout up everywhere, festooning T-shirts and album covers and gimme caps. Once pot merchandise was only sold in head shops with names like the Jolly Joint or the Gas Pipe, but now it's available in finer boutiques everywhere. Rob Innes, a clerk at Seattle record store Roxy Music, told *Newsweek*, "It's not the hippie types buying the pot shirts. It's a lot of the clean-cut student types." The nation is concerned about these clean-cut youngsters—pot T-shirts are gateway fashion, leading eventually to suit jackets emblazoned with syringes.

The cannabis leaf wasn't the only emblem ornamenting *Ecch* wardrobes. The crimson-and-white logo of the old-guy's-favorite cigar, Phillies Blunt, showed up with regularity. But except for a few creepy Patrick Bateman types, *Ecch* wasn't smoking stogies. Actually, blunts are hollowed-out cigars stuffed to bursting with ganja, a process that creates a larger-than-life superdoob. According to *The New York Times*, a blunt in combination with a forty-ounce bottle of malt liquor (aka the 40-dog) is referred to in urban street parlance as "milk and cookies." Elucidating the popularity of this combination, one young gentleman explained, "It gets you *nice!*"

Although spokespeople for Hav-A-Tampa, manufacturers of Phillies Blunts, have expressed displeasure with the "abuse and misuse" of their fine product, the company happily licensed its logo to three young designers calling themselves Not from Concentrate. In no time, streetwise rap royalty like Beastie Boy King Ad-Rock and Cypress

The Freed Weed

Hill's B. Real were appearing on MTV with the Phillies seal. "It just, like, took off," the troika's Stash remarked to *Newsweek.* "It's like Warhol's Brillo box." Alas, the Concentrate crew weren't the only hipsters down with the entrepreneurial spirit, and excessive counterfeiting bootlegged their designs into the zeitgeist.

Phillies phashion and pot pholiage have replaced X as *the* hip-hop accessories for black and white alike. *Ecch* kids (i.e., white kids) have always found rebellion in absorbing black culture. For white hipsters, smoking hoochie has always been inextricably linked to digging ragtime, reggae or rap.

*Esquire*'s John Berendt cites a 1932 jazz tune, "Smokin' Reefer," which explains the weed's outlaw appeal: *It's the stuff that dreams are made of/It's the thing that white folks are afraid of.*

"All There'll Be Is Smoke," swore Sony's advertising campaign for *Black Sunday,* the second record by Cypress Hill. These rappers deal with two very basic topics: offin' pigs and smokin' cheeba. As popular as killing cops may be, the dope factor is undoubtedly what made these pothead gangstas' rep. Due to the power of marijuana marketing, *Black Sunday* leapt to the number one slot of the *Billboard* 200 album chart the first week of its release. Apparently, white folks aren't afraid of marijuana anymore.

Even Cypress Hill's logo, a skull pierced by an arrow graced with a large green marijuana leaf, declares their fixation with dope. Check out these lyrics from a little number called "Hits from the Bong": "Inhale, exhale, just got a ounce in the mail/I like the blunt or a big fat cone but my double-barreled bong is getting me stoned. . . . Goes down smooth when I get a clean hit/Of the skunky funky smelly green shit." *Black Sunday* features other smoke-oriented songs, including "Legalize It" (not the Peter Tosh song of the same name) and "I Wanna Get High," while the liner notes helpfully include eighteen fun (and *High Times*-originated) hemp/marijuana facts.

"I can honestly say that if they sold marijuana like they sold cigarettes, I'd be smoking a pack a day," the Hill's B. Real claimed in *Tower Pulse!* "You should able to walk into any supermarket and they should have weed right next to the coffee." *Yeah, maan—wake and bake!*

The marriage of muggles and music is nothing new, but with the obvious exception of the Rasta scene, it's always been the love that dare not speak its name. These days, Cypress Hill are by no means the only pop act to extol the virtues of the weed. Dr. Dre's Top 5 album *The Chronic* was titled after street slang for way-potent stuff. Redman has a phunctional little number called "How to Roll a Blunt." Tone Lōc followed up his smash hits "Wild Thing" and "Funky Cold Medina" with "Cheeba Cheeba." Jersey redneck grungesters Monster Magnet penned an ode to "Ozium," the air freshener designed to remove the reek from your room. The ever-wary-of-controversy Sinéad O'Connor declared in *Rolling Stone* that "selling marijuana is one of the most respectable things anyone could do. I think everyone should smoke it." Once and future rock god David Lee Roth got himself busted copping a dime in N.Y.'s Washington Square Park, and the evil Valerie Bertinelli–Van Halen claimed that her hubby's former partner did it for *publicity*. If it's good enough for Robert Mitchum it's good enough for Diamond Dave.

B. Real and Monster Magnet's Dave Wyndorf, together with Urban Dance Squad leader Rude Boy, Sub Pop prexy Bruce Pavitt and Lunachick Becky Wreck, gathered at the New Music Seminar for a panel discussion devoted to rock stars who love marijuana and the marijuana they love. "Pot in Pop: Let's Be Blunt" was moderated by *Seconds* editor Steve Blush, who admitted to *Paper* that "everyone came to laugh at a bunch of stoners. We were all stoned, but it turned out everybody had plenty to say and did so in a relatively intelligent fashion." Smart rock stars is something of an oxymoron; *stoned* rock stars being intelligent is an even dicier proposition. Dig this pearl of wisdom: Lunachick Wreck, a longtime pot smoker, was unaware of weed's newfound environmentally correct status, but, she vowed, "Now that I know, I'm going to smoke even more."

Pot was so pervasive that it became a happening marketing tool for record companies. Even that most quintessentially straight corporation, the Walt Disney Company, saw the potential of the dope-smoking audience. But when Disney's Hollywood Records sent out bongs as a promotion for their metal act Sacred Reich, the media went nutso. (What's *truly* wack is the fact that a band called *Sacred Reich* plays on the same team as Mickey and the Mighty Ducks. Coming soon, the animated musical *Spandau!*, featuring the madcap adventures of *Obergruppenführer* Goofy, with the voice of Robin Williams as Albert Speer! What would Unca Walt say?)

To hawk retrocracker Faces wannabes the Black Crowes, Def American Records (now American Recordings) came up with official, band-approved rolling papers. Let it be said that American president Rick Rubin *is* the modern-day Walt Disney. The Black Crowes have always been closer to the cutting edge of pot proselytizing than rock'n'roll innovation, performing in front of a forty-eight-by-twenty-four-foot marijuana-leaf banner bearing the slogan "Free Us." The universal symbol for dope also appears on one side of the band's official guitar picks. Black Crowes singer Chris Robinson has long been outspoken about his undying affection for the skunky funky smelly green shit. And maybe a little defensive, too. "I use pot to heighten reality, not to escape from it," he has said. "What do you think of that, man?"

Heightened or otherwise, the *reality* is that pot remains illegal. Just as rock stars of yore banded together to protest and overcome such injustices as the imprisonment of Rubin Carter, starving third worlders and disco, so have today's rockers unified to denounce the criminalization of kif. Folks from NORML (the National Organization for the Reform of Marijuana Laws) and *High Times* like to mention that more than fifty thousand citizens came out to rally at 1992's Third Annual Great Atlanta Pot Festival, proving that a healthy number of Americans believe that weed should be freely available. What some forget to mention, though, is that a good number of those fifty thousand showed up because the Black Crowes were performing.

**O**n the other hand, there is a definite groundswell of *Ecch*tivism devoted to changing the image of marijuana: *Pot. It's not just for toking anymore.* The patron saint and founding father of these new pot activists is Jack Herer, author of the underground polemic *The Emperor Wears No Clothes: The Authoritative Historical Record of the Cannabis Plant, Marijuana Prohibition and How Hemp Can Still Save the World.* The book planted the seeds of this grassroots movement, arguing that hemp, as an alternative source of fuel, fiber and paper, has the potential to end the energy crisis, stop the deforestation of Northern California and, like, totally save the world. It's only outlawed because evil oil, drug and paper conglomerates want it that way.

Herer explained the genesis of his manifesto, which goes all the way back to the early days of decriminalization fever, to *Paper*: "When I joined the movement, the prime reason was I smoked pot and wanted it legal. Then I met some kids—this was back in 1973—who told me that hemp used to be paper, fiber, used to sew rugs. . . . Along about 1974 my partner Capt. Ed and I had a vision—we were stoned at the time—and we said, you know it really grows better than any other plant. It grows the biggest and the best with the least amount of chemicals. And it's the only plant on Earth that leaves the ground healthier for having grown there.

"I just had to say that to myself seven hundred or eight hundred times," he continued. "And once we came up with that conclusion, we came up with others." Yeah, they also realized that there was a universe in their fingernail, and some donuts would taste really really good right now.

In 1985, Herer finally published *The Emperor Has No Clothes* (incidentally, do you know *why* the emperor has no clothes? *'Cause he was stooooned!*), which had already generated something of a buzz through stoner word of mouth and bootlegged copies. Then *High Times* dealt the words of this new prophet to its sinsemilla-smoking subscribers, with a hot-selling '87 issue—hot-selling not because of Herer's brave new analysis, but because Jerry Garcia was on the cover. The book has since sold nearly two hundred thousand copies.

One of Herer's disciples is the babealicious Monica Pratt, who, at the tender age of eighteen, quit her photo-shop job to go on the road with the Dead when she realized the chemicals hurt the environment. Now, like an *Ecch* Saul of Tarsus with his traveling band of merry converts, Monica heads up the Cannabis Action Network (CAN), traversing the nation with various touring rock festivals to spread the hemp gospel. They've taken Herer's ideas and translated them into a homey display of buttons, growing tips, stickers and hemp products, a *GenEcch* general store that keeps CAN's coffers from getting too empty.

CAN activists aren't paid, but they receive room, board and expenses, and when you're traveling in these circles, there are bound to be fringe benefits. A successful summer trip can net the group ten to twelve thousand dollars, which, as Jeff Spicoli would say, is "righteous bucks!" But prices for primo bud being what they are, that ain't that much.

Pot activists like CAN constantly extol the virtues of hemp by endlessly repeating various well-known facts of hemp history and function. George Washington and Thomas Jefferson had their slaves tending hemp crops. "Make the most of the hemp seed. Sow it everywhere," the first prez said. The first U.S. flag was made from hemp, and so was the Declaration of Independence. Put *that* in your pipe and smoke it!

Hemp is a cash crop for countries all over the world. One acre of hemp can yield as much paper as four acres of trees. A single acre can also be used to produce a thousand gallons of gasoline. *Yeah, dude, fill 'er up!* During WWII, the American government temporarily allowed farmers to grow the stuff to produce much-needed rope and parachutes, including the very parachute that saved fighter pilot George Bush's life when he was shot down over the Pacific. Great, so it's all because of hemp that we had Dan Quayle, Clarence Thomas and Iraqgate.

If the emperor did have clothes, they'd be made of hemp, maan. This new grass revival spurred a proliferation of companies dedicated to the manufacture of important hemp products like caps, Velcro wallets, backpacks, shirts and cool surfer bracelets. Unlike, say, Dacron or spandex, these products make a point of advertising their fibrous origins on—if you will—their sleeves. *100% Hemp! Made in America!*

*Ecch* entrepreneurs Christopher and Robert Boucher run Hempstead, a Costa Mesa, California (of course), outfit that raked in $150,000 in 1992 from the sale of hemp clothing. They had to use raw materials imported from China, where hemp crops are legal (though in Beijing, when you get the munchies, you can't get Chinese food delivered. Go figure).

Robert Boucher says that the people who grab his goods are not just 'heads or *Ecch* fashion slaves. "They believe in it. They want something that's hemp because it's our future, it's their future. . . . We believe in the future of America, and this is probably one of the best rediscoveries of the late twentieth century." Of course, he admits, "a lot of people ask, 'Can you smoke it?' I say, 'Go right ahead. You might get a buzz when you're puking.' "

The arguments about hemp's resource potential are certainly valid. As conspiracy theories go, the notion that federal opposition to legalization stems from big-business pressure makes perfect sense. If nothing else, the government's consistent refusal to make dope medically available is totally bogus. Because cannabis is designated as a narcotic by the FDA, it cannot be prescribed by physicians, even though it's an effective treatment for nausea, pain and muscle spasms, alleviating the symptoms of AIDS, glaucoma, MS, migraine headaches, cancer and ambition. Monica Pratt told *Mademoiselle,* "I would give up my right to smoke if that's what it took to have sick people get their medicine." *Hey, speak for yourself!*

Most pot activists are like abortion activists: They don't advocate the use of drugs, just the right to use drugs if you want to. But wouldn't it be a nice credibility boost for the movement if there were a few hemp activists who weren't also smokers? Cypress Hill's B. Real hit the nail on the head at the NMS panel, lamenting that "the thing is that everyone goes to these pot rallies and we all get high and we all have so much fun and get so into it that . . . everyone forgets to sign the petitions and stuff."

For all the smoke *Ecch* is blowing about pot, the generation's cannabis kick may very well be a case of style over substance abuse. DEA studies show that 23 percent of youths twelve to seventeen were smoking pot in 1985 (*Hey, man I was smoking when I was eleven*) but only 13 percent were lighting up in '91. Seventeen percent said they may have, but couldn't remember. Among the public at large, the DEA numbers today's regular pot users at nine million, down from twenty million in 1968. *Ecch* might be wearing more pot T-shirts than its sixties counterparts, but when it comes to actually toking, we've failed to fill the grass gap left by aging boomers.

Of those that are actually smoking, it's only a rare few who are inspired to write epic poems, poke holes in the theory of relativity, cure cancer or solve the energy crisis. The rest just wanna eat and fuck. Ultimately, the lasting effects of the marijuana movement won't be about social change or outfitting the world in hemp jumpsuits. There's really only one thing about marijuana that everyone agrees on: *It gets you nice.*

# Mosh-ugganah

## or

## Not Raving

## but Drowning

Every generation gets the rock star it deserves. For *Ecch*, the idol in question was the bipolar scion of trailer trash, a dyspeptic, sanctimonious, cross-dressing, smack-shooting, self-described corporate rock whore. A man who kissed his bandmates on *Saturday Night Live* to "spite homophobia." A man who got more pleasure from receiving an autographed copy of the Raincoats' first album than the million bucks he took home in 1993. A man who would sooner die than spend the summer headlining Lollapalooza . . . literally. *Ladies and gentlemen, Ecch's flower-sniffin', kitty-pettin' superstar of choice, the Ayatollah of Rock'n'Rolla, the Duke of Dysfunction, the Viscount of Vacillation, the Marquis de Methadone, the Regent of Roipnol, the Grand Vizer of Grunge, the Suzerain of Seattle, the Potentate of Post-Post-Post-Punk, the Capo di Tutti Capi of Alternative Rock, the late Mr. Kurt Cobain.*

Kurt was an *Ecch* rock star all the way: politically correct, distrustful of ambition, way overplayed in the media, saddled with low-self esteem, dysfunctional to the nth degree and an incorrigible bellyacher. He was the very manifestation of all that is *Ecch.*

And now he's a friggin' God. Contrary to most *Ecch*sters' sentimentalized take on Geffen Records's tragic loss—not to mention the acceptable boundaries of good taste—we have come not to praise this Caesar, but to bury him. Again. It's been said that if it bends, it's funny. If it blows its own head off . . . *not funny.* On the other hand, comedy *is* tragedy plus time.

All shotgun jokes aside, the sad truth is that the tragedy of Cobain's suicide will forever be overshadowed by his legacy as a rock-'n'roll icon, which, even more sadly, was one of the many reasons why he killed himself. Kurt Cobain was confused, deeply depressed, chemically imbalanced and a stone junkie to boot. He never wanted to be the spokesperson of a generation, or even a rock star, but from the minute Nirvana became huge he was never anything but. His final act only sealed that fate. If Kurt could see the canonization that accompanied his demise it would kill him. Again.

**O**nce upon a time Nirvana was just one of the many fuzz-happy young skiffle groups that proliferated in the Pacific Northwest during the mid-late eighties. Then came the biggest explosion to hit Seattle since Mt. St. Helens, or the time the cappuccino machines backed up all at once: "Smells Like Teen Spirit." The most popular song ever to be named after a feminine hygiene product (with the exception of Don Henley's "The Boys of Summer's Eve"), "Smells . . ." crystallized the ethos of *Ecch—Our little group has always been and always will until the end. . . . Here we are now/Entertain us*—just as "Satisfaction," "Boogie Oogie Oogie," and "Don't Worry, Be Happy" marked their respective eras. It was the most significant breakthrough for punk rock since the Knack's "My Sharona," and not just for their mutual impact on the career of Weird Al Yankovic.

Megahugeness was bequeathed upon Kurt (as well as the tall bass player and that little drummer boy) in a way that 99.9 percent of the people who pick up rock instruments dream about. But not Our Kurt. To paraphrase David Mamet, success forced Kurt to forswear himself, to break every law he swore to defend, to become what he beheld: a rock star. Kurt was so uncomfortable with his role as an "untouchable boy genius" (his words) that he reacted badly, coming off as a petulant, paranoid putz. In short, just like a rock star.

It was all just a little too much for the troubled young lad who grew up rockin' to Black Sabbath and spray-painting "GOD IS GAY" on the numerous 4 × 4 pickups parked along the unpaved roads of Aberdeen, Washington. One day he was just another nihilistic Sub Pop loser, the next he was the throat-wrenching voice of a generation. "People are treating him like a god, and that pisses him off," one of Kurt's pals, Sub Pop's Nils Bernstein, told *Rolling Stone* in 1992. "They're giving Kurt this elevated sense of importance that he feels he doesn't have or deserve. So he's like 'Fuck you!'"

Kurt was always a fuck-you kind of guy, though. On the inside sleeve of *Nevermind*, well before the mania had begun, he's right there flipping the bird at anyone stupid enough to fork over money to listen to his music. Perhaps the gesture was directed at label boss David Geffen, Kurt already showing resentment for his status as an exceedingly well-paid indentured punk-rock servant. Or maybe it was a triumphant showing up of all those treecutter boys from high school, the guys in the Ratt T-shirts who used to beat him up because they thought he was queer.

**W**hen the harsh demands of stardom hit, Kurt chose to be "Like, 'Fuck you!'" smack dab in the middle of the spotlight's glare. He had no qualms about acting out on MTV and could be heard whining sensitively whenever a guy with glasses and a microphone was near, rock critic or otherwise.

Taking a page from fellow cultural revolutionaries Mao Tse-tung and Muammar Qaddafi, he delighted in confusing fact-checkers and editors by alternating the spelling of his name as "Curt," "Kurt," and "Kurdt." *Like, fuck, you!*

He spun poignant tales of the alienation he felt growing up in an unenlightened, primitive company town. "Everyone was eventually going to become a logger, and I knew I wanted to do something different. I wanted to be some kind of artist," he told *Rolling Stone*. And here we thought lumberjacks *cut down trees, skipped and jumped, and liked to press wildflowers. They put on women's clothing and hang around in bars.* Really, it sounds like just the ticket for a guy who did more for little summer dresses than Irwin Shaw.

Having rocketed to success largely because of MTV airplay, Kurt was quick to display his disdain for the vast wasteland of cable television. "I want to get rid of my cable," he told *Melody Maker* in 1992. "I've done that so many times in my life, where I decide I'm not going to have television, become celibate. It usually lasts about four months." Yeah, about the average length of a tour. Unable to go cold turkey, Curt told the very same publication a year later, "I wish I could take a pill that would allow me to be amused by television and just enjoy the simple things in life, instead of being so judgmental and expecting real good quality instead of shit."

Kurt's judgmental nature was just more fuel for the fire of his existential crises. He struggled mightily with his deeply conflicted feelings toward Nirvana's new admirers. It was hard enough to play in front of an audience that wasn't all friends and fellow Sub Pop grunts, far worse to play in front of people that you wouldn't want to share a Rainier with—even if they were buying. Nirvana had become the Guns N' Roses of grunge, and it gave Kurt more pain than those pink bellies the logger boys used to give him, the thought of having something in common with those immigrant-bashing, woman-degrading heavy-metal poseurs. Kurdt was traveling around the country making tons of money doing the thing that mattered most to him, but he was doing it in front of the very same people who once kicked the crap out of him.

Taking advantage of the endless possibilities of the CD booklet, he composed liner notes for Nirvana's odds 'n' sods compilation *Incesticide* that articulated his discomfort with playing for audiences that turned his antirape ballad "Polly" into a beery sing-along. "I have a request for our fans. If any of you in any way hate homosexuals, people of different color, or women, please do this one favor for us— leave us the fuck alone! Don't come to our shows and don't buy our records. . . . Sorry to be so anally P.C. but that's the way I feel." *Like, fuck you!* Then again, what's a well-intentioned punk to do when his politically *correct* fans misinterpret his *other* antirape song, "Rape Me," as endorsing forced entry. *Like, fuck me!*

At the height of the nation's Nirvanamania, Kurt found a way to protect and isolate himself from the unending scrutiny that a rock star endures. He would retreat into the mainstream of American society, get a dog and a gun and a house that didn't have a hitch in front of it. He would become a family man. He would get married!

But the obscure object of his desire was no one's idea of the girl next door. Curt's betrothed was Courtney Love, the outspoken, abrasive leader of the band Hole. Their romantic union was met with something less than a hearty *mazel tov.* Curt's Love interest was perceived as a gold digger, a groupie, a bitch on wheels, a *rock'n'roll Tom Arnold!*

Predictably, Curt reacted to the impugning of his not-so-blushing bride in the psychological battery that is the *Incesticide* liner notes. "The reason her character has been so severely attacked is because she chooses not to function the way the white corporate man insists," he wrote. Oh yeah—only a radical *black* man like Kurdt—a regular Gil Scott-*Heroin*—could truly understand Courtney, a mistress of media manipulation whose supposedly subversive sex-kitten image puts her closer to Madonna than Angela Davis. Unlike Curt, Courtney *wants,* nay, *needs,* to be famous.

"I finally found someone I am totally compatible with," Kurt said in *Rolling Stone.* "It doesn't matter whether she's a male or female or hermaphrodite or a donkey." Of course, Courtney is no donkey, but rather a more of less spectacular, if overly lipsticked, blonde bombshell: The perfect rock-star bride. If she had been a donkey, though, that would have been more fodder for both the press mill and Curt's neurotic expositions: *She's a donkey and I love her! Anybody who doesn't approve is a racist . . . er, a speciesist . . . er, an animalist . . . er, . . . like, fuck you!*

Kurt's most elevated praise of his beloved was not for her music, her mind, or her rebellion against Mr. Charlie. Rather, live on the Brit-pop TV show *The Word,* he gloated that Courtney was "the best fuck in the world." No big deal really, considering that British national television reaches about as many viewers as cable public access in Aurora, Illinois—but he still said it. Later, in *Details,* he proudly displayed a mass of deep red gashes on his back, war wounds from love in the trenches with the missus.

Out of the foxhole there soon emerged the first progeny of grunge, the baby known as Frances Bean Cobain, after Seattle's second most famous mental case, Frances Farmer. Curt and Courtney settled in to the life of domestic tranquillity that they'd yearned for since their wedding day. The Cobains are the "new family" that *Time* magazine predicted *Ecch* would become. Like any family, they spent quiet days at home spiking little Frances Bean's hair with mousse. They were determined to give their child the steady, loving, nurturing parental guidance denied to them by their own dysfunctional sixties-casualty kin.

Unfortunately, scientists have yet to determine the negative psychological effects of putting your kid on the cover of *Melody Maker* and writing "DIET GRRRL" in Magic Marker on her tiny stomach. But they are pretty sure that it's never a good idea for mom and dad to be heroin-crazed dope fiends. *Vanity Fair* reported that Love contined to boot up even when the Bean bun was still cooking in the Cobain oven. The couple stopped nodding long enough to swear a blood oath against writer Lynn Hirschberg, and to this day the mere mention of her name in Courtney's presence can result in a healthy bludgeoning from her extremely heavy pocketbook.

Their maniacal rage was understandable, however, as the *VF* exposé was more than just another one of Kurtney's media troubles. Their alleged negligence prompted the city of Los Angeles to investigate their suitability as parents. They forced the kid to appear on the cover of *Spin*, in a robust portrait of the indie Madonna with child (and her none-too-divine hubby) looking sane, healthy and familial as all hell, specifically designed to counteract all the bad publicity—sort of like when Clarence and Virginia Thomas did the cover-of-*People*-magazine thing after that pesky sexual harassment business. *Me and my ofay wife loves to watch Long Dong Silver movies! Like, fuck you!*

**D**amage control became the name of the Nirvana game. The fans were told that Kurt was not some wealthy, irresponsible smack-dabbler. Nope, the great *Ecch* rock star actually suffered from tummy trouble, a gastrointestinal disorder of the highest order. Apparently, the only effective palliative for his *agita in extremis* was heroin. *TUM-TUM-TUM-TUMS! Kurt Cobain, how do you spell relief? N-A-R-C-O-T-I-C-S.* Musicians like Keith Richards, Johnny Thunders and Charlie Parker did heroin because their *souls* hurt. Kurt went out on the mainline because his *stomach* hurt.

Except, of course, that it was his soul that was burning all along. *In Utero*, the not-so-successful follow-up to *Nevermind*, was originally titled *I Hate Myself and I Want to Die*. The muckety-mucks at Geffen felt that such a title might stunt sales a tad, and prevailed upon the band to not only change it, but delete the song of the same name from the LP. It finally turned up on the label's *Beavis and Butt-Head Experience*, along with Jackyl and Cher. *Huh-huh. Self-loathing is cool. Yeah! Yeah!*

*In Utero* was Kurt's big "Like, fuck you" to all the record company weasels and bandwagon-hopping metalheads who made Nirvana happen last time out. Songs like "Serve the Servants" and "Radio Friendly Unit Shifter" addressed Kurt's unhappiness with his success, while his deeper turmoil manifested itself in images of disease and disorder, with references to laxatives, antacids, broken hymens, broken water, and edible cancers (though how muching on a tumor might help your stomach remains a question for the ages . . . unless Albert Goldman has a Powerbook in hell).

The band had hired resolutely non-mersh producer Steve Albini, only to see some tracks remixed by resolutely mersh knob-twirler Scott Litt. The band maintained that the changes were made at their behest; Albini claimed otherwise, suggesting that Geffen forced the polish job in an effort to better insure the record's marketability and accessibility. Months later the band altered the CD's back cover and retitled "Rape Me" as —get this—"Waif Me," so that conservative backwoods outlets like Wal-Mart and Kmart would carry the record. Kurt's justification for this move was that, as a backwoods boy himself, that's where he bought all his Kiss records.

To promote *In Utero*, Kurt made the usual rounds of magazine interviews to further circulate his tale of woe and repentance. "I never went out of my way to say anything about my drug use," he told *Melody Maker* in 1993. "I tried to hide it as long as I could. The main reason was that I didn't want some fifteen-year-old kid who likes our band to think it's cool to do heroin, y'know? I think people who glamorize drugs are fucking assholes, and if there's a hell, they'll go there.

It's really bad karma." But every time Kurt publicly proclaimed that he was off the stuff, he apparently got back on the horse again.

That was one of the many rumors swirling around the rock'n'roll community when Kurt went into a coma on March 4, 1994. Officially, he was felled by an accidental overdose of the prescription drug Roipnol, a fairly moderate tranquilizer used to treat severe cases of insomnia that, when combined with alcohol—as Kurt did when he washed the stuff down with fine champagne—causes such side effects as "behavioral problems, slurring of speech, disorientation and occasional aggression." So what, then, was the point of his ingestion?

Everyone knew that Kurt was a teetotaler, mostly because of his tortured gut. What became clear exactly five weeks later was that the incident was a suicide attempt. On or about April 5, Kurt holed up in the room above the garage of his old empty house in Seattle and treated himself to an early morning breakfast of buckshot. *Buckshot—the breakfast Ernest Hemingway ate.* For a manic depressive, Kurt had a dangerously close relationship with guns. Courtney had had the local cops confiscate his armory in the past; on March 18, he had locked himself in a room during a squabble and she dialed 911 again. That time the cops took away a .38-caliber Taurus revolver, a Beretta .380 semiautomatic handgun, a Taurus .380 handgun, a Colt AR-15 semiautomatic rifle and twenty-five boxes of ammunition.

On the morning of April 8, he was discovered by an electrician who notified local radio station KXRX before calling the police. (Amazingly, he called said radio station right when they screwed up a Twenty-Song Music Marathon, and won himself a quick $20K.)

As a stunned nation of *Ecch*sters wept, the truth behind the events of Kurt's last month began to unfurl. Ten days before Kurt's body was discovered, the *L.A. Times* had reported that Nirvana were no more, and apparently there was some truth to this story. It seems that Courtney, the band's management and the other members of the trio staged a tough-love intervention to get Kurt back into rehab. Eerily, his roommate at the Exodus facility was Butthole Surfer Gibby Haynes, last seen staggering around the Viper Room with River Phoenix on Halloween night '93.

Other rumors abounded: that Courtney had left Kurt for alternahunk Evan Dando; that Courtney had herself been in rehab when the body was discovered; that next to his suicide note they found a copy of *The Catcher in the Rye;* that Rod Stewart swallowed four quarts of jizz and had to be rushed to the emergency room to get his stomach pumped (yeah, yeah, it has nothing to do with this story, but it's still the best rumor ever . . . except maybe the one about the hamster).

Nearly five thousand fans showed up at a Seattle candlelight vigil for Kurt, where they were treated to a new performance-art piece by Ms. Courtney Love. Speaking to the crowd via a prerecorded message, Courtney read from Kurt's suicide note, which she described as "more like a letter to the fuckin' editor," though it is also rather similar to the *Incesticide* liner notes. In addition to providing her own grief- and rage-fueled commentary, correctly noting that "this is such bullshit," she led the crowd in a group shout of "Asshole." Later, the grieving widow showed up in person and told them to "say 'You're a fucker!' and then say you love him." She also dispersed Kurt's personal possessions to the fans, allegedly to those who could correctly answer Nirvana trivia questions. *That's correct, the B-side of "Love Buzz" was "Big Cheese." You just won yourself a Daniel Johnston T-shirt.* For so long, Courtney had been vilified as a Yoko Ono figure; now she was destined to be Ted Hughes.

Naturally, all arms of the media were on the story like stink on shit, from the investigation of rumors to the comparisons to John Lennon. Sure, who could forget the time Kurt walked through the Russian Tea Room with a maxipad on his head, or that week when he and Courtney locked themselves in their bedroom to protest the war (they came out when reporters informed them that there was no war).

Kurt's mother, Wendy O'Connor, former lead singer of the Plasmatics, put on her best Heart Phoenix face and told the press that her son had joined "that stupid club," referring to past dead rockers. *Hey mom, Kurt's not just a member—he's also the president!* After all, never before had one of the biggies gone in such an intentionally grotesque manner, Del Shannon and the guy who wrote "Hey Jealousy" aside. MTV went into twenty-four-hour dead-rock-star mode, regaling viewers with endless reruns of the *Unplugged* show, as well as Kurt Loder's special report (although they also stuck to their previously scheduled coverage of babes in bikinis on spring break, for viewers whose tastes run more toward Salt-N-Pepa). As a result of the tragedy, the pop world completely missed out on such breaking stories as the death of Dr. Feelgood vocalist Lee Brilleaux and the unspeakable horror of Evan Dando's crewcut. Everybody weighed in, from *New York Times* columnist Frank Rich to *Newsweek*, which put Kurt on its cover to go along with a rumination by Pulitzer Prize–winning depressive William Styron. Even Andy Rooney got into the game, bemoaning the attention paid to the death of "someone I never heard of" before going on to rhapsodize about the paper clip.

**O**f course, the media played the Generation *Ecch* card hardest of all, eulogizing Cobain as the voice of a generation he never wanted to be. Canadian lamestain Douglas Coupland printed a "Dear Kurt" letter in *The Washington Post*, simpering that he wept like a little girl after he heard about Kurt's coma, and that the star's subsequent death forced him and the rest of the generation to "jettison irony." *Doug, meet Gibby.*

The *New York Times* called Kurt the "hesitant poet of 'grunge-rock'" in its front-page, below-the-fold obit. Yet most of the suicide note, at least the parts that were read to the "survivors," sees Kurt addressing the very issue of his distaste for stardom and soapbox:

"I haven't felt the excitement of listening to as well as creating music, along with really writing something, for too many years now . . ." he wrote. "When we're backstage and the lights go out and the roar of the crowd begins, it doesn't affect me in the way it did for Freddie Mercury, who seemed to love and relish the love and adoration of the crowd. . . . The worst crime I could think of would be to pull people off by faking it, pretending as if I'm having 100 percent fun. . . . I must be one of those narcissists who only appreciate things when they're alone, I'm too sensitive, I need to be slightly numb in order to regain the enthusiasm I once had as a child. . . . I'm pretty much of an erratic, moody person, and I don't have the passion anymore. Peace, love, empathy, Kurt Cobain." Geez, turns out the king of the punks was a hippy at heart. A hippy with a gun, but a hippy nonetheless.

On one level, these thoughts are the deluded rantings of a deeply depressed drug addict at his darkest hour, and surely only the surface reasons for his suicide. But in another sense Kurt turned out to be dead-on, if you will. It's not just that his final "Like, fuck you!" (or is that, "Like, fuck me"?) sealed his symbolic fate, providing the world with a garish ending to the Nirvana story, virtually guaranteeing years of cultural necrophilia (no doubt some *Ecch* Oliver Stone will attempt to tell his tale on celluloid—*Elijah Wood is Kurt Cobain in Quentin Tarantino's* Come as You Are!). Kurt decided that if he couldn't control his own myth he would put an end to it, and he did so with more showmansip than he ever demonstrated onstage. Blowing your head off sure beats accidentally OD'ing and doing the chicken in front of the Viper Room.

A further irony, of course, is that Kurt's ultimate act of self-destruction propelled the band's record sales back up the charts. *In Utero* experienced a 127 percent sales boost, the "greatest gainer" of the week from #72 to #27 ... with a bullet, obviously (the following week it went to #11). "Teenage angst has paid off well, now I'm bored and old," he sang on "Serve the Servants." Well ... *bored*, maybe.

The true measure of Kurt's helplessness, and his lack of strength, is in the way he allowed himself to be manipulated by larger music-business forces. Kurt was pressured, catered to and covered for at every turn. His whole life became a series of hastily faxed half-truths and shameless spin control. The deception reached Clifford Irving levels during the month between his Roman coma and his death: The evening of the Roipnol overdose, Geffen Records released a statement that said Kurt "suffered a complete collapse due to fatigue and severe influenza. . . . Complications arose after he combined prescription painkillers and alcohol." On March 26, Kurt was reported as "restored to full health and looking forward to touring the U.K." Within the next week, the tour was off and Kurt was in rehab.

After Kurt's body was discovered, it was said that Courtney was, alternately, in England preparing for a tour and in L.A. doing promotional work for Hole's highly anticipated Geffen Records debut, *Live Through This,* which, by sheer coincidence (?), was due to be released the following week. Courtney's visage was already on the cover of at least three national magazines. It turned out that she *was* in L.A., she had overdosed on Xanax and been arrested for possession and stealing a prescription pad.

With this many lies, who knows what was ever true. Perhaps "Waif

Me" was just one of the many minor sellouts troubling Kurt. If nothing else, it seems clear that he was never really free of his drug problems, let alone in "full health." Yet there was Courtney, on the Sunday after the suicide, telling MTV that he had only gone back to smack after the incident in Italy.

While the primary of all of these little cover-ups was undoubtedly the preservation of Kurt and Courtney's more than questionable rights to parental custody (there's only so much a nanny should have to do), the overall pattern suggests that Kurt was constantly handled as a lucrative asset rather than a troubled human being. Nirvana's music was supposed to mark a change in the ways of the old-boy biz, but their career seemed as stage-managed as an MTV Video Music Awards ceremony, and Kurt knew it. Kurt was a brilliant bundle of problems, and handling such a person is not an enviable job. Eventually, everyone around him tried to focus on his troubles and get him help, but the public fibbing didn't stop.

Kurt's audience was moved by his music's emotional honesty, and deserve a chance to come to terms with the unglamorous reality of his life as well as his death. It's a disservice to his memory not to tell the truth, and it should come from the people close to Kurt, not from some unauthorized biography or vicious satrical cultural overview. The fans are entitled to at least that much to go along with their CD of *Nirvana Unplugged*.

The very same year Nirvana's *Nevermind* sold a bazillion copies, thus kicking off *Ecch*'s bogus alternative revolution, the fifteen-year-old seminal punk-rock album *Never Mind the Bollocks Here's the Sex Pistols* finally went gold. There are similarities between the records, but where the Sex Pistols' title tells its audience, "Forget what you've heard about us," Nirvana's simply admonishes: *Forget us*. Needless to say, Nirvana's request was ignored.

Yes, the country had seen the future of rock'n'roll, and it was *Ecch*. Nirvana were harbingers of things to come, and Kurt was the herald, a grungy Silver Surfer for the world-devouring Galactus known as "alternative rock." Post *Nevermind*, A&R men traveled across the country and previously marginal groups became important musical commodities, from the Breeders and Urge Overkill to Helmet and the Butthole Surfers.

Part of the fun of punk rock, indeed the very reason for its existence, was that it stood in opposition to the watered-down product devoured by the masses—disco on the one hand and inexplicably popular, bland rockers like Foreigner, Styx and Journey on the other. Now disco is recognizably crucial to such genres as rap and techno, while the inexplicably popular, bland rockers are pseudoalternative groups like Blind Melon, the Stone Temple Pilots, and Smashing Pumpkins.

*Ecch* is the generation that grew up with the Clash and the Cure and R.E.M. and U2 and New Order and Depeche Mode and the Red Hot Chili Peppers. Because of *Ecch*, "alternative rock" is the new mainstream.

How do we know alt rock is *Ecch*? The media says so. *The New York Times* (though, sadly, not the Styles of the *Times*) pulled off an incredible achievement dropping all three of the most common *Ecch* buzzwords in the space of a single sentence:

> **"Although [Kurt Cobain] has been acclaimed as the voice of the antisocial slackers also known as Generation X, he is far too quixotic and opinionated for such a role. 'Here we are now, entertain us,' he mewled in 'Smells Like Teen Spirit,' mocking twentysomething passivity."**—*The New York Times,* on *In Utero*

There was a trend here—*Ecch* rock for *Ecch* people. Suddenly critics could stop falling back on "Dylanesque" "jangly" "postpunk," etc., and, with just a quick citation, make every record review into a broad observation about youth culture, just as every rock critic aspires to do. No one got it worse than Dinosaur Jr. leader J Mascis, the notoriously lethargic soap-opera head and man of few words, a college dropout who lived in his parents' house even after Warner Bros. signed him. The result: Practically every review of Dino's 1993 LP *Where You Been* was a bullcrit treatise on *Ecch* meaning and philosophy:

"J Mascis has been caricatured as a sort of slacker guru. . . . Mascis' disjointed, elliptical pleas speak for a postliterate generation with far more credibility than Douglas Coupland's *Generation X* postgrad speak."
—*Request*

"Today's *twentysomethings* . . . grew up on Kiss, Peter Frampton and Neil Young. . . . For one of the crowning glories of *slacker* culture, look no further."—*Rolling Stone*

". . . an ideal hero for a generation defined by 'Smells Like Teen Spirit,' *Slacker* and *Generation X*. . . ."—*Austin American-Statesman*

". . . singer-guitarist—*protoslacker* Mascis . . ."—*Spin*

". . . Mascis was being overtaken in two lanes: the *slack-adaisacal* road-to-nowhere was being hijacked by Teenage Fanclub, and the *slacker*-blues-meets-punk-metal fury initiative was seized by Nirvana. . . . Cobain conveyed the hurt, the castrated impotence, of the *slacker* condition. . . . On *Where You Been,* the original *slacker* gets his shit together. . . ."—*Melody Maker*

"Considering his position as uncrowned King of All *Slackers* . . ."—*Select*

"J Mascis is the guitar hero for the *Slacker* nation . . . he's matured as far as *twentysomething* ennui."—*Details*

"[Mascis's] guitar amply fills the void left by the lyrics of his suburban-*slacker* version of the blues."—*Boston Phoenix*

"The *Slacker* was born. . . . J's last album, *Green Mind,* was the peak of *Slackness.* It was also, necessarily, its nadir. . . . ***Where You Been*** **is J Mascis actually locating an attitude within the *Slacker* ethos . . . as opposed to Dylan's hobo hero, the *Slacker* knows he has it all to lose, and gains perverse pleasure in having his worst fears confirmed."— *New Musical Express***

*"**Where You Been** is like an electrified slacker The Catcher in the Rye . . . only it **rocks**."*—Jason Cohen and Michael Krugman, authors of *Generation Ecch!*

**T**he most obvious display of this new musical culture is Lollapalooza, the package tour put together by Jane's Addiction leader Perry Farrell. When the tour began in 1991, its concept was to gather together a bunch of what Dean of American Rock Critics Robert Christgau calls "semipopular bands," the theory being that teamed up they could sell out a few amphitheaters. By the next year, however, Lollapalooza bands were the big thing, and the show was packed with superstars like the Red Hot Chili Peppers and Pearl Jam.

Lollapalooza is *the* event for this generation that's dying to be led around by its nose ring. *Generation Ecch* is proud to give you, the reader, an opportunity to go on a little field trip. A virtual trip, if you will, navigated not with computers, drugs or cutting-edge technology, but with the humble power of the printed word. Journey with us now to the most ridiculous Lollapalooza yet, Lollapalooza 1993.

**July 16, 1993**
**Stanhope, New Jersey**
**2:30:00 P.M.**

*J: We were warned to leave for Lollapalooza early, as the streets were said to be reminiscent of a certain New York thruway in August of '69, with guys leaving their vehicles to scam on girls and Manhattanites peeing by the side of the road. We ignore this advice, even though it means missing Rage Against the Machine, the headline-grabbers of the tour, due to "some dispute over T-shirt sales."*

*M: Power to the people, man! Considering their rep for "radical" politics, Rage's very presence on the tour is hypocritical. I guess trying to sell T-shirts for a mere twelve dollars instead of twenty validates their insurrectionary stance. On the other hand, Tom Morello can make his guitar sound like a machine gun. And his mom is that cool old lady behind the anti-PMRC group, Parents for Rock and Rap.*

*J: Anyway, we made it just in time for . . . TOOL! Tool spent the previous couple of weeks subjugated to the second stage, but with the departure of Babes in Toyland they're in the big leagues now. Apparently Tool is the hot band of the tour, the one that will get the big record sales out of serving the corporate master.*

*M: They're political too! Tool struck me as being the most corrupt addition to the show. They share a booking agent and manager with Porno for Pyros.*

*J: But surprise, surprise, they have a hot Claymation video and we see more T-shirts for Tool than for any other band on the tour. Though not as many as for Metallica. Tool is one of those newfangled, bass-driven, punky, funky, monkey bands that make ya wonder what the difference between metal and grunge is.*

*M: They have a singer named Maynard, and a song called "Prison Sex." Ick.*

**3:37:42 P.M.**

*J: We quickly discover that it's boring watching bands at Lollapalooza. Though it might have something to do with the next band: Front 242, those fun-loving Belgian industrialists who are the only foreigners on the tour. Previous 'Poloozas helped make industrial bands like Nine Inch Nails and Ministry mega, so Sony made sure to get these Nazis on the bill.*

*M: They're* Belgian, *not French. The sun is blazing and Front 242 is using strobe lights. Feh!*

*J: They have some fans who sing all the words, and we strike up a conversation with fourteen-year-old goth girls, all braces and black clothes.*

*M: Their parents gave them a three-hour ride from Long Island— and stayed for the show.*

J: *Fortunately, one of the more daring acts is over at the second stage, where the "alternative" bands play. It's not music, though—it's the MC, Jason Woods, and he juggles bowling balls and chain saws. He said the MC slot was between him and "a guy who could blow himself. He decided to stay home."*

M: *Throughout his act, Woods spews politically incorrect humor, but because of the current atmosphere in youth culture, he feels compelled to apologize after getting off very funny lines.*

J: *Punkie-junkies Royal Trux follow Woods on the second stage. They're pretty good, but have as much business being in sunlight as they do playing here in the first place. It's time to hit the Village.*

M: *Let's go shopping! On the first Lollapalooza, the Village was a tent for activist groups, communists and the guys from Amok Press, who showed an Army autopsy video and the unexpurgated R. Budd Dwyer tapes. This year the Village is mostly devoted to the sale of those little black necklace things, y'know, with the beads.*

J: *It's like an outdoor mall for Deadheads. There's also a booth with those bad paintings of great rock heroes like Jimi, Jim, John, Stevie Ray . . . and Flea?*

M: *Stevie Ray?!? There are millions and millions of those little black necklace things. Millions of them.*

J: *There are two booths devoted to hemp, with the expected brochures, plus those excellent hemp tote bags and gym shorts. As usual, people ask if they can smoke it.*

M: *There are also lots of temporary tattoos. As yet, they haven't invented temporary piercing, but fortunately there's no law in this state forbidding a real piercing booth, so we go watch some fresh-faced kid get his eyebrow mangled. And they didn't even need a potato!*

J: *Just forceps and pliers. He looked as if he was going to cry. What's his poli-sci prof at Cornell going to say?*

**4:48:18 P.M.**

M: *There are haystacks on stage. Arrested Development must be on. They're singing about "Mama Lucien."*

J: *No, no, no, that's "Revolution"! How unique! Curious as to whether the music was inspiring the audience to overthrow the government, we interviewed a kid in a Suicidal Tendencies T-shirt who said he wasn't into revolution.*

*M: But he was psyched for Alice in Chains!*

*J: Arrested Development opted out of headlining, which is a shame. They probably could have stolen the show if they played in the evening. They're also Lollapalooza's token rap act, and they feature the only women on the main stage. So much for multiculturalism. So we went to visit the "LSD simulator," where you can picture yourself on a boat by a river for the price of a single dollar.*

*M: The proprietor, Ellis Dee Rick ("Think about it"), who may have taken some, shall we say, nonsimulated LSD trips in his day, describes the experience as "taking golden singles from our photon rays the sun, spinning them into optical palms of illusion inside of your brain." He also said it's a "binocular looking through the window into the neuroverse." It's more like rubbing your eyes really hard.*

*J: Then we went over to the "cybernet," a kiosk of Macs where you could get information about the show, send messages to the stage or—and this makes a lot of sense—have modem conversations with people standing five feet away from you. We struck up a particularly stupid dialogue with one "Vulva."*

*M: The woman in front of us sent the following message to the stage: "The Supreme Court is in my pussy and they won't get out. Support NARAL." Ourselves, we opted to promote this book.*

*J: On the cybernet, the computer messages consisted mostly of "Alice in Chains rules!" "Satan" was the most popular user name.*

*M: Similar philosophical depth is on display at the "political tent," where two guys without shirts discussed their belief that, "hey, if you're going to live by the Mississippi River, you take that risk, man. Don't go sending them my tax dollars!" Jason's liberal sensibilities were upset, and he wanted to leave, so we did.*

*M: It's too bad we missed the earlier shows on the tour: At least they had Timothy Leary there.*

*J: Yeah, and those two clowns at the "hair wrap" booth told Styles of the* Times *that Leary was a "real cool old dude" and they were very interested in what he had to say 'cause they wanted to go into advertising.*

**5:21:14 P.M.**

*J: Fishbone played. They sounded like Primus, and we could feel our IQs descending after hearing leader Angelo Moore shout, "Swim, motherfucker, swim!" The football guys in the mosh pit seemed to like it.*

*   M: They had a huge mechanical skeleton over the stage that looked like a whitefish after my grandfather had been at it. We knew it was now time for . . . SMART DRINKS! Yes, time for a refreshing, exciting dose of "Quantum Punch," chock-full of delicious choline citrate, nutritious L-phenylalanine and mmmhm-mmmhm fructose.*

*   J: Unfortunately, it tastes like old Tang.*

*   M: No, I think it tastes like Stephen Hawking.*

*   J: Tang!*

*   M: Stephen Hawking!*

*   J: Tang!*

*   M: Stephen Hawking!*

*   J: Y'know, time at Lollapalooza does seem infinite. It's like a black hole of bad alternative culture. I believe it was Schopenhauer who said—*

*   M: Boy, these smart drinks really work! Of course, Ecch is the first generation that actually needs them. We pass Cell on the second stage and proceed over to the main stage, where Dinosaur Jr. are performing.*

*   J: Uh.*

*   M: I get it, it's your J Mascis impersonation.*

**6:53:02 P.M.**

*M: It's time to go boot up, Alice in Chains are coming. I'm psyched!*

*   J: Boot up?! That fake LSD trip was more than I can handle. I think it's time to leave.*

*   M: If you take the sex and drugs out of rock'n'roll it ain't always that interesting. The Lollapalooza fest has become inert, anesthetized and mind-bogglingly safe, from the bands themselves to the no-genitals policy at the piercing booth. I've been to a lot of outdoor festivals in my day, and this was the first one where I didn't step in vomit. No fights, nobody thrown out.*

*J: Plenty of littering by the green-happy audience, though.*

*M: For all the talk about adventurousness, the most exotic thing here is the really bad Pad Thai.*

*J: I like Thai food. They put peanut butter on everything! Primus are playing later too, so we all have an excuse to beat the traffic. Ultimately, I didn't really expect Lollapalooza to be groundbreaking, but I wasn't prepared for the stultifying dullness of the whole affair. Aside from Marla, the woman with forty-seven different pierces ("Think about it"), even the people-watching was mundane. And I honestly don't think the audience was any more enthusiastic than we were. On the whole—*

*M: I'd rather be in Philadelphia.*

*J: That's not what I was going to say. On the whole, the Lollapalooza experience is worthwhile if you don't go for the music. Making smug comments about it is much more fun.*

*M: And rewarding, too! As we leave, Speech and the rest of the AD posse walk by, without anyone noticing. They leave through the front entrance, just like us.*

*J: Hey, given the overall conservatism of Lollapalooza this year, I'm surprised they don't have to use the back door.*

*M: Think about it.*

Incredible as it may seem, there are still great caravans of scraggly-haired hippies climbing into decrepit microbuses and trekking down the nation's blue highways, and yes, they too are *Ecch*. Alas, these modern gypsies and vagabonds are not traveling for the same reasons as their sixties forerunners. They go on the road not to experience the beauty of the American outback, not to have exciting new adventures and meet interesting new people unlike themselves, not even to simply get from here to there. Nope, these days *Ecch* ventures forth for the most vapid, inconsequential, mind-bogglingly meaningless reason of all: *The Dead do a different set every night, maan!*

The continuing popularity of the Grateful Dead (a *Fortune* 500 company) is yet another tribute to *Ecch*'s astounding sixties fetish. Deadheads will tell you, "It's the *music*, maan!," but if that's the case, why aren't other bands who play long-winded country-jazz psychedelia raking in the megabucks? The Meat Puppets, for example, have been playing long-winded country-jazz psychedelia for years, with little or no profit.

The bizarre truth is this: It has nothing to do with music. *Ecch* kids will worship at the altar of just about any sixties survivor. For *Ecch*, the sixties represent a happier, better world: a giddy time of campus unrest, drug abuse, armed conflict in the streets and in the rice paddies. *Maan, that sounds soo coool!* Since they see their everyday life as superficial and pointless, *Ecch*sters have excessively idealized the boomers' coming-of-age decade. As if they were caught in some strange sucking hole in the time-space continuum, *Ecch* heads have disproportionately based their worldview upon the sixties, even though, for all intents and purposes, *they weren't there!* These crusty buggers view the hippy-dippy era as a time when kids grasped the reins of power and stopped a war, a time when grass was cheap and plentiful, a time when rock'n'roll *meant* something, *maan!*

As such, this is the first generation to accept pop stars who are old enough to be their stepparents, as long as they played at Woodstock (the exception, of course, is Ten Years After, whom no one ever dug). If you started performing anytime around the Summer of Love, and through some miracle managed not to die in the years between now and then, you too can be a successful nineties rocker! Could there be any other explanation for the continuing careers of grizzled old hacks like David Crosby and Sting?

**E**cch's unrequited nostalgia has turned those turbulent times into a sort of free-spirited, dope-crazed *Happy Days*, starring clean-cut Bob Weir as Richie Cunningham—*Gee, Dad, what a long strange trip it's been!*—and Jerry Garcia as a bearded, bloated Fonzie (with the leather, not the windbreaker, obviously). *Aaaaaaaaayy!*

But on the road with the Dead, we are all *Pot*sie, dig? Drug culture has always been a big part of people's GD fixation. Big part? Hell, damn near the whole enchilada. In order to truly be one with the Dead thing, you've got to spend a lot of time doing the *numero uno* sixties drug, Bear's Choice, LSD-25. Other hallucinogens are cool, but not as. Many *Ecch* heads partake in psychedelic experimentation, only they aren't attempting to reach into the depths of their very beings, to open the windows of perception and look through binoculars into the neuroverse. Actually, they're dosing because it gets you totally fucked up! *I see Christ on the cross and he looks just like Jerry! The colors, maaan, the colors. Feels like my head's 'bout to bust open.* (Hey, they said the brown acid was not specifically too good—somebody better get this clown some Thorazine! The medical tent's in the back, right near the T-shirt concession).

*Steal Your Face* was a precognitive Dead LP title, for many *Ecch* heads have sacrificed their identity for the common tattered look. Most of them see themselves as standing out from society, separate from the world because of their unyielding allegiance to *the band.* To assert their individuality, modern Deadheads differentiate among themselves through, get this, wacky T-shirts! Every frat in the land has a T melding the Greek and the Dead. More advanced pop culturists inventively juxtapose modern icons with their elderly hero: Ben and *Jerry,* Ren and *Jerry,* Calvin and *Jerry,* Bugs and *Jerry, Jerry-Acid Park.* You get the point.

Eco-friendly potheads who read a lot of bad sci-fi and like to dance with no shoes on, Deadheads are perfect *Ecch* specimens. They've successfully delayed adulthood and created a perfect communal life for themselves, except there are no crops to tend, only tapes to dub. All other time is spent interfacing about how the Dead jammed for *sixteen minutes* on "I Know You Rider" last weekend in Buffalo. *Maan, I haven't heard Vince go off like that since the second set of last New Year's show in Oakland!*

Speaking of Vince, the keyboard seat in the GD is perhaps the most dangerous job in showbiz. Three, count 'em, three Grateful Dead ivory ticklers have kicked the bucket over the group's twenty-odd years, yet *both* drummers live on and on . . . and on and on and on and on and on. Most recently, hack songsmith Bruce Hornsby was offered the gig after the passing of keyb 3, "Stumpy" Brent Mydland, but he wisely declined. Better no bread than dead. When *Jerry* finally eats the peach, the outpouring of grief in this country will make the combined reactions to the deaths of Abraham, Martin and John look as small as a Desert Storm protest. When the hero falls, little Mexican women in Juárez sweatshops will begin cranking out velvet Jerrys faster than you can say, "Aoxomoxoa." The streets will run purple with tie-dye, anarchy will reign, and the prophesied revolution will come at last.

Fortunately, or, to tell the truth, *un*fortunately, there are plenty of hirsute *Ecch*sters ready to take Jerry's place. Twenty Years After Woodstock, give or take a few, *Ecch* developed some sixties groups of its very own, finally filling the band gap created by two decades of death and has-beenism. Trouble is, bands like the Spin Doctors and Blind Melon churn out substandard blues-rock so dull and derivative even Alvin Lee laughs at them. For all the Deadheads with time to kill between road trips, as well as kids who dream of the sixties but can't drop out ('cause their parents would just *freak!*), these awful new groups hit the road, filling campus bars with scruffy little beards and peasant dresses.

To capitalize on the emergence of the Lollapalooza mentality (that is, if you put a bunch of bands who don't sell many records together on tour, all the fans of each band will show up and sell out stadia across the land), the retro-groups went out as the "H.O.R.D.E.," which translates to, get ready, *Horizons of Rock Developing Everywhere.* To the naked eye, there's very little difference between the Lollapalooza fests and this aggregation. Little boys and girls in tie-dyes and temporary tattoos get together and groove out on crap acts like Blues Traveler or, God help us, Widespread Panic, while spending hard(ly)-earned bucks at the Counter Culture Concourse. The same junk jewelry and peacenik bumper stickers seen at Lollapalooza's Village are available here, and again, most of the audience spends more time milling about the designated sale area than in front of the music. One enterprising entrepreneur built himself a life-size stand-up Jerry, so the kids could have a photo of themselves with their hero. So what if it's not the living, breathing Jer, it's the thought that counts. Besides, when you get back to school in the fall, who's gonna know?

There's a peculiar, rather dated theory that claims this junk is "natural" music, as opposed to inhuman stuff like . . . well, just about anything recorded after 1975. *Except the Dead, maan! "Touch of Grey" rules!* While the boundaries have crumbled and the lines between most genres have blurred, pretty much everyone who listens to

Not Raving but Drowning

music of the GD ilk cannot deal with grunge/hip-hop/metal/punk/industrial/etc., and vice versa. For fans of the Dead, there is no difference between the Sex Pistols then and Nirvana now. *Hey, maan, they can't play their instruments! A guy like Big Head Todd, now there's a musician. Look how fast he's running his fingers up and down the fretboard.* But why is he doing that? *Whaddaya mean? Look how fast he's moving his fingers, maan!*

Next to the H.O.R.D.E. horde, the Dead are more adventurous than Ornette Coleman. (*Jerry jammed with him, maan!*) For all their self-indulgent chops, and the less productive self-indulgence of the fans, the Grateful Dead have actually given the world more than a few hours of innovative music. What's more, for a bunch of hippies, Jerry, Bob and Co. are a pretty forward-thinking bunch of guys, as preoccupied with activism, culture and philosophy as the average Lollapaloozer.

Deadman Mickey "Leakey" Hart moonlights as an anthropologist, producing indigenous music from New Guinea, overseeing the world-music collective Planet Drum and penning the scholarly tome *Drumming at the Edge of Magic*. In this book, Hart investigates shamanism and the concept of rhythm as a tool to create spiritual trance states, which explains a lot (sounds like he's rationalizing his and Bill Kreutzmann's job, as well as the dopey half-hour drum solos that continue to mar GD shows.)

Bob Weir has done the Sting/Don Henley thing, serving as a famous environmental spokesdude. He has clashed with Senators Max Baucus (D-Montana) and Conrad Burns (R-Montana) over prodevelopment legislation in his home state—hey, we wouldn't want our homes to be too close to the other famous people's retreats. *There's got to be at least twenty miles between me and Tom McGuane, dammit!* Now that many Deadheads pack the rug rats into the van every year, Weir has also ventured into the ever-profitable field of PC children's books. With his sister Wendy he's coauthored *Panther Dream*, about a boy in the African rain forest, and is currently working on a book about the Great Barrier Reef.

John Perry Barlow, the man who puts lyrics to Weir's music, might be the hippest of them all. He is the Dead's main conduit to the world of high tech, serving as a contributing editor at *Mondo 2000*, a sort of *Spin* for computer/sci-fi wankers. He is also a founding member of the Electronic Frontier Foundation, a group on the cutting edge of new information technologies that has largely been dedicated to protecting the civil rights of hackers who have been constitutionally fucked by the evil government conspiracy against free access.

Taking a cue from Barlow's world (better him than Robert Hunter), the Dead have been traveling around with a virtual-reality dealie and a smart bar backstage. When you're one of the richest bands in the world, you can afford to be forward-thinking. With a combined age of 2000, who better than the Dead to lead us into the new millennium?

This strain of futurism animating the Dead is not necessarily shared by the band's devotees. But elsewhere in *Ecch*'s cultural quagmire, the marriage of sixties messages and modern machinery is in full—albeit fully simulated—flower. Thousands of *Ecch*sters have become virtual hippies, enthusiastic believers in the possibility of unleashing Gaia's primordial energies through computers and hallucinogenics. It's a philosophy that gives whole new meaning to the tab button.

For these kids, the miraculous microchip that will dominate the future is nothing like *2001*'s fascistic HAL. Rather, it's *Knight Rider*'s genial, helpful KITT. Computers are not just *Ecch*'s friends—they open up a whole new world of human relationships. Bulletin boards like the WELL and America Online turn interpersonal communication into impersonal experiences. Mostly folks carry on inane little conversations about *Star Trek: The Next Generation.*

> klingn @xyz.com
> :) *do you think picard could take kirk in a fair fight?*
>
> spck406@abc.com
> {{{*no way!*}}}

In this brave new world, science fiction has by necessity transmogrified from Isaac Asimov's robots and Martians to a world of postapocalyptic cowboys riding modems across the matrix. Known as cyberpunk, these newfangled pulp novels are mostly style and attitude—style and attitude that have empowered geeks everywhere. They've traded in their pen protectors for leather jackets, and these days, if you give them a pink belly, they'll hack their way into the ETS database and screw up your SAT scores.

Cyberpunk hypothesizes that the new technology is a gateway to God. All these years man has been mystified by the divine phenomenon of speaking in tongues, and it turns out it was just PASCAL. Add some drugs to the mix, and you've got an idyll of technospiritualism.

If this scene has a guru, it's the man Timothy Leary himself has called "the Timothy Leary of the nineties," writer and self-acclaimed prophet genius Terence McKenna. At fortysomething, McKenna is neither neo or retro in his preaching—rather, he's an actual hippy, a guy who still hangs out in Berkeley and Big Sur exploring the transcendental self-actualizing utopian possibilities of psychedelic drugs. Unsurprisingly, McKenna's solution to most global and individual problems is what he calls the "heroic dose" of psilocybin, better known as *'shrooms, dude.*

McKenna has said that the magic morels speak to him, but the revelations he experienced while drooling in dark corners under the influence are not exactly original. For one thing, they told him to take a .45 and go kill Stacy Moskowitz. *Son of 'Shroom!* But seriously . . . the talking toadstools actually delivered the shocking information that the ecosystem is in trouble! Or perhaps Al Gore was plugging his book on *Larry King Live* while Terence was tripping.

The anthropomorphic fungi have also told him that the way to solve the world's environmental crisis is *to take more 'shrooms.* Cool! It beats composting.

**I**n the wee small hours of the morning, the disciples of cybercrap and McKennan catechism can be found at abandoned warehouses and isolated meadows, where, garbed in Day-Glo rain gear, enormous bell-bottoms and Cat in the Hat chapeaus, they harmonically converge at futuristic be-ins known as raves. Bearing fluorescent pacifiers 'round their necks and backpacks crammed with Yodels, Silly

String and VapoRub, they get juiced on nootropics and find sustenance in the nourishing sugar and caffeine of Jolt cola. Other nutritional requirements are fulfilled with large colorful handfuls of crunchy yummy Flintstones vitamins. Unapologetically escapist, fatuously optimistic and barely sybaritic, these festivities meld digital technology and New Age posturing with elements of previously viewed youth culture: disco's party! party! mentality, the frenzied spasmodics of punk, psychedelic pspirituality and that old favorite, the Dionysian bacchanal.

It should all add up to a whole bunch of fucking, the inevitable nexus of disco's excess of free sex (free, but not *cheap*) and the Woodstock nation's abundant free love. But there's virtually no pickup scene at a rave. With the sexual revolution ending when *GenEcch* hit puberty—and quite a few rave kids are still mired in those turbulent years—the gatherings are something akin to safe-sex love-ins. No lambada here!

In fact, there's very little dancing at all, at least not in the traditional sense. Whether convulsing to the 180 bpms of hi-energy techno or grooving on the inside—where it counts—at an ambient hop, rave kids dance alone, boys with the boys and girls with the girls, tripping the light onanistic in individual circles of conformity. Styles of the *Times* reported that rave boys don't like it when the girls try to dance with them, 'cause they rub up against you and make the experience something other than transcendental mental masturbation.

This aura of narcissistic Victorianism is somewhat at odds with the rave scene's illicit drug of choice, Ecstasy. A hallucinogenic cocktail akin to a mild LSD compounded with high-density crank, "E" is designed to cause great happiness, long-range alertness, and serious sensual fervor, inspiring the X-clamation of utterances like "My clothes! They're killing me!" An apocryphal rave myth tells of a girl at an outdoor shindig who, while in an E-heightened state of carnal fever, capered about during a furious downpour and was brought to multiple orgasm by the pounding rain. Jan Harold Brunvand, are you listening? One version of this tale becomes a macabre nightmare in which the girl's gasps are quite literally her last, a Cronenbergian twist stemming from the ravers' fierce asexuality.

When crusading journos go on an investigative, sweeps-week-motivated excursion to a rave, the kids are quick to report that their little subculture has nothing to do with drugged-out orgies. One raver told *Newsweek* that the scene was not about getting high, but rather, "It's about forgetting who's going to be president and having a good time." If that's not a burnout mind-set, what is? *Who is the president, anyway? Are we having fun yet?*

One popular New York–area rave is named Caffeine, not so much for the word's hyperactive implications but because, unlike speed or Ecstasy, caffeine is (to paraphrase one raver quoted in—you got it!—Styles of the *Times*) "natural, maan." X-presso bongo, anyone?

In England, thousands of kids began raving because they had nothing to do. In America, *Ecch*sters rave 'cause we have nothing better to do—after all, it's traditional for American kids to do what the English kids did the year before. As a genuinely underground phenomenon on the British Isles, ravers distributed their music as bootlegs and were routinely thrown in jail, for drugs or trespassing or disturbing the peace. They wore raincoats because the fests were outdoors and it rains a lot in jolly old England. Once the scene hit stateside, the same promoters behind Seventies Appreciation Night at the Limelight were bringing rave to the *Ecch* masses, and nylon slickers became a stylish indoor accessory.

No matter which side of the puddle you're on, one of the main tenets of rave culture is to break down the barriers of celebrity. Here the people in the raincoats are the stars of the movie, while the sound track is provided by faceless technicians with names like Moby, the Psychick Warriors ov Gaia and the Aphex Twin. Rave has completely changed prevailing notions of how music is consumed, and the result is a postmodern noise even more disposable than any previous pop. There are no stars, or artists or art, just an ever-accelerating rush of sound.

It's the kids who participate who make it vaguely interesting, with their goofy fashions and even goofier notions of community. They see their convocations as more than jubilations—they are revolutionary gatherings, geared toward a psychic advancement of their terra-bound *Ecch* lives. Ravers say there's real unity to the scene, that there's no closed-mindedness or cliquishness, but they're only looking from within. It's kind of like the Trilateral Commission saying it has no closed-mindedness or cliquishness—everyone who's on the Trilateral Commission is welcome!

Occasionally, however, regular folks bust in. Journey with us again, gentle reader, as we here at *Generation Ecch* Central venture forth on an anthropological observation of *Homo raveus* in their natural habitat.

**October 23, 1993**
**New York, N.Y.**
**Midnight: Outside the Roseland Ballroom**

*M: Here we are, ready for an Adventure Beyond the Ultraworld with the Orb, England's leading proponents of ambient rave. This should be a big event in the lives of the rave kids. With the exception of Moby, who's been called the "human face" of rave, Dr. Alex—*

*J: He's not a real doctor, but he plays one on CD.*

*M: —is the closest thing this music has to a rock star.*

*J: We spend the hours before the rave mystified and nervous. What's it going to be like? What are we going to wear? We don't own anything that isn't black, gray or olive!*

*M: Fortunately, we're immediately reassured when the first thing we see walking down Fifty-second Street is three young girls in full-on flannel, fretting that their grunge couture is inappropriate for a rave.*

*J: The mass of people ignoring the bouncers' "single-file" commands all seem to be friends, hugging and kissing and swooning as if they hadn't seen each other in a while. Probably since the rave last weekend.*

*M: We are about to enter a foreign land, totally adrift from our usual musical/cultural frame of reference. Because the Orb have been on the cover of Melody Maker and such, they are sort of known, so there are actually quite a few people here adrift from their usual frame of reference: the curious, the trendy and the people who don't participate in the rave scene but know about the Orb.*

*J: Speaking of frame of reference, here we are at Roseland's "Dancin' Shoes" Hall of Fame. Joan Crawford has very tiny feet.*

*M: Ray Bolger, on the other hand, has very big feet.*

*J: You know what they say . . . big feet, big shoes.*

*M: I think he'd feel quite comfortable with these kids. It's like a profusion of Brobdingnagian Lollipop Guilders.*

*J: Still, I don't think we'll see any signs of the Roseland Ballroom of yore tonight. I wonder what would happen if I went up to one of these teenage girls and offered her ten cents to dance.*

*M: Ah, the glory days of Paul Whiteman and his orchestra. I remember back on V-J Day I met this beautiful taxi dancer here.... Sigh.... At the stroke of midnight she kissed me. I never found out her name.... Sigh.... Hey, there's a guy in a Marcia Brady T-shirt!*

*J: I would buy doody from her!*

*M: Remember the episode where Alice comes to pick up Marcia and Greg at a rave and gets dosed?*

*J: I don't know how to respond to that.*

*M: Neither did Sam the Butcher.*

### 12:37:42 A.M.

*J: The DJs are doing their thing before the band goes on, playing some house mix that sounds like a perfect cross between Brian Eno and Teddy Pendergrass.*

*M: Teddy Pendergrass?*

*J: Yeah, you know, a mix of ambient music and soul/dance music.*

*M: Oh. I thought you meant it resembled the sound of wheels creaking.*

*J: That too. The back of Roseland is a little techno flea market, just like the Village at Lollapalooza or the bumper-sticker shop at the H.O.R.D.E. But there's no line at the piercing booth, probably because most of them already had their belly buttons perforated.*

*M: I love that.*

*J: A lot of these merchants are just DJs selling tapes and promoting their own raves.*

*M: The smart drinks here come in bigger, brighter colors like blue, but we're not about to make that mistake again.*

*J: Tang!*

*M: Shut up.*

*J: We pass by the de rigueur pro-pot table. Of course it's our good friends from CAN, taking names for the movement and assuring* kids that all information is confidential. Hey, I don't care if the FBI finds out, I just don't want my parents to know.

M: Their flyer compares pot to alcohol, an argument that's purely about getting fucked up in the healthiest possible way. Aside from the fact that alcohol causes more death and disease, CAN points out that "marijuana is a much less violence-provoking substance."

J: But what happens if you drink and smoke pot?

M: It gets you nice.

J: One table is selling futuristic jewelry and they have this little light gadget that looks like something in the back of Spencer Gifts. They're also selling that all-important sugar rush—candy, Blow Pops and those excellent Fun Dip sugar-powder thingies. Whoopee!

M: I always liked to eat the sticks without the powder. What were those things made of anyway? And where are the Pop Rocks?

J: They banned them after Mikey died. Hey, a girl in a cool G.I. Joe shirt just passed us.

M: There are also lots of T-shirts for seventies products—Tide detergent, Bounce fabric softener. Warhol's legacy lives on like never before.

J: Except these kids probably don't know it. Maybe it's weird nostalgia for the time when commercial products represented the promise of a clean, good life.

M: More likely it's because of the really bright cool colors, like orange, pink and yellow.

J: Put those together with the weird display of whirling multicolored light circles, and the place is like a pomo psychedelic laundromat.

M: These people are very clean.

J: The whole place is on spin cycle—this is the Orb, after all.

M: Seventies sneaker apparel is also a big thing. Of course, we had already read in the Styles of the Times that the comeback of blue suede Puma Clydes was closely related to rave culture, but adidas was the more dominant logo here.

J: Shouldn't "adidas" be capitalized?

M: No, it's like e. e. cummings. But that's very meta of you to ask.

J: In the sixties, the only retro item you wore was a Confederate army jacket. You found it at the thrift shop on the Haight and painted really cool fluorescent peace signs on it.

M: It reminds me of the design room at MOMA. The adidas thing kinda works as a futuristic look—the three stripes, the minimalism. It's very pure, in a 1920s Russian sort of way.

**12:48:18** A.M.

J: *I've been on the lookout for Ecstasy t-shirts. The only thing I saw was a guy wearing an "E" T-shirt, but the "E" was an Elektra Records logo. I don't think he knew. Or he works there.*

M: *We actually interviewed one guy—well, really he just grabbed the mic from us and started rapping. Then he spoke out ironically about how the media portrays the rave kids:* **"So I wanna say about rave, oooh, I just took some Ecstasy, I'm tripping my face off, ooooh, this is the place to do drugs, man, it's the greatest place to do drugs, that's all it's about. Raving changed my life drastically! That's what all you writers write."** *The only way we could respond to this little tirade was to ask him what he would* really *say. He paused for a moment.* **"What would I really say? Hi!"** *An Ecchemplary member of this most articulate generation.*

M: *I thought people were supposed to be dancing. The guys in the front are just waiting for the "band" to go on.*

J: *Everyone else is just standing around, shaking a little bit. It's ambient music and ambient dancers—it's benign, meaningless. Ambient music means you don't have to listen to it.*

M: *Everybody's looking bored and sort of glassy-eyed. It reminds me of those old pictures of Warhol's Factory, all the girls looking waifish and glazed, filled with restless ennui. That sort of silent-movie thing, like Edie Sedgwick (or Kate Moss).*

**1:21:14** A.M.

J: *We head for a spot near the stage and ask somebody who seems to know about this shit to explain how the Orb's "music" works in live performance. It has something to do with a couple of twenty-four-track mixing boards with each track containing another twenty-four tracks, so they can sound-collage their little hearts out and create different music every night.*

J: *I'll be curious to see how people react when the DJs stop and the Orb goes on.*

*M: It's basically disco, and fashion. This is where they hang out with their friends, it's about the scene, it's about going to the disco. We're going to see one of the biggest rave-oriented bands in the world, but there's still no star quality.*

*J: They say the audience is the star, but it's more solipsistic than that—it's "Me and my friends are the star, and this is where we hang out with each other in our striped T-shirts and purple hair and pigtails. There's no place else to go at four in the morning."*

*M (pointing): Though any scene that attracts transvestites is bound to catch on eventually.*

*J: Yeah. Actually, like disco, it has a strong gay presence. But unlike disco, there's this overall vibe of ambiguous androgyny. They say raves aren't pickup places, and that seems to be true. It's more about hugging.*

*M: There's a guy in front of us now with this cool paisley Day-Glo sequined blazer that looks like wallpaper. He's a real rebel, because we live in a world where you wear a tattoo and get your eyes and your nose pierced and it's no biggie. We're dealing with a crowd where you can wear a jester hat and nobody will laugh at you. But if you walk down the street in wallpaper, people still go, "Hey, look at the freak!"*

**1:53:02 A.M.**

*J: There's this little series of noises that sound like springs popping and people start applauding.*

*M: I lean over to our friend and say, "Hey, the band must be going on."*

*J: He tells us that the Orb have been on for more than twenty minutes.*

*M: That's it, we're out of here.*

**2:17:07 A.M.**

*J: So the question is, How does this connect to Ecch?*

*M: It's a scene based around nothingness, around ether, around air.*

*J: Rock'n'roll has always been a primal scream, and this is more of a deep sigh.*

*M: I never liked Pink Floyd then and I don't like them now. Screw "Shine On You Crazy Diamond." "Black Diamond," on the other hand . . .*

*J: For these kids, basically it's disco, it's fashion, nothing more. The majority of the kids don't own the records, they own Lemonheads and Smashing Pumpkins records. What fifteen-year-old girl is listening to this in her room?*

*M: It's the only place to hang out with your friends in the middle of the night. It's about the scene, it's about going to 2001 Odyssey and hanging out with Tony and Vinnie and Angie. It's life and death and the new Saturday night. It's a place for people to come hang out at night. That's really ultimately it.*

*J: Let's go get the* Times *and go home.*

*M: Yeah. Who's on* Meet the Press *tomorrow?*

**A**nd then there's Eddie.

No, not the cover ghoul of countless Iron Maiden records and baseball jerseys—Eddie Vedder, the screwed-up frontboy of Pearl Jam. For all of Nirvana's impact on the mainstream, it was Pearl Jam that got drenched with the greatest success from *Nevermind*'s wake. It makes sense, too, seeing how Pearl Jam is the one band that exemplifies all aspects of the *Ecch* world: the sappy liberal politics, the sad victim mentality and the classic rock meets grunge sound. Oh yeah, and they're from Seattle.

Pearl Jam rose from the ashes of Mother Love Bone, itself formed from the ashes of Sub Pop's flagship band Green River. That band dissolved when its members clashed over one of life's great questions. No, not *to be or not to be?* or *is man inherently good or evil?*, but rather, *should we sell out?* Mark Arm and Steve Turner said *Unh-unh!* and went off to be in Mudhoney, who have yet to sell out—except at various 500-seat clubs across the land. Jeff Ament and Stone Gossard, on the other hand, put together MLB with singer Andrew Wood and got signed to major label Mercury Records. Mother Love Bone were hyped as the band to make Seattle's supersonic hard rock sound palatable to the masses, but unfortunately, Andrew Wood hyped himself a little too heavily, succumbing to a heroin overdose in 1990. It's hard to achieve rock stardom when your lead singer is otherwise occupied being dead.

After Andy's interment, Stone and Jeff, like AC/DC and Van Halen before them (*Hey! Diamond Dave's not dead!*), regrouped and went shopping for a new lead singer. Their lyricless demos found their way to the sandy shores of San Diego via former Red Hot Chili Peppers drummer and all-around Left Coast scenester Jack Irons, who passed them along to Eddie Vedder. The frustrated artist/surfer was toiling at one of the primary *Ecch* vocations: nightwatchman—the better to catch the sickest, raddest most tubular waves when your shift is up. After the tide went out each day, he had lots of time on his hands, so he wrote some lyrics, sent them back to Stone and Jeff, and was hired immediately (just think—somewhere in San Diego *right now* a young surfer is preparing to send his songs to Krist Novoselic and Dave Grohl. Though Ed "Fromohio" Crawford is also available). Vedder hopped on the next Greyhound to Seattle and the band, which had also picked up guitarist Mike McCready and drummer Dave Krusen (later replaced by Dave Abbruzzese), was aborned.

The combo christened themselves Mookie Blaylock, after one of Jeff's favorite basketball stars. Upon inking with Epic Records the band were basically told, "we love everything about you except the name." Thus Mookie Blaylock joined the ranks of long-forgotten band monikers, along with "the Quarrymen," "Soft White Underbelly," "Mud Crutch," and "Fotomaker."

The etymology of the name Pearl Jam purportedly lies with Eddie's great-grandmother, said to be a genius with mason jars and various fruits. At least that's the story the band told during its first wave of press. *Puh-leeze.* Obviously it was another hoops reference, and Great-Grandma Pearl's concoction was just that, something cooked up by the band to amuse themselves during interviews.

In September of 1991, the same month that *Nevermind* was unleashed on an unsuspecting world, *Ten,* Pearl jam's debut, was released. Nobody cared.

But then the *eau de* teen spirit swept the nation. Nirvana's good timing broke things open for other bands, *especially* if they happened to be from Seattle (and weren't named Mudhoney). Kurt, who shared the rest of the Sub Pop crowd's distaste for Stone and Jeff's careerism, was not very happy with his own role in Pearl Jam's ascension.

He declared to *Rolling Stone* that Pearl Jam were "corporate, alternative and cock-rock fusion.

"I do feel a duty to warn the kids of false music that's claiming to be underground or alternative," he continued. "They're jumping on the alternative bandwagon." Never mind the fact that Kurt was the one pulling that train, and Pearl Jam had even opened for Nirvana in some cities. The hardened indie-punk community, shaken by Nirvana's fabulous success but not willing to condemn them, needed a target for their righteous rage, and Pearl Jam were it.

But aside from Kurt and his disciples, no one has a single bad thing to say about Mr. Vedder. From all accounts, to know him is to love him. As one highly placed Seattle insider puts it, "Eddie is a saint." Kurt was eventually forced to reconsider—he and Courtney got to know Eddie through their mutual involvement in the pro-abortion rights collective Rock for Choice, and he found that the "alternative and cock-rock fusion" icon was in fact an exemplary human being, even by their lofty standards. By the time the 1992 MTV Music Awards rolled around, the two men were tangoing about the backstage area, and according to Kurt, "I stared into his eyes and told him that I thought he was a respectable human. I did tell him straight out that I still think his band sucks. I said, 'After watching you perform, I realized that you are a person that does have some passion.' It's not a fully contrived thing. There are plenty of other more evil people out in the world than him, and he doesn't deserve to be scapegoated like that." Since the Ceauşescus were dead, and thus not presenting an award that evening, Curtney redirected their venom at two of the other people they viewed as "more evil," namely, Axl Rose and Stephanie Seymour. Kurt tussled with W., while Courtney responded to Stephanie's friendly "Are you a model?" with, "No, I'm a brain surgeon." *Hi, Axl!* The Cobain-Vedder reconciliation did not last, however. When Curt OD'ed in Italy, Courtney told *Select*, "I wish it had been Eddie. They'd have had a fucking candlelit vigil for him." *I-IIIII'm, I'm still aliiiive!*

With the "revolution" won, Pearl Jam and Nirvana were like the Lenin and Trotsky of alternative rock. But now as then, there was only room in the Kremlin for one. Both bands had their all-important follow-up records scheduled for release on the same September '93 day, but Pearl Jam, out of the kindness of their hearts, bumped their record back a few weeks, choosing not to stick the icepick in Nirvana's ear just yet. Because of Pearl Jam's graciousness, *In Utero* topped the *Billboard* chart in its first week of release, but ultimately its sales were merely a fraction of Pearl Jam's *Vs.*, which broke all records for a new release. *Vs.* stayed near the top of the charts, duking it out with Frank Sinatra and Meatloaf, for months to come, while *In Utero* dropped out of the Top 20 before the year was up. By the end of 1993 Pearl Jam were the biggest rock band around. Pre-tragedy, Nirvana just didn't matter that much in the post-Nirvana world.

**E**cch had crowned a new king—call him Eddie-pus Rex. The very first lyric Vedder wrote for his future band was "Alive," a gothic psychodrama that can only be explained in the *artiste's* own words: "The story of the song is that a mother is with a father and the father dies," he told Cameron Crowe in *Rolling Stone*. "It's an intense thing because the son looks just like the father. The son grows up to *be* the father, the person that she lost. His father's dead, and now this confusion, his mother, his love, how does he love her, how does she love him? . . . she wants *him*. . . . the second verse, I'm saying, 'the look, the look,' everyone thinks it goes with 'on her face.' It's not on her face. The look is between her *legs*. Where do you go with *that?* That's where you came from."

Where Eddie came from is his major preoccupation. He grew up under the excessively forceful hand of a quintessentially evil father. His work makes it sound like he was the last son of *Dër Bingle,* beaten, berated, and belittled to the point of no return.

Young Eddie took off before he finished high school, and hasn't spoken to the man since. It wasn't until much later that his mother revealed that his *real* father was someone else entirely, Edward Louis Severson II, the famous author of *Treasure Island.* No, actually, he was an MS-stricken musician who Eddie had met a few times in the past as "a friend of the family," but Severson had already passed on by the time Eddie learned the truth. *"While you were sittin' home alone at age thirteen/Your real Daddy was dyin,'"* Vedder would sing in "Alive." *Sorry you didn't see him.*

Abuse! Abuse! Abuse! All of Vedder's lyrics are basic variations on a single theme:

**"Daddy didn't give attention . . . to the fact that Mommy didn't care. . . ."—from "Jeremy"**

**"Maybe someday another child won't feel as alone as she does. . . ."—from "Why Go"**

**"She holds the hand that holds her down. . . ."—from "Daughter"**

**"Unfuckingbelievable to think I came from you. . . . Get out of my fucking face"—from "Leash"**

**"Was the beatings made me wise. . . . Tried to endure what I could not forgive. . . ."—from "Rearviewmirror"**

**"Hell, hell is for children . . . and you know their little lives can become such a mess. . . ."—from "Hell is for Children"**

Oh, sorry, that last one is a Pat Benatar song.

Eddie is the conduit for *Ecch*'s generation-wide feelings of victimhood. He voices the emotions of an audience *sooo* fucked by family and society that they cannot express themselves in any other way but their Tower Records purchases. "Troubled souls unite," he sings on "Leash." He's *beeeen* there, *maaan.* "I fully vow to help people out with whatever comes my way . . . because I went through the ice myself once or twice," he told *Melody Maker.* Who does this guy think he is? George friggin' Bailey?

**H**aving established himself as the world's most powerful wounded child, Eddie's subsequent fame and fortune gave him a chance to see the world and expand his horizons. "See, I never finished high school. So I guess I've had to educate myself," he told *Melody Maker.* "I learn about, like, geography, language and history while I'm traveling and I write down what I learn in my notebooks."

All this new book learnin' prompted Eddie to take advantage of his rock star's bully pulpit. On *Vs.,* he widened his lyrical focus from abused children to the politics of the abusive world they live in. Unsurprisingly, Vedder's politics run toward the correct. On "W.M.A.," which stands for White Male American (or Asshole or Authority or Agrarian, for all we know), Eddie informs his audience that powerful white people are bad. On another song, "Rats," he proclaims that the loveable little disease-carriers are a superior species: *"They don't scab they don't fight/Don't oppress an equal's given rights."*

When *Time* put Vedder on the cover without the band's cooperation, Eddie disclaimed the feature, seeing it as a subterfuge to distract America from real news: "We're on the cover as entertainment," he pronounced from the stage one night, going so far as to wipe his bum with the weekly newsmagazine. "Am I paranoid by thinking that we're just a decoy? Do you know we're declaring war on Haiti?" *Actually, we placed an EMBARGO on Haiti. Write that down in your little book.*

But then, like his friend Kurt, Eddie is one of those newfangled rock stars, the kind who says things like: "I'm being honest when I say that sometimes when I see . . . a picture of my face taking up a whole page of a magazine, I hate that guy." He has a propensity for wearing stupid rubber masks in photos, on the street and even on-stage—*Hey, who is that guy with the devil horns and pig's snout? Where's Eddie?*

When Pearl Jam appeared on *Headbanger's Ball,* back when Epic was trying to sell them as a metal band (before they got big), Eddie demonstrated where his true allegiance was by doin' the *Ecch* revolutionary thing: writing words on his flesh with Magic Marker, in this case the name of the archetypal punk DIY band Fugazi (proving that somebody is reading *The Baffler*). The more successful Pearl Jam gets, the more Eddie wants to be an indie-boy; on the initial legs of the *Vs.* tour, Pearl Jam refused to play arenas and dragged Eddie's heroes—Henry Rollins, American Music Club, and the Butthole Surfers—out on the road with them. "The audiences are suddenly getting bigger," he told Gina Arnold in her book *Route 666.* "And when they get bigger, I get smaller."

While Kurt Cobain tried to escape this trap by making a less accessible record, Eddie and Pearl Jam cannot distance themselves so easily from rock history—as a personality, preacher and amanuensis to a generation, Eddie Vedder is a rock star through and through, and Pearl Jam are a populist rock band that have more to do with Led Zeppelin, the Who, and R.E.M. than Minor Threat.

The band Pearl Jam might have the most in common with is U2, for the unironic way they inspire and uplift their fans. The music is stirring but not difficult, the lyrics thoughtful and moving yet obscure enough to inspire multiple meanings. U2 and Pearl Jam are BIG bands, bands that wouldn't work outside the context of mega-stardom. The huge *Ecch* audience that U2 and Pearl Jam share are sheep, following the somewhat sanctimonious Bono and Eddie into the breach, into the fray.

While it's possible that Eddie would only throw televisions out of hotel windows because he recognizes them as the controlling instruments of the evil ruling class, he's become rather good at most of the other rock star behaviors. He even got tossed into the New Orleans clink after teaming up with a fellow millionaire, White Sox pitcher Jack McDowell, in a full-on drunken bar brawl. He's rarely seen without a bottle of dago red in his hands, and in concert he's constantly stage-diving and hugging audience members. You would almost think he's *Jim Morrison,* for chrissakes! In fact, unsatisfied with his career replacing one dead singer, this new Lizard King sat in with the (barely) surviving Doors at the 1992 Rock'n'Roll Hall of Fame induction ceremonies. *He's hot! He's sexy! He's NOT dead!*

The Lollapalooza legion is further evidence of how *Ecch* has blurred conventional categories of musical fandom. Time was, you were either a disco kid, a punk, or a Deadhead. Now the lines have blurred—kids listen to Soul Asylum and also check out "rave night" at the local clubs. Grunge fashion, that patchwork of old flannel and torn denim, is nothing more than what Deadheads have been wearing for twenty-five years (though those snazzy J. Garcia ties could change things). Lollapalooza is essentially a Dead concert with rap, feedback, and moshing, an elitist tribal gathering of modern hippies who will do whatever they can to piss their parents off and call it revolution.

For *Ecch,* there's little difference between classic rock and alternative rock. Zep is cool, and so is Soundgarden. There's no real difference between Blind Melon and the Marshall Tucker Band. And Pearl Jam, the biggest band of them all, are like an alchemist's blend of the sixties, seventies, eighties, and nineties—a little Who, a little Doors, a little Pistols, a little R.E.M., a little Bono, and a little Oprah, all in one hard-rockin' package.

This broken classic/alternative boundary raises a troubling question. In the future, when *Ecch* are old and gray, will "easy listening" stations offer up really sick live versions of "Tales of Great Ulysses," followed by "the mellow sounds of My Bloody Valentine" to soothe you while you're sitting in the dentist's chair?

Since the release of *Vs.*, this musical alchemy that passes for the "new mainstream" has continued apace. While their stint at Lollapalooza had no immediate effect, Rage Against the Machine grew in popularity as '94 wore on. With a hard-funk sound that can only be described as the Chili Peppers with more metal, more hip-hop, and more politics, RATM have galvanized the youth of America with such articulate rallying cries as "Fuck You, I Won't Do What You Tell Me!" They also made a really sanctimonious video about wrongly imprisoned AIM activist Leonard Peltier. Watching it is kind of like watching *Incident At Oglala* while listening to the Red Hot Chili Peppers.

Reaching for the brass ring of Cobain and Vedder status in '94 was an enigmatic Los Angeles youngster named Beck, whose sound can only be described as the Allman Brothers with a little more hip-hop and a little more punk. Since he separated from his former partner, Jeff, the twenty-three-year-old Beck has watched his popularity soar, first getting radio play without a record deal, than picking the best of the quickly tendered contracts (with Geffen, of course).

Beck quickly proved himself to have the stuff that *Ecch* greatness is made of, making his national television debut as the object of Thurston Moore's probing questions on *120 Minutes*. Mostly he threw things. Actually, this New Dylan bears a startling resemblance to the gawky, gangling Sonic Youth leader—so much so that it seems as if he's spent his twenty-three years gestating in Kim Gordon's womb. A dedicated potsmoker whose original independent release of "Loser" came out on Bong Load Records, Beck's rapier wit and loquacious charm makes J Mascis look like Alistair Cooke. Hell, he makes *Russell Baker* look like Alistair Cooke!

Beck made a whole album, *Mellow Gold*, winning critical praise and the crucial support of Sonic Youth and Nirvana's management company. But the odds of his becoming a lasting artist are no more or less than the odds of his turning out to be an alternative-rock Vanilla Ice. For just as "Satisfaction," "Boogie Oogie Oogie, "Don't Worry Be Happy," and "Smells Like Teen Spirit" marked their respective eras, Beck's big hit, "Loser," became the ultimate *Ecch* anthem, taking the generation's penchant for pop-culture references, postmodern ennui, and low self-esteem to its inevitable, and, it should be stressed, most welcome conclusion. *"I'm a loser, baby,"* he sings, over a catchy little acoustic guitar riff with a hip-hop beat, *"so why don't you kill me?"*

The line starts here.

**1**968:

The spirit of activism and anarchy raged in the streets of the Windy City, as Mayor Richard Daley's police force clashed with hippies, Yippies and Black Panthers at the Democratic National Convention.

On the silver screens of America, a more fanciful sort of revolution transpired. In *Wild in the Streets*, the youth of the nation *really* flexed their political muscle.

In the *Wild* world, young Max Frost (Christopher Jones) survives the dysfunctional upbringing of an ineffectual weeny dad and an overbearing, played–by–Shelley Winters mom to become a groovy millionaire garage rocker.

Max gets drawn into the political arena by Senator Hal Holbrook, who is trying to get the voting age lowered to eighteen in a semisincere, semidesperate ploy to grab the youth vote. (Which, if you think about it, doesn't make any sense, because there wouldn't *be* a youth vote until he put the legislation through.)

Nevertheless, as the powers-that-be soon realize, America's young are not to be taken lightly. Recognizing the massive political clout of a youthful baby boom comprising more than half the country, Max has himself a little epiphany. Being a millionaire garage rocker, he sings a song about it:

> **We're 52 percent, they write the TV shows**
> **for us**
> **We're 52 percent, they design the clothes**
> **for us**
> **We're 52 percent, they play the songs we dig**
> **We're 52 percent and we make big**
> **business big**

Emboldened by his pop-star power, Max turns on the senator politically (later, he turns on the whole Senate *chemically*), taking things

**P**olitical

*Ecch*tivism

or

Johnny,

We Hardly

Knew Ye

in his own hands by galvanizing millions of teens with the suffragette battle cry "Fourteen or Fight!" With the help of his guitarist and aide-de-camp, Billy Cage, a fifteen-year-old Yale Law School grad, Frost mobilizes his 52 percent via a rock'n'roll TV campaign. The Senate, thanks to that little lysergic nudge from Max and his followers lowers the minimum age for Congress and the presidency to fourteen.

The party of Ronald Reagan recognizes an unstoppable media force when it sees one. Max becomes the Republican presidential candidate and a landslide ensues, set to the psych-rock anthem "The Shape of Things to Come."

In a world run by teenagers, "Never Trust Anyone Over Thirty" becomes law, with mandatory retirement at that age. At thirty-five comes permanent interment in camps. Once they're in the camps, no one complains—the bug juice is spiked with a steady calming dose of LSD.

**W**ith the youth movement at a fever pitch back in the real world of Vietnamization and Richard Nixon, the terrified country could at least reassure itself that *Wild in the Streets* was only a movie, and a Samuel Z. Arkoff exploitation special at that.

But what they didn't, couldn't, would never know was that the Max Frost presidency would someday become a reality.

All it took was the passing of twenty-four years—time enough for Max and his fellow boomers to grow up and actually resemble Republicans—and the participation of the latest crop of music-worshiping, media-crazy, politically alienated youngsters, a crop known as *Ecch*. The numbers are smaller these days, but "52 Percent" is an uncannily prescient description of what makes *Ecch* go, and what makes *Ecch* media and *Ecch* marketing the major preoccupation of corporations and ad agencies.

**1**992:
The spirit of activism and anarchy raged in the streets of New York City, as radical right-to-lifers proffered pickled fetuses to William Jefferson Clinton at the Democratic National Convention.

On the television screen, a more fanciful sort of revolution transpired, as America's young flexed their political muscle for the first time in years.

As on film twenty-four years before, there were dysfunctional families; candidates groveling in front of outspoken, alienated youth; rock-'n'roll campaigning; mass media pseudoevents; and even some drugs.

Only this time America's young were watching an actual presidential election. And they were watching it on a cable television network that, up till then, had given nothing to the country but Nina Blackwood, Pauly Shore and bad music videos twenty-four hours a day (this was pre–*Beavis and Butt-head*, mind you). The starring roles in the 1992 presidential campaign may have gone to boomers; but the campaign's style and tenor were *Ecch* all the way, mostly because of MTV.

It was an election spectacle that featured, in response to Clinton and Gore's preplanned spontaneous Merry Pranksters simulation, dozens of major newspapers abusing the headline BILL AND AL'S *ECCH-CELLENT ADVENTURE* (in slightly different form, of course). There was Ross Perot on *Larry King* and Clinton blowin' his horn for Arsenio. There was George Bush, who kicked off the campaign with his made-for-TV war. After that, he didn't do anything memorable but lose.

The youth vote has been around ever since the voting age actually did get lowered to eighteen, but kids in the eighties—that sort-of-late-boomer, erstwhile-yuppie, pre-*Ecch* bunch of college students—voted for Reagan. Clinton's campaign advisers were smart enough to recognize a developing segment of liberal young voters, and MTV was there with a means to communicate with them.

MTV's coverage, dubbed "Choose or Lose," was fronted by the earnestly perky pronouncements of Tabitha Soren, *Ecch*'s much cuter equivalent of Sander Vanocur. An NYU journalism grad, Tabby (as we think of her, with that mock affection-*cum*-familiarity so typical of our generation's relationship to celebrities) was born with the name Sornberger, but her boss at the Vermont TV station she worked at suggested the snappier, less, um . . . shall we say, *ethnic* appellation. (If it's good enough for Senator David Durenberger it should have been good enough for her).

The media responded to Soren the way it responds to most youth-driven phenomena, with a mixture of celebration, condescension and outright distress. Styles of the *Times* called her "the hippest reporter to ride the bus since Hunter S. Thompson sped across America." Compared to Johnny Apple, that's probably true, but as far as we know Tabby doesn't suck down Wild Turkey and NyQuil before filing her political reports. On the negative side, Liz Smith printed the damaging rumor that Tabby queried her rock-critic boyfriend about a jazz musician Clinton idolized. "Who's 'the Loneliest Monk'?" she asked, when obviously, the prez-to-be was talking about Thelonious Monk. Soren, concerned about her hipster credentials, denied the story, and Smith printed a retraction, but it's a good story in any case.

Any seasoned, sirloin-enhanced, liquor-swilling Beltway pundit would have gotten the bebop reference. But "Choose or Lose" was still more significant than *The Capital Gang* and *The McLaughlin Group* put together. It was on the MTV forum, with Tabby calling the shots in front of an inquisitive audience of young voters, that Bill Clinton first made his pledge to allow gays in the military. Whoops! Loser-boy George Bush stupidly avoided his shot on MTV until the last minutes of the campaign, then didn't take advantage of the appearance, failing to mask his disdain for Our Tabby. Whoops again!

Obviously, the expanding role of the mass media in electoral politics is old, old news. It's been said that Abraham Lincoln, sex symbol to Julia Roberts but big ugly dude to most, couldn't get elected in this age of the telegenic president. It's been years since party conventions were anything more than self-congratulatory bashes for delegates and dog-and-pony shows for the viewing audience. In an orthodoxy-sensitive field like politics, the proverbial smoke-filled rooms are *totally* out of the question. Now the conventions are like the Oscars, with fewer surprises but much better choreography.

The 1992 conventions were presented to America as pure entertainment. Comedy Central was one of eight networks to broadcast the action, offering up superfluous commentary like socialist limey troublemaker Christopher Hitchens cursing a blue streak and *Saturday Night Live* head "writer" Al Franken fruitlessly attempting to be funny. If we may throw out another version of what has become the lamest and most persistent political joke since Pat Paulsen ... *We know funny. Some of our friends are funny. Mr. Franken, you're not funny.*

MTV recruited actual rock stars to assist in their convention coverage. At the Democratic convention in New York City, reformed drug addict and Megadeth leader Dave Mustaine transformed himself into a respectable, bespectacled, suit-and-tied reporter, playing Maria Shriver to Tabby's Tom Brokaw. A month later in Houston, Ted Nugent—avowed animal killer, longbow shooter and composer of "Wang Dang Sweet Poontang"—reported from the Republican meeting. (Kennedy, the GOP-elephant-tattooed, frizzy-haired, *McLaughlin Group*–guesting alternachick, would have been an excellent choice, but she wasn't working at the network yet. Then again, she probably wouldn't have done the conventions anyway, because she's a VJ, not a reporter. Ted Nugent—*he's* a reporter. Though Beavis and Butthead would have been even better—*Hillary's cool. Hunh-hunh. Pat Buchanan—he sucks. Hunh-hunh.*)

The rock'n'roll/election connection continued long after convention season. After U2 singer Bono spent the summer prank-phone-calling the White House from the stage of the ZooTV tour, Clinton decided that if Bush wouldn't speak to the world's biggest pretentious rock star, he would, taking the time to dial up the syndicated radio program *Rockline,* on which U2 was guesting. "I can't believe I got U2 on the phone," the candidate enthused. "I want to say, as a middle-aged man, I appreciate the fact that you made *The Joshua Tree* and that record 'Angel of Harlem' at Sun Studios. You made me feel like I had a place in rock music even at forty-six." Then, because Bono has a larger entourage than the average presidential candidate, Clinton came to U2 personally, meeting with Mr. Vox in the band's Chicago hotel room during a break in the tour. Bush did take notice of all this, however, and in what might have been his first—and only—clever moment since Peggy Noonan ditched him, threatened voters that if Clinton were elected, "*You too* will pay taxes, *you too* will lose your job."

Later, in R.E.M.'s home state of Georgia, Al Gore picked up on this linguistic thread, telling an audience that "Bush/Quayle is *Out of Time,* but Clinton/Gore is *Automatic for the People!*" Thankfully, his advisers convinced him to delete the following passage from the speech: "The American public must quit *Murmur*ing and get down to *Reckoning* with the *Documented* issue of taxes and the deficit, for if they want to continue enjoying *Lifes Rich Pageant* there's going to have to be a *Reconstruction of the Fables* of responsible citizenship. We're all going to have to part with some *Green.*"

Unsurprisingly, the sheer weirdness of all this pop-culture politicking barely registered on the surrealism-immune American public.

\*     \*     \*

Things got even nuttier. First, Bill Clinton won. Then, after he assumed office on the traditional January 20 morn, America partied! Well, the 43 percent of America that voted for him did, at least.

Of all the bashes thrown as part of the official celebration, the hottest ticket in town was the MTV Inaugural Ball—that's right, the *MTV* Inaugural Ball. The network decided to revel in its own electoral culpability by throwing one of its patented rock'n'roll video variety shows. The grateful, hours-old Washington establishment welcomed the network with open arms. MTV reciprocated by allowing Roger Clinton to perform with En Vogue.

Whether or not MTV actually swung the election for Clinton (a claim made by more than a few perfectly reputable and astute political minds) is irrelevant—the observable facts were right there on national television for all to see: the First Family, introduced by new FOB Tabby, waving triumphantly as the hip young crowd chanted, "CHELSEA! CHELSEA!" The president promised that his young'un would remain there the whole night while he and the wife made the rounds, but Chelsea only stuck around for her favorite band, 10,000 Maniacs, who got a big sales boost out of the ceaselessly rerun affair.

The Second Family showed up to the strains of "You Can Call Me Al," the new vice-president dancing like a big gork while his wife, Tipper, the onetime scourge of rock'n'rollers everywhere, smiled evenly to the mixed chorus of applause and boos. For some reason, good-looking Canadian newsreader Peter Jennings and his soon-to-be ex-wife appeared onstage, looking like parents checking in on the kids' basement party. Jennings was condescending in the face of the flighty youngster who'd usurped his power, making some sort of innuendo to Tabby while she reminded him that they'd met before when she worked at ABC; the soon-to-be ex-wife didn't look amused. Ratty ex-punks Soul Asylum spent the grand occasion looking uncomfortable in ill-fitting sport jackets; furthermore, according to an interview with Tabs in *Cake*, lead singer Dave Pirner was a little harsh on the olfactories. On the other hand, Roger Clinton was resplendent with the great smell of Brut.

The whole thing was as much a case of *Ecch* becoming part of the establishment as the establishment coming to *Ecch*. Youth culture, in the form of MTV and alternative-rock bands, had permeated the American mainstream so completely that even the president was not immune.

Clinton is in fact Max from *Wild in the Streets*, grown up and sold out, still using rock'n'roll to sell his vision of America (though in this case it was Judy Collins and Fleetwood Mac as well as R.E.M.). His may be "America's first boomer administration," but symbolically, it's pure *GenEcch*. So is the government in general—below the forty-something White House and the seventysomething cabinet are hundreds of budding *Ecch* bureaucrats (and a bunch of boomers who haven't worked since Carter).

**C**linton's *our* first president, or at least the first one *Ecch* voted for. Traditionally, the president is America's father figure, and though Clinton is too young to seem paternal to his fellow baby boomers, he's just the right age to play pappy to the younger generation. Of course, we *Ecch*sters have a tendency to blame our father for everything: He abused us, he didn't spend enough time with us, he doesn't understand us and *he's pissing away our inheritance.*

We want one of those cool pot-*inhaling* dads—a dad who shows up every weekend with gifts but doesn't complain about our bad grades—not some stiff-necked L7 disciplinarian. We love our dad, as long as he does exactly what we want, but that's never the way it works out, so we're forced to take the death penalty and the botched gays-in-the-military plan with the prochoice stance and the somewhat liberal Supreme Court appointments.

But what *Ecch* really wants, what Americans of all ages have longed for the past thirty years to no avail, is for our president to enable the vicarious resurrection of one John Fitzgerald Kennedy.

The memory of Camelot's glory days has plagued the country every minute of every year since Dallas. *Ecch* is the first generation born after this national loss of innocence, and thus the first Americans with no firsthand recollections of those halcyon times.

When a generation's first political experience involves wiretapping, burglary, and worm-faced John Dean, it's no wonder the image of the martyred hunk president resonates so strongly. All our lives we have been told of the wondrous JFK, the president everyone loved. Like everything else from the sixties, it makes us feel like we got gypped out of something.

The truth is, Jack's legacy has affected us in very real ways. The welfare state, James Bond movies, John-John, and Ted's embarrassing political career—these are the real remnants of the Kennedy presidency. JFK, as he is now perceived, is no more than a mirage, just like the Monkees, free love without jealousy and, God help us, peace without honor.

The John F. Kennedy we think we know is just so much bullshit. According to various sources, both reputable and not, JFK's political career was bought and paid for by his Gloria Swanson–shtupping Nazi bootlegger dad's ill-gotten gains. It's been said that the noble war-hero senator didn't even write *Profiles in Courage,* a book that junior-high-school social-studies teachers still assign today. We've heard the stories about the women being snuck into the White House and the mistress-sharing with mob boss Sam Giancana and mob crooner Frank Sinatra (and what about poor Peter Lawford, who got kicked out of the Rat Pack for his involvement in that bizarre *ménage à quatre*?). JFK couldn't even make dinky little Cuba safe for American gambling interests again. Hell, brother Bobby, a real hero to many in the sixties but just another Dead Kennedy to *Ecch,* may very well have administered a barbituate-loaded enema to Marilyn Monroe. What about sister Rosemary's lobotomy? Chappaquiddick? That Palm Beach rape thing? And what kind of family calls its house a "compound," anyway?

Oddly, *Ecch* knows (and believes) these horrible things about Jack and Bobby, yet we still yearn for their return.

The JFK presidency was brought to us courtesy of that old illusion maker, the television. In 1960, Richard Nixon's putrid mug, sour expression, sopping brow and dyspeptic disposition, placed side by side with the dreamy young Dem, cost him the very first televised presidential debate, a debate that *radio* listeners thought Nixon had won. The country elected its very first television prez, albeit by a much smaller margin than most recall.

The Kennedys were more than just politicians—they were *celebrities.* America loved Jack and Jackie almost as much as Lucy and

Ricky—the birth of John-John was the biggest baby news since the birth of Little Ricky (except JFK didn't dress in a voodoo outfit at the hospital). Everyone swooned at gorgeous Jackie, with her tailored suits and pillbox hats. We watched as Jack sat in the War Room deciding what to do about the Cuban Missile Crisis—oh, sorry, that was William Devane in *The Missiles of October*, sometime later.

Then, tragically, Walter Cronkite announced the awful news to a shattered nation. But death could not stop the John F. Kennedy Show. After he got popped, the networks went to a twenty-four-hour dead-president format. John-John broke the country's heart into further pieces at the teary funeral (which in retrospect looks a lot like Elvis's, only in black and white). The assassination of Lee Harvey Oswald happened live and up close, right in front of the TV cameras.

Who knew there would be so much more after that, from the Warren Commission to Bobby's killing to all those TV movies. The shooting has become *Ecch*'s most resonant *faux* memory, thanks to the very first I Witness Video, the Zapruder film: *Check it out! His head's exploding like a melon! Jackie's got brains on her dress!* We've seen it so many times that, as with Charlton Heston parting the Red Sea, it doesn't even matter that we weren't born when it happened.

After JFK, America got LBJ, Nixon, Ford and Carter, none of whom mastered the medium quite like Kennedy (though Nixon's resignation and Gerald Ford falling off a chair and shouting "LIVE FROM NEW YORK, IT'S SATURDAY NIGHT" were pretty memorable moments).

Then came Ronnie.

Ronald Wilson Reagan is, in a very strange way, both the perfect mirror image of JFK and the anti-Jack.

Though he was all hair dye and Porcelana, Reagan was the best-looking president America had seen since Kennedy. Reagan was a celebrity before he ever got into politics, though he was only a B-movie actor, never a star. As studio head Jack Warner commented when Reagan first threw his hat into the California gubernatorial ring, "No. No. No. Jimmy Stewart for governor. Ronald Reagan for best friend." When he became president, Reagan finally got the script and direction to become *the* leading man. And ironically, Jimmy Stewart was one of his best friends.

Like Kennedy in the beginning of his decade, the charismatic old coot represented a promise of American uplift, both spiritual and economic. After the malaise of the seventies—gas lines, Bert Lance, crazy Iranians and killer rabbits—America was desperate for someone who could promise a new day. More to the point, America was desperate for someone who wasn't Jimmy Carter.

In other ways, Reagan was like the shadow of JFK. Kennedy symbolized a new generation grabbing the reins of power; Reagan took the votes of those very same people, twenty years older and money-hungry, their childish ideals battered and broken. Jack was young, spirited, full of piss 'n' vinegar—yet he had gray hair. Reagan was old, turkey-necked and had prostate problems—yet he had a black Bryl-creemed pompadour.

Where Kennedy united the nation in the spirit of public service and group participation with his "Ask not what your country can do for you" speechifying, the Great Communicator was merely head cheerleader for an anxious country's long-repressed patriotism: "USA! USA! USA!" Reagan and Kennedy also had friendships with the Chairman of the Board in common, though young Frank slept with the president's *mistress,* while, according to Kitty Kelley, *old* Frank actually slept with the president's *wife*—in the Lincoln Bedroom, no less. What this really means, of course, is that Frank Sinatra has been more or less running the country for almost thirty years. But we knew that already.

Kennedy's encounter with a gunman's bullet landed him in Arlington National Cemetery. Reagan merely spent a week in George Washington Hospital joking around with the surgeons. As with JFK, the experience made Reagan even more popular, the difference being that Reagan was actually around to capitalize on his new clout, returning to affairs of state instead of decomposing under an eternal flame. The two chief executives' bullet-catching sidekicks also went in opposite directions—Texas governor John Connally became a Republican, much to the consternation of his lifelong boss man, JFK veep and quintessential Texan Lyndon Johnson. Reagan press secretary James Brady made something useful out of his tragedy, working with his wife to spearhead gun-control laws, much to the consternation of Reagan veep and hotel-room Texan George Bush.

The parallels are astounding, almost ridiculous! Ronald Reagan had a secretary named Kennedy, while JFK had a secretary named Reagan. *Think about it!*

The Reagan era (1980–1992) was a timeless blur of ridiculous behavior that went across our television screens and through our consciousness very very fast. Donald Regan. "It's morning in America." Khadafy. David Stockman. "Read my lips." Astrology. Ten-thousand-dollar Givenchy dresses. Ketchup as a vegetable. Dan Quayle. "We begin bombing in five minutes." Operation Desert Storm. New china. Naps. Bitburg. The death of Vicki Morgan. Noriega. The October Surprise. Qaddafi. William Casey. AWACS. Bork. Margaret Thatcher. Star Wars. "I am in control here!" Scuds and smart bombs and Patriot missiles. Grenada. Ronbo. P-O-T-A-T-O-E. Silverado. Gadhafi. Lee Atwater. Saddam Hussein. "Mommy's" pearl-handled revolver. *Millie's Book.* The irritating ballet-dancer son and the equally irritating *roman à clef* novelist daughter and the even more irritating banker thief son. Sununu. The Keating Five. El Salvador. Junk bonds. The line in the sand. Clarence ♥ Anita. A hundred-some indictments. A thousand points of light. Ray Donovan. Jeane Kirkpatrick. The "little brown" grandkids. SALT II. James Watt and the Beach Boys. Free cheese. C. Everett Koop. Ronnie Headrest. Teflon.

Oops, almost forgot Iran-Contra and Iraqgate. But then, who hasn't?

The country rooted for the Gipper to take America's team all the way to the Super Bowl of economic prosperity and imperialist domination. The fans chose not to notice that their quarterback kept forgetting all the plays, the tight ends all had felony records and ticket prices kept going up. Thanks to some savvy supply-side field-goal kicking, Reagan led his boys through the economic playoffs and then kicked the crap out of the Russians in the big game. The team's owners profited considerably from Reagan's winning season, but unfortunately the Super Bowl prize money went fast, leaving the workaday players with nothing but a big garish ring.

*The football metaphor, ladies and gentlemen. Let's hear it! Thank you, you've been a great audience! Good night!*

Reagan's America is the America *Ecch* grew up in. He was the dad who made all sorts of new rules around the house: "You *cannot* have an abortion," he said. And "I'm sorry, we'll have to tighten our belts—we've spent all our money on antiballistic missiles." He kept having friends like Jerry Falwell and Ed Meese over for dinner, leaving us to fend for ourselves. He was a cold and uncaring father, much like . . . well, Ron and Nancy with their *real* kids, only on a far grander scale.

Then he ran out on us right when the bills came due, and we got a creepy new ex-spook stepdad; one who laid down similar rules, but didn't have any of Ron-Dad's aw-shucks charm. He didn't approve of our art, so he took away our art supplies. His own son did all sorts of bad stuff and never got into trouble, but if we did anything wrong, he threatened to slap us in jail. He was mean to our gay friends, our women friends, our black friends. His own pals, like Pat Buchanan and Marilyn Quayle, were even scarier and more unctuous than the people who used to hang around. And despite his patrician background, he wasn't very well mannered—one time, when we went with him on a business trip to Japan, he even hurled at dinner. *Daad, you're embarrassing us.*

When 1992 rolled around, *Ecch* was finally old enough to take a stand. There was only one president who could save America in 1992. And that man was . . . John Fitzgerald Kennedy.

Bill Clinton is no different from any other American in his wistful feelings of attachment to the JFK mystique. He didn't hesitate to exploit those memories for his own benefit. If America still wanted to elect JFK President, then Clinton would be JFK.

The icon of Jack was a presence throughout the campaign. We were constantly told of the parallels between the young and beautiful St. Johnny and the equally youthful, but not quite as pretty or thin Clinton. In a fortuitous twist of fate, there was even film of the adolescent candidate shaking hands with President Kennedy in the Rose Garden.

For a generation whose Kennedys are either jokes on *Seinfeld* or just plain jokes, Clinton is as close as we'll get, the crucial difference being that Clinton's personal failings and dysfunctions are public knowledge, not to mention part of his charm (unlike the last Democratic presidential candidate who attempted to pinch-hit for the Kennedy corpses, Gary Hart).

*Ich bin ein Ecchster,* Clinton declared by going on MTV. He made us believe in the system for the very first time. "It's the economy, stupid!" may have been the overriding theme of the Clinton campaign, but it was his liberal-social pitch that won us over. Here was a presidential candidate who skewed close to our own beliefs. He wasn't perfect, but we've learned to accept that in our politicians.

The only hitch with Clinton is that, unlike his predecessors, we voted for him. If he screws up and disappoints us, *Ecch* will have to accept the hard truth: If you want to be part of the political process, you have to accept some blame—never an easy thing for this generation. With great power comes great responsibility.

As a political actor, *GenEcch* is facile, confused and very far behind. "Question Authority" is a badge to wear, not a way to live. Good liberal *Ecch*sters are antiapartheid or prochoice because they know it's right, but they don't necessarily know why. Platitudes like "Smash Racism" and "Keep Your Supreme Court Away from My Body" suffice, usually on the bumper of the new Stanza Dad paid for, right next to those Grateful Dead dancing bears.

Many of those who pass for today's politically aware couldn't carry on an intelligent debate with someone who disagreed with their stand, let alone come to terms with the subtleties and ambiguities of an issue. You just can't fit that much information on a Ben & Jerry's Peace Pop. Saddled with a lifetime of fuzzy politics and manipulatin' politicians, *Ecch*'s activism is a triumph of spirit over substance.

In defense of the generation, this has as much to do with what came before them as it does with *Ecch* itself. In the eighties, most young people were uninterested at best. The only collegians with any political energy at all were Young Republicans, who had reasons to be cheerful:

**1.** Ad pages at their school's version of the *Dartmouth Review* were up.

**2.** Huey Lewis had two brand-new songs on the sound track to that new Michael J. Fox movie with the De Lorean.

**3.** They had postgraduate fellowships at the Heritage Foundation or a lucrative gig selling worthless stock certificates for Drexel Burnham awaiting them.

Folks just couldn't be moved to mass resistance and denouncement against humdrum evils like Gramm-Rudman or low capital-gains taxes. America failed to put on a good, meaty, violent imperialist action for young progressives to get bent out of shape over. The nuclear-freeze movement fizzled faster than Jackson Browne's career post "Lawyers in Love." Reagan's dirty little wars—El Salvador, Nicaragua, Grenada, Panama—were either too secret or too speedy to engender any kind of opposition. Apparently the country was too stupid, too cynical or too Republican to get worked up over Iran-Contra, while only William Safire and *The Village Voice* really know what Iraqgate was.

Even Vice President Bush's major accomplishment was a washout activismwise. Okay, before Desert Shield became Desert Storm there were polite rumblings of antiwar sentiment on the stone steps of America's campuses, but those assemblies were peaceably met by flanks of prowar demonstrators. (Yes, *prowar* demonstrators, a pretty odious idea—some of the people were just showing support for "our boys," but they still gave off a healthy strain of "America—Right or Wrong!")

Ultimately, Desert Storm just wasn't divisive enough—witness the large number of former sixties lefties turned columnists (the ones who *hadn't* become neocons) who agreed that the skirmish was a just and necessary one, agonizing at great length about how agonizing it was to be former radicals in favor of a war. Besides, the whole thing was too abstract and electronic to protest—it would have been like speaking out against a video game.

It took twelve years of the repressive Reagan regime before *Ecch*'s bottled-up impulse to speak out popped its stopper. America's education system left us too inarticulate to say anything recondite, but we sure liked the sound of our own voice. Some chose to worry about the rain forest, 'cause Sting told them to. They've got a copy of *Earth in the Balance,* but they don't know who Rachel Carson is. After rallies, they head out for lunch at the off-campus McDonald's, scarfing down Big Macs ground from cattle grazed on deforested Brazilian land. The vegetarians get those nifty nonbiodegradable plastic boxes of salad.

F or all the talk of political involvement, the most prominent *Ecch* mobilization involved the most basic means of influencing policy: voting. Our activist muscles had atrophied to the point that we had to start over entirely—how can we address specific issues or take action if we don't go to the polls first?

Again, it was just like *Wild in the Streets,* only now the kids needed Max Frost to come back and sing on TV not to get us the *right* to vote, but to get us to take advantage of that right. A coalition of students, pop stars and record-company guys, galvanized by the persecution/ prosecution of reprehensible First Amendment poster boys 2 Live Crew, took it upon themselves to make a generation believe that they could change things. In order to do that, they had to make them believe voting was hip: hence, Rock the Vote.

Obviously, there's a certain amount of justifiable cynicism in *Ecch*sters who don't see any reason to vote, but nonetheless, has there ever before been a generation that required voting to be "hip" before they were willing to do it? Who had to be told, by people like Megadeth and Aerosmith, that they had a voice in the system, and it might be a good idea if they raised it? Not that pop rhetoric is that much worse than the usual politician's jive talking: *Yo! MTV Raps* cohost Ed Lover could have been pumping up the crowd at any old political rally when he urged a New Hampshire audience, "Put your hands in the air if you're registered to vote." *Whoot! There it is! Political participation!*

Rock the Vote had gotten off to a shaky start when it was revealed that some of its 1990 spokesmodels, specifically Madonna and Lenny Kravitz, weren't registered to vote themselves. They were too busy collaborating on "Justify My Love" (and screwing Ingrid Chavez). Besides, absentee ballots must not have been in the Blonde Ambition tour riders.

By 1992, however, RTV was in full gear, registering eight thousand people for the New Hampshire primary while proceeding with a class-action lawsuit that eventually led to election-law reform there. One of the founders of Rock the Vote, former Virgin co–managing director Jeff Ayeroff, acknowledged in *Rolling Stone* that *Ecch* activism was still in its birth throes. "Next to us marching against LBJ at the Pentagon, this is just a ripple . . . [but] at least now there's a ripple."

More successes followed, as the synergy of MTV's election coverage and Clinton's campaign kicked in. Touring bands like R.E.M., U2 and Guns N' Roses set up registration booths at their concerts. R.E.M. printed a postcard supporting the Motor Voter Bill, which would automatically register anyone who had a driver's license, on the longbox of their *Out of Time* CD. (Those days are over, however, because another big music-industry cause was banning the environmentally unsound longbox). By the end of the campaign, young people all over America were not only registered, but actually pulling the levers. The election of President Clinton was proof that Rock the Vote worked—they tipped the vote over!

**P**ostelection, the rise of political awareness among the generation prompted *Ecch* to start doing things for *Ecch*.

The pseudoinsurgency of Ross Perot's campaign spawned his secular televangelical ministry, United We Stand, which in turn begat Lead or Leave, basically a Li'l United We Stand. Seemingly bought and paid for by the elephant-eared Texas zillionaire, Lead or Leave is a sort of Perot Youth, concerned about the deficit but for the most part evincing the "Throw the Bums Out!" reactionary stance of the Perotistas.

The latest presumptive *Ecch*-PAC is Third Millennium, a group whose whole existence is based on generational identity. Cofounded by a Kennedy that no one's ever heard of, Bobby progeny Douglas (*Douglas*?!?), with some help from a few of the Lead or Leave clowns and one of the fortysomething authors of *13th Gen*, Third Millennium wants to bring the generation together as serious, meaningful American citizens, proving all those *Ecch* bashers wrong in the process.

"We've put our finger on the tone of who we are as a generation," Kennedy, twenty-six says. Yep, they sure have—the "preamble" of the *Third Millennium Declaration* namechecks Looney Tunes to talk about the national debt, comparing *Ecch*'s meager prospects to "Wile E. Coyote waiting for a 20-ton Acme anvil to fall on his head." Hey, at least they spell it right.

Even Tabby told *Time*—she's in their Rolodex under V, for "Voice of a Generation"—that she thinks the group has "simplified very complex problems." Like she would know—Jerry Orbach kicked her ass on *Celebrity Jeopardy!* But the people at Third Millennium aren't necessarily trying to solve problems—they merely want to make a statement, while getting as much publicity as possible in the process.

Sure, they want to pay off the national debt and get rid of governmental abuse, and they identify all the usual crock of reasons for *Ecch*'s intense political anomie. It seems as though the *real* reason for their agitation can be reduced not to the financial problems facing the country as a whole, but to the financial problems facing each individual *Ecch*ster's wallet. We are nothing without our disposable income.

The *Third Millennium Declaration* implies that the reason *Ecch* is so financially troubled is that the government is wasting our tax dollars making mortgage payments on Granny's Century Village condo: "Social security is a generational scam.... Raise the retirement age." Until Willard Scott announces your birthday on the *Today* show, you best be punching the clock.

It's been pointed out, though, by both *Psychology Today* and *Business Week* that boomers at the peak of their earning powers are the ones responsible for *Ecch*'s diminished economic standing. We're being kept down by the ex-yuppie *wunderkind*s and the forty-year-old CEOs, senior account executives, production chiefs and VPs of A&R, all of whom plan to keep the good jobs for another couple of decades. Perhaps *lowering* the retirement age is a better idea.

Third Mill's self-directed declaration of impudence is the true stuff of *Ecch*tivism—not environmentalism, not abortion rights, not even plain old liberalism or simple political participation. Nope, it's that old truism about *Ecch*—the crushing tragedy that we're the first post-WWII generation faced with the possibility of living less prosperous lives than our parents. Government-funded housing projects for upper-middle-class ex-slackers—y'know, like Melrose Place—could be in our future if *Ecch* doesn't find some cash or career prospects soon.

So fight the power, fuck the pigs, down with the Man, join the revolution. We have nothing to lose but our Visas.

**I**n lieu of old-fashioned revolutionary stances, *Ecch* has taken up something far more insidious than the generic anarchy and communism of the past. The national low-self-esteem crisis gave rise to a multitude of twisted pedagogues lumped together under the presumptuously definitive misnomer of political correctness. Sure, they care about the whales and stuff—in fact, some value the sensitivity of other species more than *Homo sapiens*—but their main concern is themselves, or, rather, the world's perception of said selves.

Once upon a time, race and gender politics were complex issues, worthy of extensive debate and rational discussion. Now, they're E-Z! There are no more issues, only an ideology that says all truth is received and relative, unless it's truth that people of PC approve of. Either you agree or you are part of the problem.

According to PC dogma, all people who aren't ATFMSYWMs (Attractive Tall Fully Mobile Straight Young White Male) are victims of society, whether they're female or Latino, short or ugly. Oppressed for all of European and European-American history, these people—never mind if they know it or not—are yearning for empowerment. Their rights need to be restored, their position in the dominant culture needs to be improved and, most important, they don't ever want to hear anybody say bad words about them. You know, words like "girl," "black" or "cripple."

The real victim is the way today's culture thinks. Philosophy has been replaced by therapy, self-sufficiency by self-esteem boosting. *Ecch* has managed to change the world to the point where it is no longer acceptable to tell Polish jokes. Hey, did you hear the one about the starlet of less-accentuated intelligence? S/he fucked the screenwriter. [*Editor's Note: Hi, Dave again. As the representative of Fireside Books, I would to like to abdicate any responsibility for the above joke. While the authors' attempt to satirize/ sanitize the ethnic content of the joke and the careful use of the "s/he" noun is apparent, myself and the rest of the college-educated staff of Simon & Schuster still believe that the joke is racist and sexist. Yet again, we apologize to any readers who might take offense.*]

There are many questions raised by PC's practice of—pardon the overly ethnocentric expression—whitewashing. For instance, if the female of the species wants to be called "Vaginal Americans," should that be further expanded to "Vaginal *European*-Americans" and "Vaginal *African*-Americans"? Are white womyn exempt from the ancestral crimes dumped onto white males? And what's the plural of "womyn" anyway—"womyns"?

Good questions, but don't even consider asking the staunch PC advocate. S/he will likely tell you that merely subjecting her to this inquisition is an assault against her long-oppressed womynhood, before having you hauled off to a student tribunal on sexual-harassment charges.

What makes the PC loons so scary is their knee-jerk disdain for intelligent discourse and moral ambiguity. In order to form a more perfect union, and rid society of evils like elitism and racism, little things like the First Amendment might have to be sacrificed. The Bill of Rights is just a hindrance to their utopian vision. As a button worn by a group of New York prochoice activists says, "FUCK FREE SPEECH." After all, the Constitution was written by a bunch of slave-owning European-American People of Penis.

The best place to view these schmendricks and morons is in their natural habitat, the tweed-'n'-tenured world of academia. Legitimate attempts to make the American university system reflect the diversity of society have resulted in a briar patch of bizarre disputes and extreme solutions.

The kids are in a tizzy about an unjust but undeniable truth: History is handed down by the winners. At Stanford, disputes over the core curriculum prompted impassioned young PC disciples to exercise their basic First Amendment rights and assemble on the lovely Palo Alto campus bearing placards and candles. It was raining, and the candles under the umbrellas made them glow like Japanese lanterns—the moment was *devastating*.

"HEY, HEY! HO, HO! WESTERN CULTURE'S GOTTA GO!" they shouted, in the tongue handed down to them against their will by bourgeois ruling classes of old.

The battle over collegiate curricula basically boils down to this: too many balls in the canon. White balls, that is.

Shakespeare, Dickens and Hemingway are out. "Spear" and "Dick" are patently phallocentric, and Papa alone is responsible for an inordinate amount of literary balls (though two are conspicuously missing from *The Sun Also Rises*).

Prevailing notions of what constitutes great art have been devalued. The "classics" are no more valid than representative work from more disenfranchised groups—even those groups who were so disenfranchised that they couldn't afford papyrus.

The result? Books like the *Odyssey* get eked out by the lesser work of underclass artistes. Learning about Christopher Columbus is just as bogus as reading the *Protocols of the Elders of Zion*. The PC students wind up segregating themselves into specialty departments, reinforcing cultural differences instead of overcoming them, replacing the liberal arts with nothing but liberal rhetoric.

Never mind whether the work in question is any good or not—aesthetic standards and formal analysis are just oppressive elitist constructs. Artistic quality is perceived and therefore meaningless—what counts is victim status. Robert Hughes suggests that "in the same spirit, tennis could be shorn of its elitist overtones: you just get rid of the net."

This nonsense has permeated American education to such extremes that it's trickled down to the nursery schools. Okay, perhaps Sleeping Beauty is an outdated role model for today's women, but is it really necessary to teach toddlers to consider the viewpoint of the Giant in "Jack and the Beanstalk" before condemning his villainy? *The Giant's excessive size can be seen as a disability, while Jack is just another white guy systematically stealing and destroying the assets of the Other.* Clearly, today's kids should be given a steady diet of *Free to Be . . . You and Me* and not such hegemonic white fantasies as "Goldilocks and the Three Bears."

Truth is more relative than ever, so why not take what's been said about history and literature and apply it to something like science? A group of collegiate born-agains could insist that graduate-level biology courses give equal time to Creationism. Serious feminists could argue that there's really no such thing as gravity—it was a law invented by European white male scientists to keep womyn down.

**H**ey, quit chortling! Didn't you know that the University of Connecticut has banned "inappropriately directed laughter"? Your amusement at the moment is tyrannizing others who aren't as entertained. And for those of you who've taken offense and stopped paying attention, please, please—rejoin us. We wouldn't want to deny anyone's autonomy by excluding him (or *her*, natch) from our conversation, another no-no up there in pastoral Storrs, CT.

These are two of the goofiest examples of an otherwise egregiously common, seriously scary PC trend: university speech codes. Largely because of a gaggle of fraternity assholes in blackface as well as a few honest-to-goodness racists, horrified academic administrators were forced to do what they do best—hold committee meetings and make up rules, disallowing everything from the utterance of the usual offensive epithets to the telling of Rock Hudson jokes.

Most public schools have already seen their codes struck down as unconstitutional by various levels of the state and federal court systems. But private universities have no binding obligation to American law.

One such school is the University of Pennsylvania, where in January of 1993, after trying a plain old "Shut up" in an attempt to quiet down a group of noisy black female students outside his dorm room, Israeli-born freshman Eden Jacobowitz used an English translation of a derogatory but nonspecific Hebrew word. "Shut up, you water buffalo!" he yelled, approximating the word *behaymah*, which means "cattle" or "beast" but is commonly used as a colloquialism for "fool." A complaint was filed, and he was told by a university administrator that "water buffalo" is a racist term because buffaloes are black and water buffaloes are native to Africa (yeah, African countries like China and Malaysia). By the same token, the word could be seen as anti-Semitic, because, as everyone knows, like water buffaloes, Jews have horns. For that matter, would young Eden be branded a sexist had he said "Be quiet, you schmucks!" or "Put a lid on it, you putzes!" to the young women?

Jacobowitz was eventually exonerated of the harassment charges and the threatened disciplinary probation was never wielded against him, but the case created nothing but bad feelings on all sides, with a protracted period of meetings, protests, policy revisions and student-faculty hearings. The truth is, Jacobowitz may well be guilty of some sort of racist intent in his utterances, but even if he had yelled out, "Pipe down, *schvartzes*," since when is that grounds for any kind of punishment in the United States of America? The First Amendment allows for free speech no matter how trivial or odious. Everything from colonists calling for King George III's head to the American Nazi Party marching through Jacobowitz's lush Long Island hometown is protected.

But that's a message that doesn't wash with the politically correct people of *Ecch*. "We don't put as many restrictions on free speech as we should," the black student-body president of Stanford told the media, and no doubt George Wallace and the Grand Wizard of the Ku Klux Klan would agree with him. Yes, these bright young activists are the future of our nation.

The onslaught of campus codifying hasn't ended with speech. Why stop at regulating what people do with their brains and their mouths when you can exercise control over their whole bodies? The acknowledgment of date rape as a problem facing all women has resulted in fear, over-the-top paranoia and increased miscommunication between the sexes. "Since you can't tell who has the potential for rape simply by looking, be on your guard with every man," Cornell professor Andrea Parrot is quoted as saying in *New York* magazine.

Working through fear, paranoia and miscommunication between the sexes on your own, once a crucial part of the college experience, is now *verboten* by these sexual McCarthyites. It's been decided that such matters can be resolved only by committee meetings and paperwork.

Antioch College has taken the situation by the balls—pardon the French—and drafted a set of rules governing the sexuality of its charges. The policy, reported by the Associated Press, says, "Verbal consent should be obtained with each new level of physical and-or sexual contact or conduct in any given interaction, regardless of who initiates it.

"Asking, 'Do you want to have sex with me?' is not enough. The request for consent must be specific for each act."

One twenty-four-year-old male Antioch sophomore was quoted as saying the policy is "well cushioned in common sense" and "not radical." While allowing for the possibility that this person is merely an idiot (he is a *twenty-four-year-old* sophomore, after all), it seems more likely that such an observation is reflective of how pervasively normal PC orthodoxy has become. Incredibly, there are only 650 students at Antioch, which means that in the old days pretty much everyone had everyone else by sophomore year, and further permission was implicit.

"Under the policy, students can be removed from campus within twenty-four hours if accused of sexual offenses," AP further reported.

Apparently, for reasons of unenforceability, the policy does not apply to sex with animals, produce, townies, or faculty members.

This policy obviously cries out for further explication, especially when violating it can lead to the interruption of one's academic career without anything resembling due process. After a twenty-four-hour grace period to grab your favorite CDs and kiss your friends good-bye (but not without asking, mind you) you are *removed from campus*, without bail or a grand-jury hearing. All of this raises some questions Antioch freshpersons might want to ask their hall advisers before they enter the dangerous terrain of college romance, just to be sure:

After kissing and sucking a woman's breast, do you have to ask before you move on to the other breast? Similarly, if you've received permission to give "a blow job," is oral stimulation of the scrotum implied, or is that a "new level"? What about tongue-tickling the taint?

If two people have just finished a vigorous session of lovemaking and they're lying there exhausted and sloppy, is the mutual asking and receiving of permission required for another go? More to the point, is the asking and receiving of permission for *each new level* required the second time around? What about new positions? (These rules do open up exciting new postcoital freedoms for men. *Girl:* "Hold me?" *Boy:* "No.")

Along the same lines, while sexual intercourse with a person on one particular night doesn't necessarily imply automatic permission to commit mutually satisfying sex acts until further notice, does the each-new-level stuff still apply in an ongoing relationship? If you've nibbled an earlobe six times in a week, is it a crime to assume it's okay the seventh time?

Clearly, the Antioch policy doesn't go far enough. It discourages intelligence, mystery and genuine interplay between the sexes, but only in the area of physical intimacy. Two college students in the early stages of dating who have to ask "Can I put my tongue in there?" obviously require further guidance in all areas of their romantic and interpersonal lives.

To that end, we suggest that Antioch adopt this handy predate consent form to cover all potential trouble spots. It is to be filled out and agreed upon by both parties before commencing the joyous adventure of Love, Antioch Style. Now dating can be as easy as SAT, so bring a condom and a #2 pencil, and remember, there's no proctor—here at Antioch we're on the honor system.

Antioch College
Yellow Springs, Ohio

*Office of the Dean of Nookie*

*Student Interaction Consent Form*

### Section 1: The Date

**1.** Would you like to go out with me?: **Y/N** (circle one)
(If **N,** please sign and return for entry into your permanent record.)
**2.** Acceptable dining options (circle one or more):

    **A.** Vegan
    **B.** Nonvegetarian restaurant
    **C.** Burger World
    **D.** Let's go hunting!

**3.** Can I buy you a drink?: **Y/N** (circle one)
If **Y,** how many drinks before sexual consent is no longer valid?_____
**4a.** Permission to dress alluringly without implying immediate sexual availability: **Y/N** (circle one)
(If **N,** please sign and return for entry into your permanent record.)
**4b.** Permission to make nonthreatening complimentary remarks about my appearance: **Y/N** (circle one)
(If **N,** just forget the whole thing already.)
**5.** Permissible topics of conversation (women check off Column A, men check off Column B, pick as many as you like):

| A | B |
|---|---|
| Norman Mailer | Jane Austen |
| football | horses |
| Howard Stern | Kahlil Gibran |
| Henry Miller | Sylvia Plath |
| Katie Roiphe | Susan Faludi |
| Guns N' Roses | Bikini Kill |
| Camille Paglia | Camille Paglia |

## Section 2: Sex (*Note: Condom rules are non-negotiable*)

**6.** Please list **1, 2, 3** or **+** to indicate first date, second date, third date or more:

| | |
|---|---|
| holding hands | arm around |
| nuzzling | kissing |
| tongue-kissing | lobe nibbling |
| neck biting | copping a feel |
| over the bra | under the bra |
| dry hump | crotch squeezing |
| crotch fondling | unzipping |
| hand in undergarments | pants at ankles |
| fully naked | fellatio |
| cunnilingus | 69 |
| taint | intercourse: man on top |
| intercourse: woman on top | intercourse: side by side |
| intercourse: doggy style | third input |
| mild bondage: dominant | mild bondage: submissive |
| spanking | pearl necklace |

(*Note: Dirty talk is no longer permissible under any circumstances.*)

**7.** Postcoital behavior

**A.** Cuddling: 1 hour; 30–45 minutes; 15–30 minutes; 5–15 minutes; please leave! (circle one)
**B.** Smoking: **Y/N** (circle one)
**C.** Left side or right side of bed (circle one)
**D.** Sleep over or not sleep over (circle one)
**E.** Leno or Letterman (circle one—if Leno, please leave)

## Section 3: Post-Sexual-Intimacy Behavior

**8.** Will you respect me in the morning?: **Y/N** (circle one)

**D**espite *Ecch*'s efforts to remake the political arena in its own shallow and sanctimonious image, the status quo remains the status quo. The deficit continues to grow. The First Amendment still exists, at least for now. The guy from the sixties we elected as president isn't exactly Country Joe. (*Give me an N! Give me an A! Give me an F! Give me a T! Give me an A!*) And Congress continues to do next to nothing for gun control but makes a big televised show of concern over TV violence, real, or imagined. (They don't like the Brady Bill, but the Brady Bunch is okay.)

One of the leaders of said smokescreen is Representative Joe Kennedy (D-Mass.), son of Bobby, who proposed some futuristic *faux-*cyberpunk thing called the "V chip." This device, when installed in a television, regulates the flow of violence coming over the family set. (It's a lot like the thermos—*how does it know?*)

But what does it matter? With anti-incumbent fever crossing generational boundaries, *Ecch* is likely to rule over a time of single-term presidencies, continuing in 1996. The president is so overexamined at this point that it's impossible for him to do anything right. The Republicans, having gotten over the maniacal xenophobia of the '92 convention, should change strategies and capitalize on this by running Bill Clinton against himself in '96.

That is to say, they will run a young economic conservative who's open-minded on social issues—a Republican clone of Bill Clinton, a moderate. That's the way to reach *Ecch*—protect our pocketbooks while condescending to the false consciousness of our social conscience.

Early favorite Jack Kemp has the JFK hair and the good looks, plus he used to be a big-deal professional football quarterback. Problem is, he played for the Buffalo Bills, and everyone knows they can't win the big one. The Bill most likely to come due is Massachusetts governor Bill Weld, a Republican who believes in gay rights as strongly as he believes in supply-side economics. According to G. B. Trudeau and Joe Queenan, Weld is the only politician ever to answer the critical boomer qualifier "Who's your favorite Beatle?" correctly. In fact, Weld is so hip that his favorite band is Seatrain, a reference so obscure that even *we* feel compelled to explain it. (So here: Seatrain were a late-sixties/early-seventies San Francisco folk-fusion band led by onetime Grateful Dead/David Grisman cohort Peter Rowan.)

Of course, when *Ecch* finally supplants the baby boom as America's political power brokers, the criteria may be a teensy bit different. In the future, ABC anchorperson Tabitha Soren will be asking the candidates, "Who was your favorite member of Soundgarden?"

(The correct answer, by the way, is Ben Shepherd.)

**W**here does it all stop? Well, for the sake of this book, right here, obviously—that's why it's called an *Ecch*-ilogue. But for the generation itself, however, there is no end in sight. Andy Warhol's fifteen minutes—the Boomers' standard parameters of fame—shrunk to about 7.5 minutes long ago. At forty-seven million *Ecch*sters, that works out to *six million* episodes of *Late Night with Conan O'Brien*. Since that seems unlikely, consider the seemingly infinite profusion of magazines, TV shows, bands, comics, movies, and cyberspace rest-stops, and it is clear that *Ecch*'s domination of our culture has only just begun.

There's *Time 2 Generate*, a syndicated news magazine that was initially presold with the name *Generation X*. The producers dumped that notion around the same time they replaced Christine Craft with a fresher-faced *Ecch* anchor. Attempting to be a teenybopper cross between *Mademoiselle* and *Details* is the new magazine *Mouth 2 Mouth*—Prince's etymological influence on *Ecch* should never be underestimated.

Our friends at Marvel Comics have a new mutant title called *Generation X*, finally latching onto something that's been right under their hypersensitive noses for some time. Unlike their X elders, this Lycraflanneled crew—Slacker Lad, Video Rental Girl, Irony Man, Pavement Boy, Sonic Youth, and Miss Thang (the black woman, natch)—has no leader (and no anthems, no style to call their own). When they aren't downtown sipping cappuccinos at the Film Forum, or battling baddies like Dr. Workethico, they live in New York's luxurious Baxter Building, in a penthouse paid for by MTV. When they are out of costume (which is rarely), they're in bands, they make independent films, and do spoken-word performances, No wonder none of them have the time to do the dishes. It's like the latest edition of *The Real World*, only better drawn.

Actually the real *Real World* has been rolling around the steep hills and bohemian enclaves of San Francisco, the no-smoking-allowed petri dish for the show's third *Ecch*-periment. The demographic make-up of this gang is pretty much what you'd expect, except this time producers Pavlov and Skinner are shooting the works. To the usual loft full of jerks and morons, they've added a "Person With AIDS," whose presence changes the dynamic considerably. For some reason, there are a lot less fights over leftovers (Nobody ever says to the PWA, *"Hey, are you going to finish that sandwich?"*) and bathroom etiquette (*"Um . . . which one of you has been using my toothbrush?"*). No doubt the puppetmasters at MTV have planned for the poor martyred *Real World*-er to exit (literally) by episode six so that they move in a new white-male guitar player.

Though you still won't see it on MTV, pot smoking is now *officially* back. Thanks to Cypress Hill, the Black Crowes, and other hemp activists, recent statistics show that actual doob usage has caught up to the T-shirt sales. This rise in the nation's toke factor is a possible explanation for the utter lack of new, trendy *Ecch* fiction. On the bright side, however, there's a chance that director David Cronenberg will soon be bringing *American Psycho* to the silver screen. *Judd Nelson, if you still have one, call your agent!*

On the political front, it appears that the generation doesn't find Congressional elections to be nearly as rockin' as the Presidential one. Rock The Vote's nonexistent profile in 1994 could give the Prez it helped elect two years of turbulance that will make Whitewater look like a week on the Colorado River. (Though Tabby's *Choose or Lose* forum with the dishonorable representative from Chicago was truly enlightening: *Congressman Rostenkowski, have you smoked Indo? Can you introduce me to Chelsea?*)

*Ecch* activism has never been too convincing, anyway. Its solipsistic brand of liberal secular humanism is offset by their consumerist obsession, so that following Graduation Day, most *Ecch*-tivists dive headlong into the running-dog capitalist world. *Ecch* is the generation that wants to be both Jerry Rubins at once.

Perhaps the *Ecch* crush will end someday, but what finally has to be noted is that while the generation's pop-cult ubiquity might be a figment of the media's imagination, its forty-seven million members are not. They're here to stay, perhaps stuck with one of those pesky sobriquets (we're partial to *Ecch*, but that's just us) for all eternity—after all, who expected "boomers," "hippies," "yuppies," and "New Romantics" to become permanent additions to the lexicon?

Cultures may change, but kids don't. The characteristics ascribed to *Ecch* could just as easily be applied to a certain melancholy Prince of Denmark. *Lookit, a new label! "Hamlets."* But of course, with the exceptions of River Phoenix and Kurt Cobain, all young people eventually grow up to complain about "kids today." It's both a rite of passage and a vicious fucking cycle.

Our own thoughts, then, have little in the way of predictive power, and jack-all to do with over-intellectualized hand-wringing. Nonetheless, the message has a certain elegance, and its truth is undeniable.

And that is:

**THESE**
**PEOPLE**
**ARE**
**IDIOTS!**

# **K**udos

**Where**

**Kudos Are**

**Due Dept.**

**A**s much as the authors would like to take sole responsibility for all that is contained within, it's time to extend greetings, salutations and gratitude to the many wonderful people who assisted us in our hellish task. You can blame them if you want to.

The following folks contributed to the research, writing and production of *Generation Ecch* in one way or another: Marilyn Abraham, Michael Azerrad, Lori Berk, Evan Brownstein, Kathy DiGrado, Gavin Edwards, Mary Bess Engel, Dennis and Dean Feeley (who let us turn their house into our personal Yaddo), Daniel Fidler, Yvonne Garrett, Mark Gompertz, Melissa Kapustey, Mindy LaBernz, Bonni Leon, Brian Long, Leslie Lyons (for photos and the introduction to our agent), Steve Messina, Barbara O'Dair, Kevin Rioux (who lent us his copy of *Generation X* and never saw it again), Melissa Rawlins, Cathy Watson and Sioux Z.

A few sections of *Generation Ecch*, in slightly different form, appeared previously in other publications, and for that we would like to thank Mark Kemp and Scott Becker at *Option;* Rob Patterson, Louis Black and Nick Barbaro at the *Austin Chronicle;* and Wally Stroby at the *Asbury Park Press*.

Lacking a bibliography, we also wish to acknowledge the people whose work influenced ours. Thanks are due to them all: Mr. Agreeable, John Aldridge, Sven Birkerts, Elizabeth Caveney and Graham Young, David Edelstein, Robert Hughes, Joe Queenan, Ira Robbins, Howard Stern, and John Taylor.

These people, places and things are also cool: the Appletree Grocery, Gina Arnold, Davin Auble, Brian Berger, Pat Blashill, Eric Bluhm, Randy Bookasta, Sarah Cohen, Susan Cohen, Mark Coren, Ben Davis, the Dentists, David Fricke, Karen Glauber, Jonathan "Monkeyboy" Gordon, David Gottstein, Rob Gottstein, Brent Grulke, Hater, Bob Hellman, David Howard, Jake's/Aunt Martha's/Su Su Yum Yum's, Karen Johnston, Nora Kim, Kitty, Cary Knopp, Craig Koon, Paul Kopasz, Stuart Lodge, Nina Malkin, Frank Marchionne and the rest of the guys at Sleuth, Craig Marks, Amanda McManus,

Margaret Moser, Mountain Dew, Paddy, Parliament Lights, Debbie Pastor, Pavement, P.B. Crisps, Scott Schinder, Naomi Shapiro, Dave Sprague, Spud, Roland Swenson, Roy Trakin, Ed Ward, Erika Weinman (wherever you are) and Luann Williams.

The extraordinarily talented, and extraordinarily botz, Mr. Evan Dorkin.

The cartoonist would like to thank his parents, Howard and Jayne Berger, and his collaborator and best friend, Sarah Dyer. I am also grateful, of course, to the authors for this gig, and to all the television sets I've watched. Without them none of this would have been possible. I was also going to try to be funny and thank my agent, the Academy and Yahweh, but I won't. Hi, mom! Look—my name's in print!

Finally, extra special thanks to:
Sue Murray, tireless researcher.
Betzy Iannuzzi, the most powerful woman in the industry.
John Paul Jones: He didn't write "No Quarter," but his cooperation down the final stretch was key.
Superagent Gordon Kato, who earned every penny and shared his editorial insight as well. More important, he never failed to have a good CD on when we came to the ICM office.
Regina Joskow and Ken Weinstein, there at the book's inception (Regina even paid for dinner!) and two of the swellest people we know.
We would both like to thank Laura Haff for being the most tolerant woman on the planet. (Note from MGK: Thanks, Sparky!)
Our parents: David and Cynthia Krugman, Marilyn Cohen, Martin Cohen.
Last, but certainly not least, the most tolerant *man* on the planet, Dave Dunton. When he wasn't busy playing with his organ, Dave proved himself to be an exceptional editor and a good friend.

Jason Cohen and Michael Krugman use Apple Macintosh Power-Books, Cary Torkelson's Action-Strategy Baseball and Zildjian cymbals.

Now give us the goddamn Jean Hersholt Humanitarian Award and let's get the fuck outta here!

KUDOS WHERE KUDOS ARE DUE DEPT.

**Jason Cohen** lives in Austin, Texas. He is currently working on a history of American indie-rock labels.

**Michael Krugman** is a writer and journalist. He lives in Brooklyn, New York, and does not know how to drive a car.

**Evan Dorkin,** America's Cartoon Sweetheart, has had work published in *Esquire, Reflex,* and the U.K.'s *Deadline.* He is currently producing three ongoing comic series—*Dork!, Hectic Planet,* and *Milk and Cheese*—all of which lose money and are published by Slave Labor Graphics in San Jose. A Brooklyn native with an accent to prove it, our hapless cartoonist is now planning his escape from Staten Island. He wrote this bio himself, and it shows. It would've been funnier, but he found out you don't get paid for bios, so why waste material?